HITCH YOUR WAGON TO A STAR

Terri W. Majors

HITCH YOUR WAGON TO A STAR
PROLOGUE

The thing about Melba was her "smarts". She knew more than most kids her age, but she believed knowledge should be carefully guarded. Why let them in on her secrets? After all, she reasoned, the only good thing to come of being smarter than the boys was keeping that secret to herself. The morning of June 4, 1926 was no exception to her rule. As a matter of fact, there would never be an exception to guarding certain secrets. After all, American women had just earned the right to VOTE the year after she born, a fact that made Melba fume! She believed in secrecy regarding SOME things, and that belief would be the key to future successes for this Texas girl...

> *"Our true history is scarcely ever deciphered by others. The chief part of the drama is a monologue, or rather an intimate debate between God, our conscience, and ourselves. Tears, grieves, depressions, disappointments, irritations, good and evil thoughts, decisions, uncertainties, deliberations --all these belong to our secret, and are almost all incommunicable and intransmissible, even when we try to speak of them, and even when we write them down."*

(Henri-Frederic Amiel, Philosopher)

CHAPTER 1

"**Stop** it, Brother! You NEVER play fair, but I'll show you, just you wait and see!" At that, seven year old Melba, with mud splattered all over her one play outfit that was now ripped in two places besides being a filthy mess, gathered her two cornhusk dolls and ran toward the house. Brother and Lindell laughed at her and threw more mud balls as they continued their "war" game in the wooded spot they called their hideout.

Brother was 12, Lindell 10, and they weren't really bad boys; they were just playing, after all! Both the boys knew Sister was always getting mad at them, but she was constantly pestering them to let her tag along. Sometimes, they told each other, it was just too much! Now she was bound to tell Mama, and Mama was sure to be upset about Melba's dress; they'd get it, but Mama would likely get over being mad real quick. Lindell and G.W. were her boys, and they were accustomed to getting lots of attention and hardly any real reprimanding. Mama honestly believed "boys would be boys", and she had a soft spot in her heart for her male offspring. Mama was more likely to get after Melba for ruining her dress by acting like the boys. Melba ran away from her brothers with one thought in mind: show them she could handle whatever they dished up! She was no "sissy"; she could take care of herself!

Life in Damon, Texas was simple; in 1926, poverty was king. Melba's dad, Oscar Lee, worked in the oil fields discovered in Damon nine years earlier by Sinclair Oil. He worked for Sinclair as a roughneck, doing whatever messy, dirty job available. Times were tough. So when Melba ran into the oil-field shanty they called home, Oscar was in no mood to be sympathetic. Annie, Melba's mother, was equally unmoved by her oldest daughter's angry cries, telling Melba, "Get to the water barrel and clean up your clothes! Then get the needle and thread and fix those rips. I'm tired of you chasing after Brother and Lindell! You need to act like a girl, stay at home, and help me with the chores."

Melba felt her face flush, more with frustration and resentment than with embarrassment because of the mess she was in. It seemed Mama never took up for her, and Melba hated it! Why didn't the boys have to clean and sew? Coming home dirty and with ripped pants was just fine for THEM, Melba fumed as she trudged to the water barrel. With every step, she plotted a way to get even with her brothers. She'd catch them by surprise one of these days and teach them a lesson!

CHAPTER 2

Mama and Papa had moved to Damon from Corsicana right after news of the newest oil find in southeast Texas had oil workers rushing to this small town. They had high hopes of making life better for themselves and their family. Cecelia Anne and Oscar were both 29, sharing the birth year of 1896. Oscar's early life had been unsettled since his birth in Alabama. His father, Andrew Black, and his mother, Missouri Stephens, married in 1893 in Tennessee and moved to Birmingham, Alabama in 1895. Oscar was born to them the next year. That same year, Andy was killed in a "shooting incident" that was never explained to anyone in the family, and Missouri was left alone to care for baby Oscar. She eventually made it to Texas and found refuge with her mother, Adaline, and her brother, George Washington Stephens. Oscar had no memory of his biological father, a fact that always caused him grief.

Within a year of her move to Texas, Missouri met and married a widower named George Paul Aycock and took on the raising of his two children, Carroll and Winfield, along with Oscar Lee. George was not a loving stepfather to Oscar, preferring his biological sons and treating Oscar like an outcast. Oscar and Winfield were the same age, but George doted on both Winfield and Carroll while mostly ignoring his step-son. As a result, Oscar left home in 1912 at the age of 17, and set out to live his own life far away from the demands of George Aycock!

4

He migrated from Rogers, Texas where his mother and stepfather lived, to Corsicana. He'd heard about the discovery of OIL there, and he determined to see what kind of job he could get by showing a willingness to do "whatever". The Corsicana oil field was accidentally discovered in 1894 by water prospectors hired by the Corsicana Water Development Authority. It was the first commercially significant oilfield find in Texas. Within a few days, Oscar was hired by the Cullinan Oil Company to work as a roughneck; he would do all sorts of harsh manual labor to assist with the drilling of newly discovered oil. For Oscar, the dirty, physically challenging work was just what he wanted! It helped him get over the loneliness of being away from his family, and it helped heal the bitterness of life with his stepfather.

Surprisingly, it was on a trip back to Rogers to visit Missouri that Oscar met the woman who was to become his wife: Annie Cecilia Meissner. Following a short courtship, Oscar proposed and Annie became his wife on October 23, 1915. They made their first home in Corsicana, but soon moved to the little town of Damon for a "better" job.

CHAPTER 3

Things did not work out in terms of money and a better place to live after the move to Damon, but Buster (as Annie called her husband) and Annie still managed to be happy. G.W. was their first-born child, arriving in 1917. Mama was still nursing him when she discovered she was pregnant again. Ten months later, Lindell joined the family. Melba's birth in 1919 added the first girl, and two years later Anna Jean was the new baby.

They loved their kids and enjoyed simple things. Sitting outside at night and telling stories became a family tradition, and everyone participated. Oscar was a great storyteller, and he loved to entertain his brood with tales of adventure and fantasy to which he always added a great deal of humor. Even on days when Melba was mad about the "fairness" thing, she liked Papa's stories, especially when they were "Tall Tales". One of her favorites was the story about how the Mississippi River came to be, and Papa said it was the best tall tale ever told by a famous story-teller, Gabby Hayes. Here's how Papa told it:

> *Brrr! Listen to that storm blow out there, buckaroos. I wonder if that snow will ever stop fallin'. Shore glad I'm sittin' here inside my cabin with a warm fire goin' back of me! Of course, I know you young'ns can't wait for it to stop so you can get out there and get to sled ridin' and skiin' and throwin' snowballs and buildin' snowmen. Yep, I reckon*

that's real fun!

You know, whenever I'm out after a snowstorm and see young'ns buildin' snowmen, it reminds me of my uncle, Snowball Hayes. Snowball know'd more about buildin' things with snow than anybody in the whole world AND Texas! There was nothing Uncle Snowball couldn't build with snow. Why, he even learned them there Eskimos to build Iglooys! But when it comes to buildin' snowmen, I reckon he built the greatest snowmen the world has ever know'd. Looked jest like they could walk and talk, yes sir-ree bob.

One time he was way up there in Minnesoty and he decided he was goin' to build hisself a snowman, and this un'd be bigger than any one he'd ever built before.

Well, he worked for three years, nine months, twelve days, two minutes and thirty-five seconds jes gittin' the snow together. Fact of the matter is, he used up all the snow in the whole state of Minnesoty. When he got through, his snowman stood, oh, maybe four, five-hundred feet high. Couldn't see the top of his head on a cloudy day. Of course, folks come from all over the countryside to see it. You might not believe this, but that snowman looked so real that folks used to talk to it and wait for it to talk back to them.

One day a couple of young'ns come by and started makin' snowballs right in front of my uncle's snowman. Well sir, that snowman took one look at what was goin' on and he started a runnin'. He took outa there like a scared jackrabbit. He run jest as fast as his legs could carry him. Fact is, he run all the way from Minnesoty to the Gulf of Mexico.

Course, as he run South, it got warmer. And the warmer it got, the smaller he got 'cause he started meltin' and leavin' a trail of water behind him. And by the time he stopped runnin' he'd plum disappeared.

But, and you can believe this or not, that
trail of water he left behind is there to this very day.
Folks call it the Mississippi River, yes sir-ree bob.

The kids all loved that story; they'd never seen snow and it was always fun to hear Papa tell about "his" Uncle Snowball! Papa's funny use of bad grammar and back woods dialect kept everyone giggling while they listened to the amazing (and very "tall") tale about America's greatest river. After Papa got them started, G.W., Lindell and Melba tried to outdo each other with tall tales THEY made up. Even Mama smiled during those evenings, no matter how tired she was. Life wasn't all bad…!

CHAPTER 4

Of course, some things never ceased to irritate Melba, and the fact that Anna Jean was "the baby" and spoiled beyond what was right by Mama and Papa was definitely one of those things! Sister had to admit Jeannie was an especially pretty child, but it was sometimes hard to admire her because everyone did! At five years of age, Jeannie's soft brown eyes and long, curly eyelashes beneath a beautiful cascade of light brown curls, paired with dimples when she smiled, guaranteed "oohs and aahs" from all who saw her. All that attention did very little to appease Melba's (clearly justified!) jealousy. Jeannie was the delight of the family while Melba felt like Cinderella before the ball! It just wasn't fair.

Any attention Melba got was generally connected with a long list of "Sister Do" demands such as, "Sister, watch Jeannie and don't let her get hurt." It was exasperating! Melba fumed silently, thinking how unfair her life was since Jeannie was ONLY two years younger. She'd soon be in school, too, and then she'd see what Melba had to put up with. That thought kept Melba from getting TOO frustrated with Mama's demands about Jeannie. It would be nice, though, Melba couldn't help thinking, if things could be a bit fairer!

On top of the issues with Jeannie, there were problems at school. One of the worst things about having to go to school, Melba mused, was the embarrassment of not fitting in and being rejected by lots of the other kids. It was one of the secrets she buried deep inside, never sharing her misery with anyone. Even though Melba had no trouble learning and often received praise from her teachers for her unusual abilities in the classroom, she struggled with making friends and feeling like she belonged. The "rich" kids made fun of her when she wore Mama's high-heeled shoes and too-big coat. Melba felt ashamed, but Papa couldn't afford to dress her any better. She understood, but couldn't help how she felt. Hand-me-downs came from cousins that lived in Needville, near Houston, but they were usually tacky and patched, at best. Sometimes, Mama used flour sacks from the feed store to make her a new dress, but Melba had never owned a real "store bought" dress. She was always told that they had to make do. There were no options. That fact didn't make life any easier at school. One morning during recess, one of the older girls, Patty, started taunting Melba and singing this made-up song: *"Melba Smell-ba came to class wearing her mama's coat, the silly lass! Silly Melba-Smell-ba; silly Melba-Smell-ba!"*

Melba could feel the blood rise to her face and it was all she could do to keep from either crying or starting a fight. She ran back into the schoolhouse and hid in the broom closet until the teacher called everyone back inside. Melba knew no one would understand her humiliation and no one would punish the mean kids, so she kept everything to herself... but she secretly vowed that someday she would be both well-dressed and respected by everyone who knew her. Achievement, recognition and respect seemed the only future goals that were worthwhile, and thoughts about how to do something important and worthy became another of her deeply buried secrets.

CHAPTER 5

Despite the poverty the family and most of their oil field neighbors endured, the excitement of the "Roaring Twenties" was contagious! Everyone talked about the new motion pictures with stars like Mary Pickford and Douglas Fairbanks. It was amazing and awe-inspiring to learn about the lives of the movie stars, how they lived like kings and queens and were rich beyond imagining.

These early movies were shown in theatres called Nickelodeons, and gorgeous actresses like Greta Garbo, Theda Bara and Louise Brooks fell in love with the likes of Rudolph Valentino and Francis X. Bushman, both great lovers on the silent screen. Popular, too, were zany character actors like Charlie Chaplin and Fatty Arbuckle. Mama and Papa talked about how Chaplin was raised in London. He was even poorer than them, and he was sent to a horrible, abusive workhouse when he was a young teenager. Even with such a terrible background, Charlie Chaplin had become both famous and wealthy!

Mama loved to hear about Chaplin, and she and Papa listened to stories on the radio whenever they could. They told the kids that Charlie came to America in 1908 when he was 19. By 1914, Chaplin was performing as his most famous character, the "Tramp". Papa always said he wanted to take Mama to see a Chaplin movie at the nickelodeon in Richmond, but he never did. It was just too expensive. But Mama still liked to dream about seeing a "live" movie in one of the theatres someday, and when her sister, Aunt Dorleita, came to visit, they giggled like teenagers as they talked about the movies and the stars they adored.

Melba and her friends talked and dreamed about the most popular movie stars, too, and sometimes got to see pictures of them in newspapers or magazines. Even though Damon was a small town, the local paper usually had stories about new movies. Mama and Aunt Dorleita whispered about the "risqué" movie starring Greta Garbo called *Flesh and the Devil*. The newspapers wrote about Greta and her leading man, John Gilbert, having a real and very romantic love affair during the filming of the movie. It was even rumored that the two were living together in Paris! Mama and Aunt Dorleita really giggled about that! According to Hollywood gossip columnists, Gilbert actually proposed to Garbo; she accepted and a fabulous wedding was arranged. The next time rumors were circulated, the stories were all about Greta changing her mind and calling off the wedding.

Mama and Aunt Dorleita acted scandalized by this news, and the whispers and exclamations made Melba extra-curious; how could her MOTHER and AUNT act so silly and be so smitten with all the Hollywood chatter? It just proved that even though Mama made a big deal about never gossiping or spreading rumors, the truth was SHE didn't always follow her own rules! Melba felt good about this "epiphany"; it enabled her to talk about "Hollywood stuff" with her friends without feeling guilty!

The papers kept on writing about the Garbo/Gilbert love affair, but when Melba or the boys asked questions about it, Mama said it was "inappropriate" for the children to even hear words like "hot" or "steamy" that the papers used to describe the romance between Garbo and Gilbert. Of course, that comment by Mama caused G.W. and Lindell go out of their way to find out WHY Mama thought it "unfit" for their eyes! It was really funny. Almost all the kids in Damon knew a lot about this "off-limits" movie and its famous stars! Melba decided that SOME things were, well…just plain old copacetic to know about, regardless of what Mama said! The scoop about movie stars definitely made her smile!

By 1928, the newest "craze" in film making, animation, brought Mickey Mouse to the theatres. Mickey was created by an up-and-coming film maker named Walt Disney. Melba, Lindell and G.W. began to draw pictures of Mickey and had great fun coming up with their own "Mickey adventures". Mickey's role in *Steamboat Willie*, written about in the newspapers, gave all the kids something "crazy" to talk about, and songs from the film, played on the radio station, were whistled and sung continuously. Melba's favorite was "Turkey in the Straw". The music and lyrics just stayed in her head, making her smile even while she did her boring chores!

When *Plane Crazy*, the second Disney movie starring Mickey, was released, all the kids were talking about getting tickets to see it. Truth be told, though, none of them managed to see the film; it was just for the "rich" kids. But it was always fun to dream about such adventure! Just talking about the "big screen" made life more bearable for all of them, and Melba enjoyed the banter as much as anyone. Maybe, she prayed, she would get the chance to go to movies when she grew up and left home. There just might be someone special out there who would take her away from the drab life she lived right now! It was those dreams that made life bearable… and, secretly, deep in Melba's soul she KNEW her life would be very different from life as it was in this little oil town.

CHAPTER 6

Despite the lack of material things, life in Damon did have its perks. School was easy for Melba. She liked to learn and had a fantastic visual memory; once she read something it stayed with her like a photograph. She could close her eyes and "see" the pages of books, remembering all the details without really even trying. She liked to read a book with lots of facts, close her eyes and visualize the pages. She could recall everything on the pages, even the "fine print" underneath pictures! Melba's teachers were sometimes irritated with her since she usually knew the answers to all their questions and sometimes was bored with assignments she was forced to complete. She liked to be the "teacher's helper", and often tutored other kids when they struggled to learn something new.

Even though helping the teachers gave Melba something to do when she completed her own work early, she often got bored and restless. Classrooms were crowded, and teachers had no time to come up with special assignments and projects to entertain the quick learners. Sometimes Melba felt like a fish out of water, but she tried to fit in and rarely misbehaved. She really LIKED school and learning, but it just seemed unfair (again!) that the teachers expected her to accept boredom and do what all the other kids did, no matter what. Even when Melba knew all the answers and wanted to learn more, her teachers let her just sit in class and wonder what else there was to know...

Recognition for "fast learning" was often given in the form of "skipping" grades, so when Melba completed first grade in 1926, her teacher recommended she be placed in third grade for the coming school year. Melba was okay with the plan and considered it didn't matter if she moved ahead of her classmates since most of the kids were less-than-friendly to her, anyway. There was no incentive to stay with her age group, and Melba figured maybe she'd make new friends by moving on. At the end of that year, though, another skip was recommended by the school and Melba found herself in fifth grade in 1928. She was only nine years old! G.W. and Lindell were her only real playmates, and Melba was a rough-and-tumble "tomboy". She had no trouble keeping up with her brothers, and was, in fact, frequently the ring leader in activities usually reserved for boys. After all, Melba always thought, being smart worked in many different ways. Sometimes, "smart" was a ticket to doing the things that mattered most to HER.

CHAPTER 7

"Let's go to the creek and swing on vines", G.W. suggested after school. The children were walking home, but the thought of getting there only to do chores and homework was not exactly appealing.

"Okay, let's!!" Melba and Lindell agreed. They'd deal with Mama's disapproval afterward.

It was October 10th, but still hot and muggy in Damon. The threesome took off at a run, going past the football field and down the dirt path that ran behind the bus barn. The "creek" was really just a drainage ditch hidden in a grove of trees, but it was a favorite spot for the kids. They'd found an old oak tree that had trailing vines, and using the biggest vines like ropes was great fun! Melba managed to run ahead of the boys and grabbed the end of one of the vines...

"Wheeeeeeeeee!!!" she hollered as she swung over the ditch. Brother and Lindell caught up and, determined to outdo Sister, took running leaps as they grabbed vines and hurtled across the ditch.

"Yeowwwwwwww!!" they screamed, laughing so hard they could barely keep a grip on their vines. The higher the boys careened, the more determined Melba was to "beat" them. She really was quite good at competing with her male siblings. Years of rough play had toned her muscles, and she had no fear. After about fifteen minutes, Brother and Lindell were ready to say Sister won their contest. They needed to get home before Mama started worrying about them, but just then

Melba's hands slipped and she flew through the air, hitting the ground with a loud thud and a scream that made the boys cringe.

"Owwwwwwwwww!!" Sister rolled to her side, grasping her left arm and moaning in pain.

"Oh, great!" G.W. muttered to Lindell. "Mama will KILL us for letting her get hurt."

"Okay, Sister, calm down. You'll be fine. Let me see what's wrong", he said in a soothing voice. "Is it your wrist again? Do you think it's broken?"

Melba started bawling. "I think it IS, and I just broke it in the same spot last year…and it really hurts…and Dr. Farmer told me to be careful because my wrist is already weak. Oh, Pooh! Mama's gonna be extra-mad this time!"

At least Melba could feel good about her two brothers. They helped her get up and made sure she was able to walk before starting home. Brother and Lindell each put an arm around her waist and gave her lots of sympathy on the way to face what was sure to be a stern reprimand and two very unhappy parents. Oh, well, they figured. Sometimes you had to pay a hefty price in terms of family "peace" in order to have fun. Melba's most-likely-broken wrist would heal. Those thoughts helped give the siblings the courage needed to get Sister home…

The kids were right about Mama and Papa's reaction to their afternoon's entertainment that had ended so badly. All three of them were worse than "in the doghouse", and Melba's trip to see Dr. Farmer was a bummer. He set the break but told her she had permanently damaged her wrist. He said she'd probably break it again if she continued to act like a boy. Papa let Melba know the dollar he had to pay Doc was taking food off the table, and his disappointment in her behavior was hard to take. After all, she didn't break her arm on purpose! As usual, G.W. and Lindell were almost instantly forgiven for THEIR "misbehavior". Mama's scolding of the boys was mighty soft, Melba fumed. She muttered some not-so-nice words under her breath and felt absolutely frustrated with the way things were going. Besides being upset about all the unfair reprimands from both Mama and Papa AND Dr. Farmer, Melba's wrist really did hurt. Tears rolled down her cheeks as she went to her bed to rest; it was easier than being around the family! Her bad attitude was reinforced once again.

After the day's unexpected turn of events faded into evening, Mama and Papa were a little bit less upset with the three siblings. In fact, things at home got slightly better for awhile, even though Melba's wrist was splinted and wrapped so she couldn't move it. Mama let her skip some of the usual chores, and the boys had to help with things like sweeping the floor and hanging out the clean clothes. It was kind of nice because Melba got some of the attention usually reserved for the boys and Anna Jean; Mama actually rubbed her back some nights and even "fussed" over her. Melba reveled in feeling loved.

Life was much the same for the family over the next months. Money was scarce and there was never anything left for extras. School was okay, but Melba's lack of friends was always upsetting to her. More than anything, she wanted her classmates to treat her like one of them, but that just didn't happen. Melba relied on Brother and Lindell for companionship like she'd always done, but she fantasized about playing with girl friends. After all, the boys cared less about "girl" stuff and only wanted to be outside doing "boy" things: fishing, running races, climbing trees, hunting snakes, having dirt fights, collecting bugs, and lots of other things that Melba did without much effort. Sometimes, though, she wished for a friend to talk to about, well, BOYS. She'd like to giggle with a female friend about movies and the movie stars that Mama and Aunt Dorleita talked about. She missed having someone to share ideas about how to fix her hair and how to take care of her skin and nails. And to have a confidant to talk about really nice, fashionable clothing that Melba dreamed of seemed like one of the most important things in the world. Someday, thought Melba, someday…

CHAPTER 8

Melba was a sixth grader in 1929. When school started in September, lots of people were talking about something called a "recession". Melba heard Papa talking to Aunt Dorleita's husband, Melvin, during one of their visits just before the fall semester began at Damon Elementary. They got into an argument about President Herbert Hoover because Papa said Mr. Hoover should be doing more to help people get jobs and to see that they got paid "a solid amount of cash for a day's work". Uncle Melvin said Papa was wrong.

"Look, Buster," Melvin insisted, "Hoover knows things will get better for all of us. How can things be bad when the price of stocks keeps going up?"

"You know I don't own any stocks, Melvin! How can rising stock prices help me? Besides, what I hear is the huge increase in stock averages is a bad thing. What's making them go up? If you ask me, there's just a bunch of lies being told all of us by the government! And that's why I think we're in for even worse times" said Papa in a weirdly calm voice. Melba heard the underlying anger, though, and it made her want to ask him to explain "recession" and "stock averages". She would, too, as soon as Uncle Melvin and Aunt Dorleita left to return to Needville.

That very night, Melba, Brother, Lindell and even Anna Jean sat on the front porch with Papa and asked him to tell them why he said those things to Uncle Melvin. Papa explained that lots of people had been losing jobs over the past 10 years, but the government had done nothing to help maintain job opportunities. He told the kids to think about all the friends they had whose families had to move away because their dads lost jobs. He reminded them about food lines they saw every time they went into town and not having money for anything except things they absolutely had to buy. Papa told them that just a few citizens in the whole country were rich, that the rich only made up one percent of the entire population.

"When we first moved to Damon", Papa explained, "the oil boom here made me think I'd be able to make good money and provide a really good life for all of us. I was wrong."

"Why, Papa?" Melba asked. "Why were you wrong?"

"Well, Sister," Papa said, "I didn't know how much money the country spent during World War I, or that we didn't have enough tax money being collected to pay for all we spent. Of course, America had no real choice. We had to help our allies during the Great War!"

"Anyway," Papa continued, we got into the FIRST recession because of the War costing so much and the government cutting back on spending to try to balance the budget. Now we're in a SECOND recession and more than half of the wage earners in the country are either not able to find work or are working, like I am, for a paltry, below poverty level, paycheck. Even Anna Jean knows we don't have enough money! While most people in the country are starving, a few are getting rich because the value of their stock investments has tripled or even quadrupled in the past year. It can't continue like this! Things are out of control!"

With that, Papa said, "I've said enough about problems for one night. Off to bed, all of you!"

CHAPTER 9

Two months after school started, the terrible thing Papa seemed to know would happen became news headlines. The stock market, whose averages had continued to rise, faced one of the worst events in the history of America, indeed in the history of the world: it CRASHED! October 29, 1929 was dubbed "Black Tuesday", and losses for the month totaled an unheard of SIXTEEN BILLION DOLLARS! America was about to enter the Great Depression.

For the next few months, fortunately, things seemed to be about the same in the little town of Damon. Most of the folks remaining there still had jobs thanks to the oil field. National news trickled down, but the huge problems facing people living in cities like New York and Chicago seemed truly far-removed. By late spring, however, it had become clear that President Hoover could not save the country. Thousands of American citizens seemed without hope.

"What will happen to us, Brother?" Melba asked.

"I'm afraid Papa will lose his job, too, and we'll be living in a tent or worse", G.W. stated in a hushed tone of voice. Melba and Lindell were huddled with G.W. outside the house. They didn't want Mama and Papa to know what they were talking about. Papa would just "shush" them and be upset. The last thing the kids wanted to do was cause MORE trouble for their parents, but they couldn't help but worry. They knew money was even tighter than in the past and bad news was all the adults in town ever seemed to talk about these days. Even Anna Jean was cranky and out of sorts...

As the next weeks and months passed, the "Great Depression" would begin to affect the entire world. There were problems all over Europe. G.W. and Lindell always seemed to find out more about stuff in the news than Melba, so she was constantly questioning them.

"Why can't the government fix the money problems?" Melba demanded to know.

"I know President Hoover is smart. How can he let so many people lose their jobs and have no place to live? It just doesn't make sense!" Melba had no patience with what she perceived as a refusal to ACT. She believed that leaders should be able to handle problems and make things workable.

CHAPTER 10

The summer of 1930 was frightening: cotton crops failed to thrive in the hot, dry atmosphere; the five-year drought had wreaked havoc on almost every type of agriculture. News about what was called "the crash" was in every newspaper headline, and the news was worse than bleak. Melba's intense curiosity was in high gear and she asked questions constantly. Sometimes Papa was too busy to talk, but sometimes he'd sit at the table and explain why so many folks were jobless and starving. He said he was lucky to have his job with Sinclair and didn't mind his pay cut; it was just good to have work. Papa said President Hoover was trying to keep American's spirits up by remaining confident in an impending recovery from the crash. Mr. Hoover, Papa explained, believed the economy would regain the vigor of the 20's as long as people didn't panic. When Melba asked if Papa thought the President was right, she sensed his fear and uncertainty even though he tried to make her and her siblings believe everything would be okay.

As the summer days passed in Damon, signs of trouble were everywhere. Most men working the oil field got lower wages. One night, Melba heard Papa and Mama talking.

"Buster, what's Sinclair gonna do? I've heard about more lay-offs and you know we'll starve if you lose your job!" Mama whispered this with a fearful-sounding voice that scared Melba.

"Annie, I've told you to stop worrying about us; we'll be okay." Papa almost growled. Melba just tried to be silent   as she lay in her bed, listening. She was frightened, like Mama, but she wanted to believe Papa when he said they'd be alright.

After a few minutes, Papa told Mama part of his worries were because of the President. "I think Hoover should ask the federal government to provide relief for our citizens who can't find jobs. It makes me sick to know families are literally starving on the streets because unemployment just keeps skyrocketing. It's just not right!"

"Why do you think President Hoover won't help all our homeless people, Buster?" Annie questioned Papa. She was clearly upset; her voice was tremulous and she sounded almost sick.

"Hoover keeps insisting relief should be handled by the private sector. He believes people should get help from foundations like the Community Chest, United Way, the Salvation Army, or their churches. He says local help is more democratic, cheaper and less government controlled", Papa explained and added, "But Hoover's plan just isn't working."

Melba's eavesdropping, though unintentional, had her head spinning as she mulled over what Papa had said. She knew people were afraid to spend their money. She understood "economy". After all, hadn't she learned about capitalism in school? She "got it" when store owners closed their shops because no one could purchase their wares. She "got it" when families began to leave, following an often foolish quest for jobs "somewhere else". Sometimes, Melba wished she was stupid and unable to understand all the terrible things this Depression was doing to people all over America! It would be less painful than KNOWING there were worse days ahead. There was no more sleep that night; she lay awake and tried to think of something that might help…

The next day, Melba confessed what she'd overheard Papa and Mama discussing when Lindell and G.W. were outside and she could talk to them privately. The brothers agreed with Melba that things were not good…

CHAPTER 11

Summer turned to fall, but the cooler days did nothing to make things better. It seemed days and weeks went by with no hint of good news. By December 1930, it seemed that the world was coming to an end. Unemployment increased to almost 20 percent as more and more families faced the unthinkable. Everyone was affected and stories about "bread lines" made all who had jobs even more grateful and willing to "pinch pennies". Papa talked about people who had lost their homes living in "Hoovervilles" which were shanty towns built with scrap materials, boxes and tents. The worst of places grew up on vacant lots and were just crude shacks cobbled together with scrap metal, tarpaper, cardboard and old wooden crates. There was no plumbing, no electricity or gas, and no way to cook meals. These horrible places, named after President Hoover, scared Melba and her brothers; what if THEY lost their house? Mama had heard tales of "Hoover Stew" handed out in "soup kitchens" for the homeless and unemployed. For some reason, she told the kids about this "free food", saying it was disgusting, but better than starving to death. Melba really tried to be appreciative of what her family had; she didn't complain. After all, Papa had a job! Unfortunately, even her wildest imaginings did not come close to predicting how much worse things would get in the next two years.

Lindell and G.W. were just as curious about "world events" as Melba, and the three of them read newspaper articles whenever they got the chance. At school, some of the teachers sometimes brought newspapers that were a week old to their classrooms, and reading them was a real treat! The three siblings discussed everything they read. What they read scared them, but they wanted to know what was really going on. It was hard to believe how many Americans were jobless and homeless! Mama and Papa had little to say about the way things were, and the kids knew they were trying to protect the family and keep them from worrying.

"Do you really think Papa could lose his job?" Melba asked Brother after one of their reading "sessions". She was afraid to tell her siblings how scared she felt, and she certainly didn't want them to know about her nightmares! They would probably just laugh at her, and she REALLY couldn't handle that right now! Sometimes Melba was SURE she was crazy to worry so much, but the last thing she wanted was her brothers telling her to dry up and scram... She understood things, but in this case knowledge was not a friend. The awful imaginings became part of Melba's "secret thoughts".

One evening, G.W. surprised his sister with these words: "Sis, Papa's not gonna lose his job, but, if anything DID happen, me and Lindell would take care of you. Please don't worry."

Melba almost lost her temper. She had to make a big effort to keep from yelling at G.W. that she could take care of herself. "He thinks I'm a weakling, a little sissy-girl!" she steamed inwardly. "That's what I get for letting him know I CAN worry about things!"

And so Melba determined to squelch her fears and be a big girl. She knew, intellectually, that she was lucky to have two older brothers who could take charge if need be and help the entire family. The siblings still spent a lot of time reading whatever news articles became available, and what they learned certainly did nothing to stop Melba's nightmares. She kept all her bad dreams to herself. It was impossible NOT to be worried with so many terrible things happening all around them. Sometimes even Brother and Lindell admitted the things they learned were frightening, but such admissions were few and far between. Buster's "oldest" were very good at hiding their true feelings.

CHAPTER 12

The three siblings read about hobos who rode on railroad cars without buying a ticket. They'd wait until the train started moving, leaping onto empty cars for a ride to the next town...or even further. One afternoon, Melba found a days-old newspaper. What she read was horrible! The reporter talked about injuries and deaths caused when people took to the rails; hobos were among the thousands of citizens who became lost, displaced and forgotten. The same article told an unthinkably terrible story about a family from Oklahoma with six kids. All of them died when a train they attempted to ride was moving too fast; the father tried to help his children get on the moving train car, but none of them made it. They fell to their deaths with their father screaming for them to hold on.

The story was one of the worst things Melba had ever heard about; she was sickened by it. The rest of the paper's news articles were almost as shocking. They spoke about other horrors that Melba found hard to believe, but she realized were true. Almost half the children in the United States were hungry, homeless and unable to get medical care. A lot of schools had closed because teachers couldn't be paid and buildings had no lights or heat; kids were not even learning the basics. Melba suddenly understood with great certainty how lucky she was to be going to school, to have a house to live in, and to have food to eat. Now she knew things COULD get worse...

It was the first week in January, 1931, only a week since Christmas. School was still closed for the holidays. Melba missed her teacher. She liked to pretend Miss Johnson was her fairy godmother who would turn her into a beautiful queen. Then Melba would show the mean kids who called her names like "Melba-Smellba" and "Ratty-Tatty" that she was as good as them, maybe even better!

Christmas had been a reminder of how poor the family was: an orange and a peppermint stick in her stocking along with a set of "Jacks" were the only gifts, not that Melba failed to appreciate them. In fact, she was happy with her gifts and only wished more for her brothers and Anna Jean. Papa's job as a Roughneck for Sinclair Oil paid only enough for food and shelter. Gifts were special, indeed. Melba was grateful to Papa, and she loved him dearly, but she liked to dream about plans for a different future as a "grown up". She liked to dream that the depression would be over and people would have jobs. She liked to dream that things like shantytowns would go away. In her dreams, she'd have a fine house, real China dishes and sterling silver dinnerware. Her furniture would be Henredon or Broyhill like she'd seen in the windows of Robinowitz and Bul's on Main Street. Her sofa and chairs would have matching upholstery in rich shades of chenille and chintz, and her side tables would be hewn from dark rosewood, not pine... Her bedroom furniture would include a big four-poster bed carved in mahogany and beautifully "dressed" with fine linens and a pink silk duvet. Life would be grand...!

"Sister!! I thought you said you'd play cards with me!" cried Anna Jean. "And you promised to teach me how to play

Jacks!"

With that, twelve year old Melba's daydream came to an abrupt halt and reality flooded in. Mama really needed her to keep Anna Jean occupied, no matter what else, and that's just the way it was. Being the oldest girl meant "little sister duty" as well as lots of chores, and that left no time for daydreaming. It really did infuriate Melba that Jeannie was allowed to be such a "prima donna"; she was a spoiled brat! So much for wishful thinking about her future, thought Melba.

CHAPTER 13

That night, she lay awake listening to Papa and Mama. Voices rose and fell, mostly with excitement. Papa said, "Annie, I met a man today, a Kenneth Powell, who just traveled back to Damon from East Texas to get his family. He's taking them to the new "wildcat" oilfield we heard about that's north of the Daisy Bradford farm near Joinerville. There are JOBS to be had and there's money to be made! We need to pack up and join the Powells. This is BIG! We have a chance to get rich! This time, it will really happen! The Depression be hanged! East Texas is filled with black gold!"

Melba had never heard Papa sound so excited, but Mama just sounded upset and scared. She was crying when she asked, "Buster, how can we go? You can't go without a job! How will we feed the kids? And what about this new baby I'm carrying?"

Papa's reply would stay with Melba the rest of her life. In a strong, firm voice he said, "Annie, we must hitch our wagon to a star! I'm sure this is the chance of a lifetime! Now stop that crying and trust me!"

Melba could not sleep the rest of that night. (Sleepless nights were becoming a pattern!) Her life was about to change; fear and excitement gripped her heart and made her hands shake. She clenched her teeth as she imagined going to this strange place that seemed so very far away from the only town she'd ever known. What was this "black gold"? Could they really get rich?   What did Papa mean about "hitching our wagon to a star"? How did Papa know this was the right thing to do? What about Mama? Melba couldn't stand to hear her crying; Mama's tears were scary and upsetting. Melba lay awake and worried about what would happen. Was Papa really going to make them leave Damon?

The next days were simply "crazy", and Melba felt like her whole life was coming to an explosive end. Papa left to travel to East Texas, telling Mama to start packing up. Mama was frantic with worry, and she cried all the time. Her pregnancy was in its seventh month, and she was moving slower with every day. Not only was Mama distraught about the move, but now she worried constantly because there would soon be another mouth to feed! Melba was forced to help Mama with the packing, AND put up with G.W. and Lindell acting like ornery older brothers. Even though they were full of themselves, Melba knew both her brothers were unhappy, too. None of them knew what would happen when they actually got to this new place in East Texas. Papa had said he planned to look for work in Kilgore, a town just north of Joinerville. He thought Kilgore would be a good place for his family because it was a farm town that already had railroad service, a post office, and schools. All Melba knew was the chaos of this sudden change; she just knew her life would never be the same. Maybe Papa was right, maybe not, but change was surely coming.

CHAPTER 14

Just three weeks later, Papa returned to Damon to get the family. He was filled with excited anticipation because he had found a new job in Kilgore! Gulf Oil needed workers to handle the pumping jacks on the new oil wells and Papa's experience with Sinclair helped him secure one of these jobs; he was ecstatic! He would no longer have to "roughneck"; the new job was a big promotion for him! Gulf had lease houses for the oilfield workers, and Papa had one ready for the family. There would be no tents or shanties for HIS family! Mama was appeased, but still unhappy about leaving her friends in Damon. She seemed to worry constantly about the new baby that was coming soon. Melba thought she needed to stop being whiney and get a grip. After all, Melba was never allowed to whine and cry and she really had little patience for Mama's histrionics!

On February 12, 1931, the family left Damon with all their belongings piled into a borrowed pickup truck. The kids all sat in the truck-bed and helped hold everything in place during the bumpy 6-hour drive. Despite Mama's advanced stage of pregnancy, she was actually in good spirits as they set out on the newest adventure.

That afternoon, Mama and the kids saw their new town for the first time. Kilgore was nestled in the beautiful, hilly, piney woods of East Texas, but its formerly pristine streets were muddy and black with oil. People were everywhere, and all seemed to be in a huge hurry; the town was bustling. Wooden oil derricks, hurriedly constructed, set on land just off the streets, and the noise of pumps filled the air. There were derricks crowding stores and businesses. Papa drove down the main street in town which was lined with small businesses interspersed with derricks, torches, separators, storage tanks and all sorts of oil field debris. Melba tried to take it all in, wondering how so much could be going on in one place. Flares blazed with burning natural gas as what she would soon learn were "separators" directed petroleum into pipe lines after removing it from the natural gas flowing from the wells. The air was thick with smoke and the ground was charcoal. Jeannie was in awe because of all the people and frenetic activity, but she whined about the "dirt". This new town was nothing like Damon, even with the oil wells they'd grown up with. Damon was quiet, settled and, Sister thought, civilized. Brother and Lindell pretended to know all about "wildcatter" oil production and their cockiness made Melba want to punch them for being such smart-asses! They refused to act impressed with the crowds of people and the craziness of this town named Kilgore! In spite of G.W. and Lindell's irritating behavior, Papa's excitement was contagious. Even with the anxiety of being in a new town and of having a new baby on the way, his energy infected all of them. When they arrived at the small and rapidly constructed oil field housing area, everyone was in high spirits despite the glamour-less dwelling they encountered. They had a house to live in; they were home!

CHAPTER 15

Within a few days, the family was as settled as possible. Mama and Papa bought groceries and life once again became "normal". Mama learned the name of the town doctor from one of the neighbors, and made an appointment to see Dr. Allums the following week. Papa went to work early each morning, walking the four miles into town to tackle the rigs.

The kids were registered at Kilgore Elementary and Kilgore High School and days at school took most of their time. Anna Jean was in 5th grade at Kilgore Elementary, so she was still in just one teacher's class; Melba thought she was lucky! Of course, Melba was already in 9th grade because of her "grade skipping" in Damon. At just 12, she was younger than any of her classmates (and the youngest kid in Kilgore High!) and was, as usual, having trouble making friends. Most of the other kids just ignored Melba, but there were a few who went out of their way to belittle and bully her. It was this first year in Kilgore that really solidified Melba's "fighting" instincts; she was NOT going to let the "bad kids" win! (In truth, the majority of the most hurtful classmates were wealthy, or so it seemed to her. They came from houses in town and their fathers were in charge of the growing oil fields. Some of them loved to make fun of Melba's clothes and hair. It was not much different from the treatment she'd had in Damon.) Each morning, students gathered outside the school building to talk, play around, tease and gossip. Melba always wished she could hide somewhere until the bell rang for classes to begin, but, sadly, there was no place to go.

"Hey, Melba!" one of the rich girls said with a snicker. "Do you wanna join our group? We're talking about the sale at Jordan's Dress Shop and the outfits we plan to buy after class today." This question was met with laughter from the other girls surrounding Lydia. Melba looked away and pretended not to hear them. She was SO mad at Lydia, but she determined not to let her ruin the day. Lydia was just plain mean, and Melba wanted to punch her. Of course, she'd never really punch anyone, even Lydia. But Melba wanted to do something, anything, to get away from Lydia and the humiliation of knowing she was deliberately out to hurt her. Lydia was just a bully, Melba realized, and at the same time she knew she had no way to escape. Then, when things were looking worse than grim, a girl from Melba's English class appeared.

"Hi!" she smiled. "Let's go over by the entry and sit on the steps so we can talk. I simply MUST tell you a secret!" Melba's relief at Janice's words almost made her feel faint. She smiled back and said, "Yes, let's!" From that moment, Melba had an ally. Her school world was about to change. Janice's "secret" was especially fun to hear because it involved Lydia.

"Did you know that Lydia got kicked off the newspaper staff yesterday?" asked Janice. "Rumor has it that Mr. Lethem, the teacher in charge of Bulldog Review, accused her of making up some of the stuff she wrote in her reports about clubs. She is in BIG trouble!" With that, Janice looked conspiratorially at Melba and raised her eyebrows with a smile.

"Isn't that just toooooo bad?" Melba had to laugh; things were looking up at Kilgore High!

With Janice, school days started to be almost enjoyable. Soon, she was eating lunches with several other girls along with Janice. The very things Melba had wished for began to happen. Janice, Betty and Nancy were fun-loving and zany, so it was easy to talk and laugh in their company. It turned out their fathers, like Papa, worked the oil fields. None of them had much money, but they made up for being poor by being witty and smart. Once again, life was good.

CHAPTER 16

The month of March seemed extra short as the family settled into a routine and all of them got ready for the birth of the baby. Dr. L.L. Allums (one of Kilgore's three physicians) assigned a midwife to help with Mama's delivery; he understood Mama and Papa could not afford a hospital delivery. Mama met with Mrs. Cooper on two occasions, and they made plans for the impending birth of the baby. Melba overheard some of their conversations as the two women planned for the day the baby would be ready. Mama told Mrs. Cooper that her other children were born at home, too, and that there were no "complications". Melba wondered what THAT meant, but when she asked Mama, she was "shushed" and told to stop worrying about "grown-up" things.

That just made Melba worry even more about what was going to happen. She was left to imagine all sorts of things about having a baby, and her thoughts were scary. What was going to happen to Mama? Did having a baby hurt really bad? What if something was wrong with the baby, or what if Mama died? Not knowing much about "birthing", Melba had to rely on what she'd seen when animals had their young, and those memories were far-from-comforting! Mama had taken to her bed right after the move to Kilgore, and she complained constantly about pain and discomfort, becoming more and more demanding of attention. Melba, as usual, had to handle extra duties not expected of any of the other kids, and she spent all the time she wasn't at school waiting on Mama.   It was a relief when Mama went into labor on the evening of March 30th. Papa went to get Mrs. Cooper and he asked Mr. Jones, the next door neighbor who had a telephone in his house, to call Aunt Dorleita and tell her the baby was on the way. Melba wanted to run out of the house when Mama started moaning and screaming, but Papa told her she was in charge of Anna Jean.

"Stay put, Sister! I need you to take care of Jeannie, and Mrs. Cooper may need something, too", Papa said with a stern voice.

Of course, G.W. and Lindell got to go to the neighbor's house. As always, they didn't have to put up with any "inconveniences"!

That night was the longest Melba could ever remember because Mama's cries and Anna Jean's questions and fears kept Sister from even THINKING about sleep! Mrs. Cooper must have been really good at her job since she kept Mama at least a little bit settled in between contractions (Yes, Melba learned a lot about childbirth that night, and the timing of contractions became almost simple to figure out!). Finally, on March 31st at 7:32 in the morning, Bobby Darwin came into the world. He was a healthy 8 pound boy. Melba hoped Mama would soon be "normal" again. At least she was sleeping now, as was little Bobby! By the end of the day the whole family was back home. Of course, Melba had to cook dinner, clean up the kitchen, and take care of Anna Jean, but all that was certainly better than listening to the misery of childbirth! At least Mama and the baby were both okay, thank the Lord! Getting adjusted to a newborn baby would take some time, but they were all glad Bobby had finally arrived!

CHAPTER 17

As the spring days went by, Oscar and Annie's kids began to make the most of their new hometown. It was certainly PRETTIER than Damon, and having lots of trees packed on hilly terrain was nice! The days began to warm up, and even the long walk to school wasn't so bad! Lindell and G.W., unlike Melba, liked Kilgore High School, especially since they were both being chased by lots of girls as the "new guys". Try as she might, Melba just couldn't figure out HOW they managed to make friends and fit in so easily. It was simply easier for boys, she fumed. Besides, Brother and Lindell were already playing football and they got to stay after school to work out while Melba had to walk to the elementary school to meet Anna Jean and then get both of them home as fast as possible.

Mama's health was still bad since Bobby's birth last month, and she relied on the girls to watch him anytime they weren't in class. Melba really resented the way things had become even more irritating at home with Bobby to look after practically non-stop! Mama relied on Sister to wash the diapers, walk Bobby when he fussed, and bring him to her for feedings. It was just too much! On top of that, Melba ended up cooking most of the meals for the whole family and keeping watch over Anna Jean, too. Jeannie WAS able to help, and that was a good thing. It was just that MOST of the jobs involved things that were hard for her to handle so her "help" was minimal. Life felt to Melba like she'd been thrown a curve; sometimes she just wanted to take off on her own. As always, though, Melba kept her feelings to herself; she was determined to protect her thoughts and dreams. It was the dreams that gave her the strength and stamina to keep on "keeping on".

Fortunately, Bobby was a really good baby. He was a lot less demanding than Mama OR Anna Jean, and sometimes Melba even had time to do things just for herself. She liked to think about clothing and how she could create some really snazzy designs. The rest of her first year in Kilgore was taken up with school and with using any "free" time to develop her new passion for making clothes.

The truth was, Melba had a real talent for sewing, and this newly-discovered skill had the potential to make her life MUCH better. For Melba, sewing was easy (kind of like solving a puzzle), and it was great fun to create her own patterns. Mama even encouraged Melba's hobby, much to her surprise. Aunt Dorleita was a good seamstress, and she helped out by giving Melba fabric whenever she had any leftover material. Anna Jean even benefitted because Sister made dresses for her, too. The girls didn't have a lot of clothes, but Melba loved the few outfits she made.

What hung in her closet in Kilgore soon almost made her forget about those humiliating hand-me-downs and patched dresses she'd worn in elementary school back in Damon. Melba felt, in comparison, quite pretty! Sewing was a great creative outlet, and, for the newly transplanted pre-teen, a good way to feel special. Melba knew no other KHS kids who could design and make really cute clothes that were unique AND fashionable. Making clothes became a step in the right direction for her as she looked for ways to rise above poverty and fit in…

CHAPTER 18

By the beginning of Melba's tenth grade year, even though the nation was deep in the Depression and the family had no extra money, things began to get better. Papa had been right to move them to Kilgore because the oil boom kept the fast-growing town from feeling the worst of the Depression. He could put food on the table and could even provide a few "extras" like shoes for the kids in the winter.

Before long, Janice was looking at Melba's new outfits longingly. "Melba, how do you know what's going to look so snazzy?" she wheedled on a warm September afternoon while over at Melba's. "I'd give anything to have a dress like this!"

"I just like this fabric," Melba stated. "Aunt Dorleita had a few extra yards of this floral printed blue calico and she let me have it. I love the way it feels!"

"But the way you made the waist so slim and added the fabric-covered belt and buttons is what makes the outfit really girly", Janice insisted. "It looks cool even if it IS only cotton calico."

Melba wasn't sure the dress was a fashion statement, but she decided to wear it to school the next day, anyway. "Just let Lydia or Gaye Nell say something catty!" she thought as she got ready for bed. It WAS nice to have Janice on her side!! Her compliments really DID boost Melba's morale, and that was a rare event, indeed!

The next morning came with the usual routines at home. Melba had to feed the chickens, gather the newly laid eggs (all SIX of them!), change Bobby's diaper and take him to Mama for nursing, help Anna Jean brush and braid her hair, dress herself, eat a fast breakfast of oatmeal and hurry out the door to walk to school. Of course Lindell and G.W. had to torment her about wearing a NEW dress to school, saying, "Who do you think you are, the Queen of England?" Melba just sniffed loudly and said, "What's it to you?"

When she reached Kilgore High, the usual kids were already hanging out in their "assigned" places. Most of them ignored Melba as she walked down the sidewalk, but a few of the girls pointed and started whispering among themselves. Melba was sure they were talking about her, but she tried to ignore them as she frantically searched for Janice or Nancy or Betty. None of her friends were anywhere to be seen, and at that moment Melba wanted to run and hide. Just when she was about to bolt, Betty appeared near the entry steps calling out, "Melba! Wow! I LOVE your new dress!"

Melba was so relieved she almost started crying. She quickly joined Betty who was touching Melba's dress and repeatedly saying "Wow! That dress is swell! You look simply nobby!"

Betty and Melba were soon joined by Janice and Nancy. Their compliments made Melba feel proud of her creation, and the fear she'd felt earlier simply melted away. It was another step in the right direction for the girl from Damon. Maybe she wasn't all wet or stupid after all!

CHAPTER 19

Not surprisingly, one of the classes Melba enjoyed most at KHS was Homemaking. It was one of two electives allowed that first year, and Melba thought the teacher, Mrs. Daniels, hung the moon. Mrs. Daniels was beautiful. Her hair, makeup and fashion style were greatly admired by all the students, and Melba was simply mesmerized by the young educator.

Mrs. Daniels quickly recognized the creativity and intelligence in Melba and was delighted by her self-taught sewing skills. In fact, she was truly astonished that Melba was cutting and sewing cloth on the bias since that ability was far advanced and unexpected from a fledgling seamstress.

To her credit, Mrs. Daniels chose to mentor Melba. She made sure Melba was allowed to visit her classroom during study hall, and she spent time talking with Melba about both her creativity in clothing design and her ability to recognize high quality in fabric and fashion. She encouraged Melba to learn more about fashion by sharing such journals as *Women's Home Companion*, *McCalls*, *Pictorial Review*, *Good Housekeeping*, *Cosmopolitan*, and *Ladies Home Journal*, providing copies of these magazines for Melba to read. Even though the majority of the magazines' articles and pictures seemed to focus on keeping women at home and dressed simply, some of the articles talked about fashion trends in Europe and New York. Those were the ones Melba greedily devoured! Just seeing photographs of the newest "looks" was the only catalyst she needed to fuel her creative instincts; Melba found the magazines really juicy!

Melba told her friends, "Mrs. Daniels is the best teacher I've ever had! She understands how I feel about beautiful things. She understands Mama can't really help me achieve my dreams. She knows I can learn to be a better person and she wants to help me! I like the way she talks to me about going to college after high school and about reading everything I can get my hands on; Mrs. Daniels understands the importance of education for my future!"

School became, again, the best sanctuary for Melba. The time she spent with her homemaking teacher was the best part of every school day.

CHAPTER 20

After one of the "normal" days at KHS, the kids arrived home to find Mama terribly upset. In fact, she was crying and pacing the floor with Bobby in her arms. Papa had come home earlier that afternoon in terrible pain, and he was in big trouble. He couldn't see! Dr. Allums was there, and Papa was groaning and moaning. It was horrible! The fact that Papa was HOME at that time of day was all the kids needed to hear to know whatever was wrong was really bad.

Mama said Papa was working a new well and the sulphur gas from it was thick and strong. Although the sulphur smell was really bad, Papa said he got used to it and really didn't notice it after awhile. Some of the men got sick from breathing the gas, but Papa said he wasn't bothered by it and seemed okay. After awhile, though, his eyes started itching and then they began to feel like they had dust in them. Instead of quitting and getting away from the gas fumes, Papa kept on working. He said his hands were covered with black oil, and he had to use a rag to wipe his eyes. They kept on bothering him, though, and finally started burning like fire. No matter how much he wiped them, the burning just got worse. That was when he came home. Dr. Allums had done his best to clean Papa's eyes, and had used some drops in them, but the pain was severe.

Dr. Allums said he'd done all he could. He told Mama and us that he'd seen some bad outcomes when other oil workers got "gassed". The only thing to do, he said, was keep

Papa in a dark room and use the drops he left by his bed. Only time would tell whether Papa would lose his eyesight, and the doctor said he'd come back the next day to see how things were going. By morning, Papa looked terrible; his eyes were swollen almost shut, they were bright red and oozing pus-filled tears. We were sure he'd go blind, and it seemed Papa thought so, too. Some of the neighbors came over to check on him, and we heard other stories about "gassed" eyes. To our immense relief in the midst of all the doomsday stories, some of the workers who'd seen the affliction before told Papa his eyes would clear up in a few days. We sure did hope that was true! Meanwhile, Papa just lay in bed with his eyes shut. Opening them even a fraction was excruciating, so he had to keep them closed. Dr. Allums came to the house every morning, but none of us thought he was helping Papa since we'd never seen Papa so sick. He was practically blind and told Mama he was sure he'd never get his eyesight back the way it was before the "gas poisoning". Brother, Lindell and Melba were as distraught as Mama and had all but given up any hope.

It seemed absolutely miraculous, then, when to everyone's surprise Papa woke up on the fourth day and actually got out of bed. It was so unexpected that the entire family was astonished! Papa said his eyes felt much better and he claimed his sight was almost normal. Amazingly, his eyes looked just about as good as they had before the gas; it was hard to believe! Of course, they were still a little red, but the swelling was practically gone. That was one time G.W., Lindell, Melba and Anna Jean all felt so relieved they almost cried. They loved Papa, and the thought of him not able to see   was devastating. Besides, if Papa was unable to work the wells, they knew they would starve. He was the rock of their family; Mama had never held a job.

Against all odds, the very next day Papa walked to work. He vowed to stay away from sulphur gas, regardless of what the rig bosses wanted. If they refused to protect the workers, Papa vowed he'd speak up and demand no one work wells that were leaking extreme sulphur fumes. Melba wondered if he could really stand firm with the boss men. After all, Papa HAD to support the family. "Time will tell..." she mused.

CHAPTER 21

By the end of those first two years in Kilgore, Buster and Annie's kids were feeling like they belonged. Melba was happy with the new friends she'd made and the teachers she looked up to. Besides Mrs. Daniels, Melba loved her English teacher, Pinky Hart. Miss Hart was hard to please, and she drove her students unmercifully to be well-versed writers. Miss Hart made every student in her classes learn proper English, and all of them were required to become experts at diagramming complex sentences. Besides that, every student was expected to produce two detailed and extensive research papers each semester in addition to a plethora of essays and summaries of novels.

Miss Hart was not nice; she was stern, demanding, unyielding, and unwilling to even pretend to encourage "average". Her expectations were high, and she never accepted mediocre work from anyone. Melba did well in Miss Hart's class; her creativity in writing was in step with her creativity in clothing design, and she loved to write! Miss Hart reviewed all Melba's work with great detail, and she certainly never hesitated to use her (dreaded!) red pen. The critiques helped Melba immensely because her goal was to earn an "A" from Miss Hart. Every comment and every red mark was received with serious regard and contemplation regarding how to improve on the next assignment.

All the students at KHS had Miss Hart for English I, II, III, and IV; she was the only English teacher on the campus!

Many feared her classes and all the students talked about how hard she was. No one was immune from her demands, and a lot of students failed one or more of her courses. Some even thought they were lucky if they failed and had to take one of the required English classes in summer school. Miss Hart did not teach during the summer, thank God! The summer school English teachers were always recruited from other courses (usually from Civics or American History), and they were never as hard as Miss Hart.

Of course, the KHS students who struggled with English hated the unyielding teacher known as "Pinky" Hart. There were all sorts of rumors about this spinster teacher, but almost everyone believed she liked to party and she was reputed to frequently hang out at Mattie's Dance Hall.

Mattie Castlebury's ballroom was the most popular entertainment venue in East Texas at the time, and Mattie knew just what to do to keep her business "number one". With an undisputed reputation for having the best dance music in the area, she kept the ballroom hopping. There was no slow music played at Mattie's. She would only book the best local talent and traveling bands, and her ballroom crowds had grown so much by the early 1930s that she was starting to book nationally known acts. The yellow wood framed building was usually packed.

Mattie's Dance Hall was built up off the ground on a wooden frame. During prohibition, one of her employees, Tim Templeton, would sit in a room built underneath the ballroom and sell bootleg liquor to her patrons through a trap door in the floor. Although many city officials and authorities frequented her place, she was never busted for bootleg alcohol sales, probably because she did not tolerate "drunken patrons" and had the undesirables escorted out of her establishment at the first hint of impropriety. Even in the year of Martial Law in four East Texas counties, including Gregg where Mattie's was located, her establishment was never closed down.

Between the best music and the popular "dime a dance" taxi dancers, Mattie's was talked about across the nation. Mattie played songs like Bing Crosby's "Brother Can You Spare a Dime", and brought in artists like Duke Ellington to play such greats of his as "It Don't Mean a Thing If You Ain't Got That Swing". She even booked Tommy Dorsey who, of course, played "I'm Getting Sentimental Over You". If Miss Hart was a normal, fun-loving woman, why would she go anywhere else for an evening of "good times", brooded Melba.

By booking the most sought-after national bands and orchestras, Mattie was rewarded with crowds of fun-seekers at her dance hall on a nightly basis. But in 1932, the year Melba was in ninth grade, Mattie's Ball Room would have to prepare for some fierce competition! A rival from nearby Henderson saw a great investment opportunity in the Kilgore/Longview area and decided to build a spectacular "other" bar on "Honky Tonk City" row. The dance hall would be located where Highway 31 intersected Interstate 20. In this popular "entertainment" area, there were at least 12 other dance halls crowding the road. Of course, no alcohol was officially served due to prohibition, but plenty of "bootleg" booze made the scene. The new club was dreamed up by entrepreneurial genius, Hugh Cooper. His first dance hall had done well in Henderson, especially after the oil boom brought so many new folks to the area. Reportedly with the help of a few "butter and egg men" from Longview, Hugh Cooper bought land two miles outside of town and started to build his new honky tonk. It was the buzz of Kilgore High, and Melba heard all about it, especially by listening to her brothers and their friends! Lindell and G.W. shared lots of stories about the up-and-coming Palm Isle Club; they heard all about the cool establishment going up just outside the city limits, and told Melba how much moolah was going into the construction.

What Brother and Lindell said was true: Mr. Cooper's club was huge by local standards. It was a large-framed structure that was 80 feet wide and 200 feet long. The front of the building was brick and lined with over a dozen moveable windows for ventilation. Inside, the floors were wooden as were the walls, and there was a huge wooden dance floor. Near the front door on the north end of the building, there was a bar speculated to be near the length of the building all the way down the right wall. At the far end of the building, a 20 by 30 foot stage was centered with a grand stone fireplace – the type you would expect to see in a large mountain lodge – to its left. This provided the only source of heat for the majority of the building. (Central heat in the 1930s meant your fireplace or stove was in the middle of the room.) The building cost Cooper and his investors over $2,000 which was a huge amount of money at the time, and it was big enough to hold 1800 people! At the end of its completion there was no larger dance hall anywhere in Texas than the Palm Isle Club. Melba and her brothers laughed about the day THEY would go to the Reo!

Even after the Reo opened, Mattie's Ballroom remained popular, but during the next few years, conflict with the Reo Palm Isle escalated. Hugh Cooper brought some of the best talent in America to his new club, and his bookings gave Mattie's Ballroom a lot of grief!

Nationally known singers and bands played at the Palm Isle almost weekly. Among the acts brought there were the Glenn Miller Band with songs like "Let's Do It" and "My Kind of Love", Tommy Dorsey who wowed the audiences with "Boogie Woogie" and "Once In a While", Ozzie Nelson and his band playing "Everyone But Me" and "Whirligig", Ella Fitzgerald singing "A-Tisket, A-Tasket" and "All or Nothing at All", and Louis Armstrong playing songs like "That Rhythm Man". People drove for hours to the stretch of road between Kilgore and Longview to dance on the huge dance floor and listen to performers, some of them already legends in American music. The sweet success of the Palm Isle put many small competitors out of business in the Longview - Kilgore area, but Mattie's Ballroom was an exception; Mattie's still stood strong with loyal patrons.

Melba, G.W. and Lindell heard all the talk about the Palm and Mattie's. They were, rightfully, curious about what Mattie could do to keep her business thriving. Everyone in Kilgore knew Mattie Castlebury, and her spunk, tenacity and refusal to allow her club to have a bad reputation enabled her to maintain the respect of most. Melba asked, "What will Miss Mattie do if folks stop going to HER place?"

G.W. laughed and stated, "Mattie can handle ANYTHING! She won't let Mr. Cooper steal her customers. I think she'll come up with lots of 'incentives' to dance at HER ballroom!"

"I guess you're right, Brother, but I can't help but worry about Mattie. She's no twit, and it will be unfair if all her hard work is for nothing! Even Mama says Mattie's helps keep Kilgore safe since the patrons can't get drunk or use bad language in her club. I don't want that grandstand man, Cooper, ruining things for her! I hope her base of loyal customers will see to it that Mattie's stays open!" Melba clearly meant what she said; her eyes were suddenly filled with tears.

CHAPTER 22

In the midst of all the "stuff" going on in and around Kilgore in 1932 during Melba's 10th grade year, things that would profoundly affect citizens around the entire country were happening at the national level. Because the presidential election was so important, students at KHS heard a lot about it in their civics classes. Mama and Papa talked about it, too. They liked the fact that Franklin Roosevelt was a Democrat. Brother and Lindell said they liked FDR and wanted him to win. Melba liked him, too, but she had questions about some of his plans. Mostly, she wanted to know some specifics about how he intended to make things better when everyone was struggling to get food on the table. Melba had to admit it was really cool that the president-elect used one of the most popular songs that everyone loved, "Happy Days Are Here Again" as his campaign theme!

On Election Day in November of 1932, the man known by most as "FDR" defeated Republican Herbert Hoover. New leadership was definitely what the American public wanted: Roosevelt won 57% of the vote and carried all but six states. Melba and her brothers had fun talking about how he won using a SONG as his "ticket"! G.W. and Lindell joked about going to Washington to work for FDR.

Lindell said, "He's definitely cool! Let's get going with the happy days!" G.W. followed with, "It's about time to tear down all the shantytowns and listen to a leader who has new ideas! I'm on board with FDR!"

In his acceptance speech, Roosevelt declared, "I pledge you, I pledge myself, to a new deal for the American people... This is more than a political campaign. It is a call to arms."

It was true that the election was conducted under the shadow of the Great Depression in the United States, and was affected by the new alliances created during those deeply disruptive times. Roosevelt and the Democratic Party mobilized the expanded ranks of the poor as well as organized labor, ethnic minorities, urbanites, and Southern whites. Melba thought life might never be the same, and she reasoned "never being the same" would surely be a good thing! Strangely, it seemed odd that Herbert Hoover was no longer in charge, even though she never had liked what happened to people when they lost their homes during the "bad days" and had to live in "Hoovervilles".

Roosevelt began his presidency by denouncing Hoover's failures to restore prosperity or even halt the downward slide, and he ridiculed Hoover's huge deficits. Roosevelt had campaigned on the Democratic platform advocating "immediate and drastic reductions of all public expenditures, abolishing useless commissions and offices, consolidating departments and bureaus, and eliminating extravagances and for a sound currency to be maintained at all hazards."

The one thing that made the nation's citizens believe in Mr. Roosevelt was his amazing optimism about America's ability to recover its greatness. The fact that FDR was crippled by polio in 1921 at the age of 39 yet continued his life enthusiastically and with boundless energy and a positive attitude. Roosevelt determinably used his personal victory over polio to show the entire nation that giving up is never an option. He renewed the national spirit just by being himself! And the programs he started got the country back on its feet. In his first 100 days in office, which began in January of 1933, Roosevelt spearheaded major legislation and issued a profusion of executive orders that instituted what became known as the New Deal. The New Deal was, simply, a variety of programs designed to produce relief (government jobs for the unemployed), recovery (economic growth), and reform (through regulation of Wall Street, banks and transportation). The most popular of all the New Deal agencies – and Roosevelt's favorite – was the Civilian Conservation Corps (CCC), which hired 250,000 unemployed young men to work on rural projects. Word was out all over America about the "programs" started by FDR, and millions of workers enthusiastically joined the newly-created work forces.

Some men, like Papa, said the new president was making things too easy for men who needed to do things on their own. Papa argued that all people needed to do was take a look at East Texas and the use of Martial Law by Governor Sterling. Controlling the outrageous overproduction of oil that was ruining profits for the landowners had affected Papa and every other oilfield worker in the area! Even though Papa HAD supported FDR and voted for him, when the many changes instituted by Roosevelt were mandated, Papa decided the new president had gone too far. Papa thought FDR was ruining the country with his "crazy" notions. Government- sponsored jobs were just too much for Papa to accept. Melba,

G.W. and Lindell thought, with teenage smugness, Pa needed to keep his distain to himself, at least until some of the programs were in place for awhile. Maybe FDR would prove to be on the right track and Papa would change his mind…

Since FDR was so proud of his favorite New Deal Agency, the Civilian Conservation Corp, he paid a lot of attention to activities carried out by the recruits. At most of the CCC Camps, the days were long and hard. But in the evening, there was time for games, education classes, and even plays and variety shows put on by the enrollees. Most of those who adjusted to the military discipline in the camps re-enlisted when their six months were up. The men could stay in the CCC up to two years. But the biggest legacy of the agency may have been the hope it provided both the young men and their families. Unknown and unimagined by 14 year old Melba, a young man from Tulsa, Oklahoma who joined the CCC in 1930 would become her future husband, Clarence Earl (CE) Winters.

For the first few months under FDR's leadership, Americans watched and waited for more "bad" things to happen. After all, they were in the midst of the Great Depression; how could their new President work with Congress to turn things around? It seemed only the few who owned prospering businesses believed in the newly-elected administration; they were accustomed to success.

Hugh Cooper must have had some "inside information" when he kept his Reo Palm Isle open during the worst years of the depression. At least that's what G.W. (always the one with risqué news!) told his siblings when prohibition ended in 1933! The Palm Isle immediately opened its huge bar and business mushroomed. At the same time, profits at Mattie's Dance Hall soared as a small liquor shop was added onto the ballroom building. Prior to prohibition, a liquor store could not be in the same building as the ballroom, so a customer would have to go out the front door and into another room to buy liquor, then return to buy ice and setups in the ballroom. It was simply a slight variation of the way use of liquor had been handled in previous years. Of course, with the end of prohibition, all the dance halls made quick changes to allow sales of liquor on their premises. Mattie's only REAL competition continued to be the Palm Isle.

CHAPTER 23

As it turned out, seven years later events out of both Hugh Cooper's and Mattie Castlebury's control created a situation that would change everything. In 1941, Hugh received his draft notice. He was going to war. Competition with Mattie, he reasoned, might turn into a good thing. Cooper spent the next days musing over what to do with his successful ballroom. He couldn't simply close it; he still owed money on the mortgage. He determined he would have to find someone to run the club for him while he served his country, and who could handle the job better than his fiercest competitor, Mattie Castlebury?

Mattie, of course, had taken a little frame building in Kilgore in 1931 and made it world famous for the music and dancing it provided. Mattie really knew how to run a club. When you entered Mattie's Ballroom, the first person you would see would be Mattie. Mattie was always dressed in a beautiful evening gown and pearls. Her make up was "movie star" perfect, and her dark hair was accented with popular 1930s spit curls cascading from her center part down across her forehead to a small curl that looped right above the bridge of her nose. She always looked amazing! Mattie never drank or smoked. It is said she would often tell her male customers as they bought their dancing tickets from her, "I sure hope you boys aren't going to be smoking in there tonight."

Mattie was not only a very sharp business person but also a straightforward lady. Though Hugh Cooper's Palm Isle Club had devoured other competitors, Mattie's Ballroom stood strong and kept a happy crowd of revelers throughout the week that became an absolute mob on the weekends. With all this in mind, Cooper worked on a "deal" to offer Mattie. After some serious negotiations, she finally accepted his proposal to run the Palm Isle while he was overseas.

Dividing her time between the two clubs was exhausting, yet Mattie slaved to operate both her ballroom and the Palm Isle for an entire year. As the war progressed, money got tight and Mattie realized she could not keep both clubs open. She was able to contact Hugh Cooper who was in England and explain her interest in buying the Palm Isle Club. Being a strong arbitrator and a very headstrong lady, Mattie eventually succeeded in convincing him to sell his club. Cooper even financed the deal for her! Mattie purchased the land, building, and business for $5,750. She had always paid cash for her investments, but could only give Cooper a down payment of $2,875, with the agreement to pay $150 a month for the balance. As it turned out, however, the debt was paid off in six months. Mattie's Ballroom closed for good, and on September 27, 1943, the Palm Isle Club, now known as Mattie's Palm Isle, opened for business.

For a number of years, Mattie brought in large crowds of partiers, entertaining them with such stars as Elvis Presley, Jim Reeves, Ray Price, Waylon Jennings, Boots Randolf, Jerry Lee Lewis, Willie Nelson, Mickey Gilley, and many others with claims to fame. The Reo was a jewel of a club in the heart of East Texas!

CHAPTER 24

The "taxi dancers" at the Reo made good money for a night of dancing, but often the girls had other motives. While they danced through the evening, they met men who made a lot of money. Although hanky panky was not allowed, the girls did find love on the dance floor. Many times a man would come for dancing and companionship and meet his future wife. There were even several marriages at the Reo Palm Isle.

Over the next few years, Mattie's reputation grew. She became well-connected with important people and authorities in East Texas. One way she managed to do this was by changing her name from Castlebury to Castleberry. There was a predominant wealthy family with the name of Castleberry in nearby Longview, and she wanted people to associate her with them. Although the spelling of her name was a "con" of sorts, Mattie felt justified. The name change and other "good business" decisions ensured Mattie continued to do well in Kilgore. She became a respected and powerful woman in a place and during a time where business was mostly conducted by men. For an unmarried woman to own a successful dance hall was an amazing and highly unusual feat!

Mattie spared nothing in order to provide hospitality for her customers. She hired many people from the black community that lived in the neighborhood around the ballroom. If a vote came about to change a local ordinance or law, it was a good thing to have Mattie on your side. Because of her honest and fair dealings with blacks in East Texas, that population as a whole trusted and respected her opinion; she could influence an election by encouraging the black community to show up and vote.

Another business tactic developed by Mattie was advertising the Reo by printing stacks and stacks of signs that promoted the club. Like her money, she did not trust her advertising to anyone else and she personally drove around East Texas tacking up the signs at intersections, general stores, gas stations, and any other location where a lonely man might see them. Mattie's success made an impression on others throughout East Texas as dance halls and clubs sprang up like wildflowers, some in facilities not much larger than a one room storage garage.

As many of the oilfield families moved out of the small town of Kilgore, they settled in the nearby and larger towns of Tyler and Longview, making them fast growing. During all the unprecedented growth, East Texas became known as much more than a bustling oil-boom region. Its equally-touted fame included the best of the best in live entertainment. Nightlife was alive and thriving!

CHAPTER 25

Back at Kilgore High School during the pre-war years of 1932-1935, Mattie's success in the entertainment business fueled speculation about some of her customers. In fact, a group of the senior guys talked about seeing Miss Hart's car parked, of all places, at the Palm. There was even chatter about Miss Hart's often bloodshot eyes, and hence her nickname, "Pinky". She was the brunt of lots of jokes made by the "in crowd" at KHS, but Melba figured no one really knew the truth, and it made her furious that such nasty comments were thrown around about one of her beloved teachers. Why, she fumed, were people so black-hearted and mean?

Melba knew Miss Hart deserved to be treated with more respect. It was just another example of how unfair life could be. The more she thought about stuff kids said about Miss Hart, the angrier Melba got. After all, she knew first hand how it felt to be picked on! The more Melba thought about the ugly rumors, the more she wanted to do something to make them stop.

In truth, it was the lure of good music and upbeat dancing with the promise of enjoying a little time with other adults that kept Miss Hart returning to Mattie's Ballroom week after week. She laughed about her students' teasing and mockery of her after-school outings; in fact, the more some of the kids talked about Miss Hart's "extracurricular" activities, the more she ignored their gossip. Melba was SURE the really disrespectful talk around KHS was rumor of the meanest sort, and she really wanted to protect her teacher. But how?

During one of her English classes, a new idea entered Melba's head. It just might work! Melba decided to start her OWN rumor about Miss Hart. If nothing else, she determined, it would give the kids who wanted to ruin Miss Hart's reputation something to contend with that was contrary to the tales being circulated. Melba started with G.W. and Lindell that very afternoon.

"I heard something about Miss Hart today that will definitely surprise you!" Melba told them. "As you know, some of the guys on the football team are talking about her being a "boozer" and going out to dance halls like Mattie's Ballroom and the Reo without an escort. Well, I know the truth! She's dating one of the fiddlers in Bob Wills' band and even when his tours take him to other cities, Mr. Wills makes sure Miss Hart is given the best seats in the house. She's treated like a queen!"

"Who'd you hear that from, Sister?' G.W. demanded. "I really doubt there's any truth to that tale!"

"Well, I DO have a reliable source!" Melba stated with anger in her voice. "Why are you so sure YOU'RE right?"

"That's not what the word on the street tells me", G.W. stated authoritatively. "Miss Hart brings all this gossip on herself because she breaks all the rules about keeping a professional image and behaving morally."

"Ohhhhhhh, you are SO maddening, Brother!" Melba hissed. "Miss Hart is a good person and she has every right to go out and party on her own time! What makes you think spreading nonsense about her is the thing to do? She behaves with integrity in her classroom, and the examples she sets every day are wholesome! I'm glad she's my teacher; I've learned more about writing from her in two years than in all the rest of my years in school! I'm sick and tired of hearing ugly stories about her!" Melba was so upset she could barely get the words out without crying.

"Whoa, Sister!" G.W. pleaded. "Maybe you're right. Maybe we should try to spread this good stuff you've heard about Miss Hart and change things around here. I'm willing to help start some new rumors!"

"Well, for starters, I believe the one about Miss Hart dating a popular musician is true, and she should be admired for handling her relationship with him so discreetly!" Melba declared. "As a matter of fact, just check out the marquee for next week's events at Mattie's. The main attraction is 'Bob Wills and His Texas Playboys', and you can be sure Miss Hart won't miss a single performance!"

"I'll do that, Sister. And I DO hope you are right about Miss Hart and that fiddler. I guess it makes a good love story." With that, G.W. left the house without another word.

As the weeks went by, students at KHS began to wonder if the "rumors" about Miss Hart and her musician friend had merit. After all, Miss Hart certainly came to school looking nicer than usual. Her hairstyle (and color!) changed for the better, and she lost the dour expression so well-known by the entire student body. In fact, she seemed HAPPY, and that, in itself, was a huge change in Miss Hart. Maybe she and one of the musicians WERE dating, Melba mused, as some of the usual snide remarks about her began to taper off.   Melba felt gratified. Her idea to help end the nasty rumors with a different type of rumor seemed to be working, thank goodness, and what harm had her "little white lie" done?

CHAPTER 26

Even with all the incredible changes going on in the country, the spring semester of Melba's tenth grade year at KHS in 1934 would prove to be almost as unexpected in terms of "life changes". The next few months could have been considered CHALLENGING, but Melba really did not want to think she had it tougher than most of the other kids. Papa and Mama still managed to provide enough food for the whole family, and even took in Mama's cousin, Sam.

With Papa's help, 20 year old Sam soon got a job in the oil fields as a roughneck. Mama said Sam just needed a chance to make some money and grow up. She and Papa said it was a "second chance" for Sam. For awhile, the new arrangement seemed to be working. Sam shared Brother and Lindell's room; Bobby still slept in Mama and Papa's room. Melba, as always, shared a room with Anna Jean. She continued to help Mama with just about everything. Cooking, laundry, cleaning, and watching Bobby were expected. Of course, being the oldest girl meant she had to explain everything to Jeannie and help her with lots of things, too. The only good thing, Melba thought, was the fact that school work continued to be easy for her; school wasn't the challenge!

The biggest problem was SAM. He was always pestering Melba. He wanted to talk to her and he wanted her attention any time they were both at home. When she tried to let him know she was busy, Sam got angry. Sometimes he used swear words, and even though Melba had heard them before, she was startled to hear them aimed at HER. She tried to tell Mama that Sam was trouble, but Mama just got mad and told Melba to stop being such a twit; Mama believed Sam could do no wrong. Unfortunately, Mama was mistaken…

To make matters worse, Melba was about to learn what it meant to "become a woman". Some of the other girls whispered about "the curse", but Melba really had no idea what that meant. Mama never talked to her about "growing up", and Melba, the tomboy younger sister of two older brothers, never considered that SHE would have to face FEMALE issues. Even though she knew about childbirth because of Bobby, and even though she understood SOME of the things women had to put up with, Melba had managed to stay blissfully uninformed about "the change". Because of grade-skipping, Melba was only 14; most of her girlfriends were already 16. What happened during her tenth grade year when she "got her period" was, quite literally, a shock!

In America, mothers had essentially stopped teaching their daughters about menstruation in the early part of the 19th century. Victorianism made knowledge of the body shameful, especially among women, and the informal passing of knowledge from older girls to younger ones was further inhibited by changes in the school system. With grade level classrooms, pre-teen girls were only around others their own age. Physicians and moralists took over by default and the outcome was absurd! There were so many exaggerated stories about "periods" that the truth was distorted and hard to come by. After all, women were SUPPOSED to endure their monthly "curse" without complaint. It was the current cultural belief that when "bleeding", they were unclean and to be shunned. "Whatever!" Melba would later exclaim. She would never believe all the horror stories and she hated to think about it!

With Sam in the house, Melba was constantly being teased and pestered. He just would not leave her alone! Since Mama thought Sam was nearly "perfect", nothing Melba said made any difference; Mama told her to stop being rude to their house guest. Sam played around with Anna Jean, too, but even Melba thought he was just treating her like a little sister. He certainly did not treat Melba like a "sister"! One evening after everyone was in bed, things changed dramatically from being simply irritating to being totally unacceptable and frightening; her innocence was about to be stolen.

Melba was having trouble going to sleep, and after tossing and turning for what seemed like hours, she decided to slip outside and sit on the porch. It was a dark night, but Melba knew the path to the front door and had no trouble quietly getting to the porch. The night air felt good, and she sat on one of the chairs usually "reserved" for Papa or Mama. She was lost in her thoughts when she heard the door open and saw Sam. Startled, Melba gasped and stood up.

"What are you doing out here?" she demanded when Sam moved toward her without saying anything. He had a strange look on his face and didn't even look like the same man. Instead of answering Melba, Sam grabbed her from behind, covering her mouth and whispering, "Don't scream! You know you want me to touch you!"

Melba tried to pull away, tried to bite Sam's hand, tried to scream. Her efforts were futile; Sam outweighed her by at least 80 pounds, and he was determined. With his other hand, he reached under her pajama top and fondled her breasts. Melba was terrified, squirming and kicking with all her might. Sam pushed her to the porch floor, straddled her back and said he'd really hurt her if she kept fighting him. That just made Melba fight harder. All those years of keeping up with "the boys" paid off when Melba used all her strength to head-butt Sam right in the face. With a barely-concealed roar, he rolled off her back, using the sleeve of his shirt to cover his bleeding nose.

Sam shoved Melba away and hissed, "I'll kill you if you ever tell anyone about this." Then he slipped back into the house, leaving her sobbing on the porch. Melba was shaking, but it was with anger, not fear. She would figure out a way to get rid of Sam, and she would never forgive him for what had just happened.

CHAPTER 27

By the end of Melba's eighth grade year in 1931, there were lots of changes in Kilgore. The town had grown from a tiny, rural community with a population less than 800 into a bustling town of more than 10,000 residents. The growth created all kinds of problems for the town which was forced to incorporate in 1931 in order to maintain some semblance of law and order as well as to try to provide services such as clean water, a fire department and a sewage system. Roads had to be built, lodging had to be provided, stores were needed…the list of "needs" seemed endless! Kilgore's change was simply mind-boggling, and life was challenging.

One of the most frightening things that occurred was the day Governor Ross Sterling ordered the National Guard into Kilgore. The entire oilfield region in and around Kilgore had been placed under martial law! Once more, Melba and her brothers were whispering about something they did not understand, but were trying desperately to figure out.

"What's going to happen to us, Brother?" Melba asked as the siblings gathered outside the house later that night. "I'm scared!"

Papa had come home from working a well that evening and called a "family meeting". He'd told them about Governor Sterling's order and how soldiers were pouring into town in trucks and on the train. Papa explained that no one could be on the streets after dark, and that THEY were not to go into town for any reason except school.   Papa assured the kids the "uniforms" were going to protect the residents who were working the oil field and following the law.

"Don't worry, Sister", G.W. soothed. We'll be okay as long as we stay near the house and mind our own business. The soldiers aren't here to hurt us; they're trying to control all the riff-raff and thieves who're taking over the town. It's really a good thing they're here!"

As the weeks and months followed, changes mandated by the National Guard became just another part of life in Kilgore. There were lots of arrests. One of the Rangers, "Lone Wolf" Gonzaullas, was feared by anyone breaking the law; he did not hesitate to do whatever it took to control the "bad guys". His partner, Bob Goss, was also greatly feared. Considered a sharpshooter, he never hesitated to use his gun to settle matters. When these two men rode into town, the smart lawbreakers rode out!

On the night of March 2, 1931, they quietly brought a few lawmen they could trust into town. Shrouded by darkness, they raided every honky tonk, beer joint, pool hall, dance hall, domino parlor, gambling den and house of ill repute, closing them down and arresting owners, workers and patrons with no leniency. There was no jail in Kilgore, but the Rangers improvised nicely. Gonzaullas and Goss had no concerns about providing either shelter or comfort for the scalawags who had the bad judgment to bring their lawlessness to East Texas! These Rangers knew all about crime and punishment!

Without a moment's hesitation, the lawmen herded their hundreds of prisoners to a wooded corner of town and hooked them up to a makeshift, home-made "trotline" that consisted of huge chains wrapped around pine trees and locked in place. The scalawags sat or slept on the ground with no cover and no comforts. At the time, the amenities did not matter to the Rangers! A few days later, the little Baptist Church was turned into a jail which was certainly less comfortable than the "shelter" under the pine trees. The log- chain trot line was dragged from the shade of the pines into the sweltering sanctuary of the church. The chains were bolted to the walls. The heat and stench made it difficult to breathe, but Gonzaullas and Goss made it clear they did not care.

Eventually, most of the prisoners were made an offer: release from the chains and a chance to leave town within four hours and NEVER return. It was commonly said, "Lone Wolf gave them four hours and they gave back three hours and fifty minutes." Few, if any, ever made the mistake of finding their way to the Trotline Baptist Church more than once. Soon, the curfew set by the Rangers was obeyed by just about everyone. When the day grew dark, Kilgore shut down!

By what Melba secretly believed was a MIRACLE, Sam announced one night after dinner that he'd be leaving. Without looking in Melba's direction, he quietly said, "Buster, I've decided to move on. Jobs in the oil field are shut down, and I can't make any money. I've got a friend in Nacogdoches who needs help on his farm."

Annie looked upset and said, "No, Sam! You're better off here, even with the Rangers in town. I know things will change soon and the wells will start producing. When that happens, the money will come back; you can make more money in the oil business than in farming. Why don't you reconsider?"

"No, Aunt Annie", Sam said, shaking his head back and forth, "I'm tired of the kind of work here in the fields, anyway. It's filthy, and I earn no respect being an 'unrefined hooligan', like the hot shots call us roughnecks. I'm done with oil." Sam's expression was one of disgust. Melba was both relieved and delighted to hear his words. Mama had never listened to anything she said about Sam not keeping his hands to himself. Mama's only response to complaints about him was becoming irritated and hostile toward MELBA. She could not wait to see him walk out the door and keep on walking!

By the next week, Sam was gone. Even Brother and Lindell seemed pleased at his departure; Melba just hoped she would never have to see Sam again!

Meanwhile, the unrest and malicious behavior contributing to the surge of crime in the little town of Kilgore seemed to ease. After awhile, violence became less and less likely in the town that only recently was ruled by thugs. Attitudes changed at a reasonably brisk pace because the rule of Martial Law was backed by Rangers like Gonzaullas and Goss who never flinched. Their delivery of "the law" was something everyone recognized as unstoppable, and, as both men said, "A good, first-class killing is sometimes the best sermon you can preach to these kinds of people. That, they understand."

Over the next two years, legal battles raged at the state level about how to regulate the production and pricing of oil in East Texas' mega-oil reservoir. Swings in oil prices seemed as unstoppable as the rule of Martial Law had been! Kilgore's crazy drilling over the past decade reeked havoc with the oil economy and oil producers ended up at the bottom of a very deep financial hole. If twelve thousand dollars was required to drill a well, it became necessary to produce as many as two hundred thousand barrels of oil just to break even. The days of "fast riches" came to a screeching halt!

In February of 1934, the rule of martial law was finally ended by Governor Sterling. Oil producers and legislators agreed to proration of drilling which would eventually stabilize pricing. Kilgore's "lawless" era was ending with a welcome positive change toward civility and morality. As Lone Wolf Gonzaullas, himself, said, "After things got a little better organized, and they got a little better housing, the working boys started sending for their families. When they start sending for the families, and they start having churches and schools, then you know you're getting somewhere, and you're straightened out."

Early oil boom people like Oscar Black and his family who migrated to Kilgore to work the wells and survive the Great Depression were pleased to see order returned to the streets of their town. It had not been a particularly "wholesome" town when they'd first arrived, but it wasn't the lawless town it had become over the past several years. The influx of the "bad" sort had never sat well with those who brought their families to Kilgore when the Daisy Bradford well was discovered. The changes, especially over the past two years, had been hard to endure, and Oscar's worries about his children had weighed on both him and Annie. The rough-talking, gun-toting law-breakers overtaking Kilgore had caused more difficulties than the hardships they'd endured even during the "leanest" days back in Damon. In hindsight, the positive and substantive changes to life in Kilgore were welcome, and the fact that Governor Sterling had accomplished the massive cleanup by calling in the uncompromising Texas Rangers and National Guardsmen would become fodder for many future front porch tales!

CHAPTER 28

Similar to occurrences in Kilgore where problems produced by too much of a good thing happening too fast created the need for takeover and control by the Texas Rangers and National Guard, worldwide problems brought about by the Great Depression and the ongoing aftermath of World War I were creating the beginning of severe political unrest. The unrest would eventually affect not just Europe; unrest and hostilities would continue until a second upheaval of life would overshadow other disastrous events from past history. The eventual death toll would be beyond precedent. At the time, most families in Kilgore were blissfully unaware of the deadly actions taking place in Europe.

As usual, G.W. and Lindell learned about far-away news faster than anyone else, or at least that was Melba's opinion! When any rumors came to her attention, she knew her brothers would know the facts. At least, she always reasoned, even if they didn't HAVE the facts right, they managed to find the answers.

The high school kids in Kilgore had a lot of news sources since some of the students came from families with relatives in New York City and other places where world news was commonly discussed. One day, Jake Spear, one of the popular boys whose father was president of the bank, told a group of guys in the gym, "You won't believe this! My uncle called father yesterday and told him some terrible things have happened in Germany! He said that some man named Hitler who is in charge of a group called "National Socialist Germany" ordered his Secret Service to find and kill at least 75 members of his own 'Stormtroopers,' a large group of men assigned to protect him during his Nazi meetings. My uncle said no one seems to know why he ordered their deaths, but it sounds crazy to say the least!"

G.W. wanted to know more about this man named Hitler and the things going on in Germany. He asked Jake how to get more details. The next day, Jake brought a copy of *The New York Times* to G.W.. Covering the front page, an article about what had occurred stood out like a red flag in a snowy landscape. G.W. read every word, feeling more and more anxious by the minute. Under orders from Adolf Hitler, he leaned, the Nazi Party leadership called a "meeting" of the leaders of the S.A., the "Sturmabteilungen", otherwise known as the Stormtroopers. According to the *Times*, on the morning of the meeting all the men were cold-bloodedly shot. Called "Operation Hummingbird," the murders cemented an agreement between the Nazi regime and the German Army (Reichswehr) that enabled Hitler to proclaim himself Führer of National Socialist Germany and claim absolute power.

G.W. was shocked to read about these actions, and he raced home to tell Papa what he'd learned.

"Papa! I have terrible news!" G.W. slammed the door and ran into the kitchen where Papa and Mama were sitting. Papa had just arrived home from a long day on the wells.

"What's wrong, G.W.? Is someone hurt? What happened?" Papa demanded.

"Pa, you won't believe this... It's bad news about stuff going on in Europe...in Germany! They have a new leader named Hitler. I think President Roosevelt has talked about him on the radio. Anyway, Hitler managed to get Nazi leaders to KILL a bunch of his own group of men whose job has been to PROTECT him during meetings and such. Can you understand why he'd do such a thing?"

G.W. was the most upset Melba had ever seen him. She had just walked into the house and was standing at the doorway, listening.

Both Mama and Papa looked surprised but they tried to calm G.W. down. Papa said, "G.W., you know things have been pretty messed up over there. I've heard this Hitler fellow is pretty well-liked, and he's been working with the German President... Hindenburg, isn't it, Annie? What was Hindenburg doing when this supposedly happened? I'm sure there's an explanation..."

"Papa, the newspaper said Hitler declared himself the Fuehrer, the absolute dictator, and it also said President Hindenburg died a few days before the S.A. leaders were killed. To me, that sounds like an odd coincidence...! I don't like what I read, and I sure do hope it's wrong! I'm afraid things will just get worse over there with someone like Hitler in charge." With that, G.W. went out on the porch where Melba and Lindell were standing, taking in all of their brother's conversation with Pa. Unfortunately, G.W. had no idea how accurate his prediction would be.

CHAPTER 29

While these epic changes were occurring in Germany, there were also lots of changes in 15 year old Melba, now a very young high school junior. Completely unexpectedly to some observers, Melba was becoming quite a "looker"! Her dark hair was shiny and sleek and her good friend, Liz, cut it for her in the popular "bob" style. She was slender and had a nice shape; in fact, she was as cute as a bug's ear!

Lindell and G.W. noticed how good Sister was looking, and they began to notice other guys ogling their younger sibling. All that fall, friends of the boys hung out at the Black's house. They played ball in the field across the street, threw horseshoes in the back yard, and kept an eye out for Melba. G.W. sometimes told his buddies to "lay off my Sis", but he said it half-heartedly. After all, she seemed to like the attention. He told himself he would protect her from the friends who got too "friendly"!

Around this time, G.W. acquired a new friend, a guy who was a few years older and worked in the oil fields doing roughneck jobs. It was a friendship that came about due to several unlikely circumstances. Papa and this young man named Clarence Winters happened to meet during the drilling of a new well just off Main Street in downtown Kilgore. Papa liked C.E. because he was a hard worker, a fast-learner concerning the requirements of working on a rig and the issues of safety, and a man who refused to be "baited" into altercations by other roughnecks. He carried a pistol, and he made it clear that messing with him was a bad idea. Even with his rough demeanor, Papa could see a good man beneath the hype.

On one of the first days they worked together, Papa and another floorman on the rig were in the middle of changing the drill bit on a well that was already at a depth of 3,000 feet. Papa's hands slipped and he dropped one of the pipe joints into the mud, nearly losing his grip on the new drill bit. He hollered for help. Clarence was several feet away on the left side of the platform lining up pipe joints as they were pulled, but he managed to grab the edge of the board holding the drill bit. With all three men working like crazy, they salvaged the job, screwing the bit onto the last link of pipe and dropping it into the hole so drilling could resume.

From that time on, C.E. was "the man" in Papa's eyes. He made it a point to mentor this new member of the team and the two worked together for the next few months as the well on property owned by A.P. Merritt was completed. Of course, C.E. met Oscar's family and that's when he and G.W. started hanging out. They liked playing horseshoes and placing bets on winning. The bets were for a few pennies, but it sure did make for lively competitions! Lindell hung out with Clarence and G.W., as did other guys from Kilgore High School. Clarence liked the looks of G.W.'s younger sister, Melba, but, at just 15, she was a bit too young for any serious attention from the 21 year old man...

There were lots of older women in Kilgore who thought C.E. was a "dish" with his wavy black hair, strong features, nice build and cocky attitude. He certainly had looks that turned heads, and getting smiles and "come on" glances from the ladies was almost expected! During the boom-town days in Kilgore, new faces were seen on a daily basis, so there was no real glory in being a newcomer, but C.E. got more than his share of attention. For this young man, however, the goal was making money, not finding girls to date. He flirted a little, but that was about it.

In October, an invitation to supper at the Black's home was a nice "change of pace" for Clarence. He also hoped, to be honest, for a chance to talk with Buster's daughter, Melba. She had most definitely done more than catch his eye; he wanted to get to know her better than just "the sister" of a good friend! Without even a hint of an idea that supper at the Black's would be the beginning of something really big, Clarence cleaned up for a welcome home-cooked meal and began the two-mile walk to Oscar and Annie's.

Since the last two years of his life had been spent serving in the Civilian Conservation Corp (bless President Roosevelt!) in Wyoming, C.E. had been ready for more than a change in jobs. After returning home to Tulsa to check on his mother and sister, Clarence decided to take a chance and head to East Texas where news of a fabulous oil boom made him hope for good fortune.

As the son of a sharecropper farmer from Kentucky, life had never been easy and had become even harder when the family moved to Indiana so his dad could pursue a dream of making better wages. Charles Winter, C.E.'s dad, had been able to purchase a truck which he used to haul farm crops to market for the farmers who had only horses and wagons. He managed to do okay for awhile. After two years, though, Charles realized his idea of making a good living by owning a crop delivery business was not working out; he decided to move on and the Winter family ended up in Tulsa in 1922.

Charles Winter was sharp-witted, good looking and physically strong; he was quickly accepted for training in the police academy and his certification was followed by a position on the Tulsa Police Force. For the next 8 years, he worked on the force as a patrol officer. The change from farming to civil service was good for the family. It seemed that life might be a bit easier for all of them even in the midst of the Great Depression. Then tragedy struck. Charles became sick... The year was 1930, and the diagnosis of lymphatic cancer was a death sentence.

Even though Charles eventually ended up at the highly advanced Mayo Clinic in Temple, Texas, the doctors could do nothing to save him. He died three years later in 1933, never having returned to work after the initial diagnosis was made.

Clarence was 16 when his dad got sick, and he finally dropped out of school to support the family by working a daily paper route and caddying at the Oakhurst Country Club on Saturdays and Sundays. Soon after Pa's death, Clarence joined the CCC to support the family. Two years later, in 1935, he was in Kilgore and, it seemed, real change was in the air! (In fact, one decision involved changing his surname from Winter to Winters; he just liked the sound better with "s"!) He reminisced about all that had happened as he walked to the Black's for a much-anticipated evening.

Dinner was delicious! Clarence helped clear the table, raving about Mama's cooking. She'd made fried chicken (one of her specialties!), mashed potatoes, fried okra, cream gravy, cornbread (thick, rich, and buttery), and her "famous" apple pie.

"That was the best meal I've had in forever, Mrs. Black!" Clarence stated, rubbing his belly and groaning in pretend pain from being so full. Mama just glowed with his praises; she loved the attention and everyone knew she deserved it. G.W. punched Clarence's bicep and laughingly teased him, "Yeh, Clarence! Just keep on brown-nosing Mama; maybe she'll invite you back for more home cooking!"

At that point, Melba chimed in with, "You know that's what he's hoping even though he certainly didn't do without in the CC Camp. He's not looking TOO lean!"

Everyone chimed in and even Papa had to laugh. "You swells won't give CE a chance!! I don't know WHAT he thinks about our loud and crazy family. We're probably running him off and I just brought him home to get him away from all the riff-raff down at Mattie's and show him what a REAL family is like!" Papa groused. "You're making me look bad…!" With that, Papa motioned to CE and went out on the porch for a smoke.

"Sometimes my brood can be downright irritating." Papa mumbled, but C.E. just grinned as he looked back inside the house to see Melba and Anna Jean doing the dishes. The screen door opened and out came G.W. and Lindell, both clearly ecstatic about what had just happened.

"Mama's in love with you, C.E.!" G.W. said in a low, conspiratorial voice. "It won't be long before you have Sister swooning, too! It's a good thing Dell and I both like you!"

Clarence looked away, but turned back, smiling broadly, to tell the three men, "I knew she was the one the first day I met her! Someday Melba will be my bride, mark my words!"

"Hmmmm…" was the only sound from Papa, but he looked pleased.

A few minutes later, the guys were joined on the porch by Mama, Sister, and Anna Jean. Mama was trying to keep Bobby from being his usual VERY active 18 month old self, so she was holding him. They sat in the rocking chair while she attempted to get him settled down for bed. Everyone seemed relaxed and happy.

Lindell looked at Clarence and said, "So, tell us about YOUR family, C.E. Do you have brothers and sisters?"

Clarence nodded affirmatively and smiled. "So where are they?" Lindell questioned.

"My mom lives in Tulsa in the house my dad bought in 1923. She shares the house with my sister, Nellie, her husband, Harvey Watters, and their two kids, Harold and Mary. Harold's three years old and Mary's one. Harvey's 33 and a lineman for the electric company. Nellie's 28 and works part time for the Tulsa Telegraph Company. She's smart and she works hard to bring home a paycheck to help keep food on the table. Mom watches the kids when Mary's at work.

My dad died last year; it's been really hard on all of us, but especially on Mom.   She and Dad married in 1916; they were just kids, but they managed to make a good life and raise my brother, Estel, Nellie, and me. Estel's married, too, and lives a few miles away from Mom in Tulsa. He's 25, and works for the city water department." Clarence was a bit flustered after sharing so much about HIS family. He rarely talked about any of them; it was just easier to keep family matters to himself…

"That's not a lot different than us, except your family is smaller", Lindell said.

"Sounds like your mom's doing all she can to help your sister. That's keen of her" added G.W..

Papa cleared his throat. "Clarence, do you mind sharing what happened to your dad?' he asked.

"No, I don't mind", Clarence said in a low tone. "My dad was very special to me. I looked up to him and believed he was invincible. When he was diagnosed with lymphatic cancer, I was only 14. I thought he'd beat it, and he sure did TRY. It still seems impossible he's gone."

Papa looked upset when he said, "I'm sorry, Clarence."

"It's okay. My dad was a good man. He loved his family and he gave us much to be proud of. The way he died taught me the meaning of doing what's right when the chips are down. He never complained or said things weren't fair. He just did what he could to leave Mama with a house to live in and as much money as he could save for her future. I'm just grateful for what he did because without his sacrifices, we would have been out in the streets after he passed."

"I'm sure you're right about that, C.E." Papa agreed. "Were the last days really bad for him and the family?"

"Yes, they were. In fact, I hope to never see another loved one as sick as Dad was at the end. It was really awful. Mama will never get past the fact that she couldn't help Pa. It was almost worse for her than for him." Clarence said all this in a low and sad voice; he was clearly deeply affected by his father's death.

"Thanks for sharing about your father, C.E.. I know we all feel terrible for you and your family!" Papa said this with palpable sincerity. Everyone was quiet for a few minutes as the calming sounds of nature filled in for the words Papa, Mama, nor any of the kids could find a way to express.

After a few minutes, Mama said, "I think we should have another piece of pie!" Everyone laughed and agreed with her wise suggestion. There was no more talk about Clarence's family that evening.

CHAPTER 30

Even though Papa worked long hours on the oil rigs, he continued to stay connected to C.E. over the next months as much as possible. On weekends when a rig wasn't "blowing", Clarence often came by the Black's house to visit. It just seemed natural for Melba and him to talk, and the talking soon extended beyond casual "flirting". Melba began to really want to see this Oklahoma man; she hoped he felt the same about seeing her.

Lindell and G.W. didn't let opportunities for Melba and C.E. to interact get away from them. They made all kinds of excuses for "together-ness" between Sis and C.E. to occur; the entire Black Clan seemed fixed on ensuring a romantic ending to the "friendship".

Eventually, Clarence could not stand to wait another minute. On a beautiful April Saturday afternoon at the Black's when the sky was blue and the winter chills seemed gone, he walked up to Melba. His arm slid around her waist as he said, "Hey, beautiful. Let's take a walk."

They headed down a worn path that led to a pond that was near the oil field shanties. C.E. was almost breathless when he said, "Melba, I have something to say. I hope you will be okay with what I tell you. You are the most beautiful woman I've ever known. You are smarter than I can even express. You are so special to me. May I kiss you?"

Melba's smile made her face even more beautiful. She turned to Clarence, wrapped her arms around his neck, and their lips met. She would tell Clarence much later that she felt dizzy with passion when he kissed her! Her knees were weak, her heart was racing and she was giddy with happiness. The moment felt predestined; it was simply the fulfillment of Melba's dreams about romance.

During the remainder of spring and into summer, the happy couple was together as often as possible; C.E. made a point of being wherever Melba was if there was ANY way! They were clearly in love. It was no stretch of the imagination to conclude that the entire Black family was also really happy for the two "love birds".

Papa and Mama hoped a wedding would be in the near future, but Melba was still in high school, and she was only 15! It wasn't that falling in love was unheard of at her age, but C.E. WAS her first real boyfriend. Even though they both believed their relationship was the "real deal", Melba wanted to complete school. She stated that getting her diploma was a priority, and Clarence, although somewhat reluctantly, agreed. His understanding concerning Melba's determination to be "educated" was to be tested many times in the future...

Melba's June birthday, her 16th, was celebrated with family and C.E. She was SO pretty, and her happiness was clear as her eyes sparkled and her cheeks had a pink glow. It was such fun to be in love! Melba could never remember a time when the entire family seemed so close or when even the dreary days of the Depression seemed brighter.

They were all lucky that both Papa and C.E. had jobs; Kilgore was still a "boom town", and the money made with oil had enabled the town to build and fund one of the best school systems in the entire United States. To be graduating from Kilgore High School was meaningful. Both G.W. and Lindell had diplomas from KHS, and were returning to the town of Nacogdoches, 60 miles south of Kilgore, to resume college classes at Stephen F. Austin State College in September. Although Melba secretly wondered how going to college would feel, she'd decided it would have to wait for a day in her future.

When school began in September, it was the start of a whirlwind of events that almost always happen during the last year of high school, but for Melba it seemed bizarre to be included in any of them. She still felt like "Melba Smell-ba" on the inside, so it was a really big stretch to try and fit in. Those early scars would never go away, but Melba began to find a "hiding place" deep in her soul to keep the ugly memories at bay. A new and very different woman was emerging; the dirty, tattered child from Damon and those lonely first years in Kilgore were, at least temporarily, forgotten.

The remainder of her senior year was a blur for Melba; life was delightful! It was early autumn, and the days were getting cooler. Just the change in temperature seemed exciting. Although school days were spent as usual, many evenings included time with Clarence. Their courtship included attending football games and senior events, hanging out with friends and family and just learning everything they could about each other.

One of the really amazing things Melba and Clarence were able to enjoy together was attending MOVIES at the Crim Theater! Melba was transfixed by the "big screen"; she had dreamed about seeing moving pictures for a long time, and having her "prince charming" take her to see *Top Hat*, starring Fred Astaire and Ginger Rogers was just about the best thing that had ever happened! C.E. also treated his adored fiancé to *Barbary Coast*, starring the fabulous Edward G. Robinson, Joel McCrea and Miriam Hopkins, *Call of the Wild*, with the swoon-inducing Clark Gable and gorgeous Loretta Young, and even *The Devil is a Woman*, starring the sultry, sexy Marlene Dietrich (yes, Melba FINALLY got to see Ms Dietrich!) and Cesar Romero. Being a movie-aficionado just tickled Melba pink!

The couple sampled "Mexican food" for the first time at Kilgore's newest restaurant, Albert's Mexican Village. They agreed it was simply scrumptious! In fact, Albert's was to become THE place to go every Sunday. It was such a grand place to eat that even G.W. and Lindell drove back to Kilgore at least once a month to join Melba and Clarence at Albert's. What fun memories they made on those weekends! When May arrived and graduation really happened, Melba was both overjoyed and saddened. It was great to know she'd earned her high school diploma, yet leaving high school heralded big changes and saying goodbye to beloved teachers. But wedding bells were ringing in the not-too-distant-future. In just EIGHT months, Melba would become Mrs. Clarence Earl Winters!

Of course, during the entire year of the engagement, Melba and her closest friends talked about "the wedding". Melba knew it had to be small and that it would be held at Mama and Papa's home, but she still wanted a pretty dress and some of the beautiful wedding accoutrements she'd seen in an advertising insert in *The Kilgore News Herald* called "So You're Going to Get Married!" With the help of the three girls who'd been her best friends all the way through high school, the planning began in earnest.

Janice really liked the sketches Melba drew of her "dream dress", and the girls giggled for endless hours about how Clarence would be "overcome" when he saw Melba in such finery. Janice was wiping tears of laughter from her eyes when she said, "You know Clarence will simply go wild when you walk in wearing this dress! He'll probably just keel over!"

Betty and Nancy agreed, and Betty teased, "He'll be stuttering and stammering when Reverend Vermillion asks him to say his vows!"

Nancy nodded and said, "Clarence is SO smitten with you, Melba! This wedding will be something else, just you wait and see!" Melba smiled at her friends. It was fun to have them around to help with the planning, and she really did appreciate the suggestions all three friends made. Both Nancy and Betty were excited about making things like the pretty little rice bags that were to be thrown after the wedding and the decorations to make the house look its best. Even though her outfit for the wedding would be a lot less fancy than a "gown", Melba really wanted it to be as "fine" as possible.

On a particularly memorable weekend, Aunt Dorleita came to visit. The fabrics she brought to show Melba were really pretty. Melba knew about the rampant unemployment across the country, but Kilgore's oil boom kept most of its citizens protected from some of the more severe effects of joblessness that occurred in other places.

Even as Melba "oohed and aahed" over some of Aunt Dorleita's beautiful fabric samples, she knew a simple dress was all she could manage. She finally decided the dress she sketched would be made from a pale pink wool gabardine fabric in Aunt Dorleita's bag that felt soft and smooth; Melba liked the color and light texture. After she added a bit of lacey ribbon, she knew the dress would look lovely. Melba began to feel like a bride! For the first time in her life, she was able to see a tiny piece of the "other side", the life reserved for rich, important and powerful people. She liked the feeling...

CHAPTER 31

Although it seemed impossible that family members Melba only saw on rare occasions would travel all the way to Kilgore for her wedding, on the week of the "big day" Mama's extended family drove into town. Included were Aunt Elsie, Mama's oldest sister who lived in Oklahoma City with her husband Kelly Robinson, Uncle Max, Uncle Herman, and Uncle Leo, Mama's brothers along with their wives, Aunt Marie, Aunt Bertha, and Aunt Fannie Lou. All lived in East Texas except Aunt Elsie, but it was still unheard of to travel to an out-of-town wedding! The house was bursting at the seams!

The morning of February 24, 1936, was simply beautiful! With a cloudless sky, cool temperature and the feel of spring in the air, Melba's first thoughts included, "Oh, my! I'm really getting married today!" and, "How can I be so lucky?" followed by, "Is this really happening?"

It was soon apparent that OTHERS in the household were already preparing for this most special day! Mama called out, "Sister! I hope you're awake! We have to get you ready and finish the food!"

Melba practically sang, "I'm up, Mama! Be right there!"

Anna Jean was already dancing around the kitchen. When Melba walked through the doorway, Jeannie ran up to her, threw her arms around her waist and chortled, "Oh, Sister! This is the BEST day ever! I know you'll be the most beautiful bride in the whole world! And I don't know what I'll DO when you go away with Clarence!"

"Don't worry, little sis! I'm not going anywhere for awhile, and when we move away I promise to write to you every single week! We'll be back to Kilgore, I know that much for sure! Besides, you'll always be my favorite sister!" Melba smiled mischievously when she added that last statement. She HAD to keep this day happy and upbeat; there would be no tears at HER wedding!

The truth of the matter was that she and Clarence had been discussing a move to Tulsa where Melba would be able to stay with his mother while he drove a bus for Greyhound. He wanted to take the Greyhound job because it paid well and the move would solve his dilemma about how to help both his mom and his cousins. He certainly couldn't stand the thought of Melba being alone on the nights he was working, so living with Ina Belle would solve that problem, too!

The Dust Bowl coupled with the Depression had affected the economy in a very negative way; money was scarce. Even though Clarence had made fair money working as a roughneck in Kilgore, drilling new wells was slowing down. He knew it was time for a change, and the Greyhound Bus job would have him working a route between Oklahoma City, Tulsa, Little Rock, and Topeka. It was something both Clarence and Melba thought would be a smart plan. Bus travel was booming, thanks to the 1934 hit film, *It Happened One Night*, the first movie to win FIVE Academy Awards! The story centered on an heiress (played by Claudette Colbert) traveling by Greyhound bus after running away from her wealthy father who wanted to control her life. The socialite meets a fellow-passenger, an out-of-work reporter (played by Clark Gable).

Their escapades while on the bus made for a hilarious romantic comedy, and, VOILA!, bus travel became trendy. Already the largest bus carrier in the United States, Greyhound began taking delivery of 306 new buses within the next year…

Melba put these thoughts aside when Mama exclaimed, "Come on, Sister! Your breakfast is getting cold! Stop daydreaming! Shake a leg!" (She DID have a smile on her face and she actually patted Melba's arm affectionately…)

Following a relatively calm breakfast with Anna Jean and Bobby, the morning became hectic. Mama had Melba work on the chicken salad while she finished shaping the croutons from the dough that had been rising for several hours. They had fresh tomatoes from the garden. Mama was especially proud of those since it was early in the growing season. The cake was Mama's special surprise for Melba, and it was simply beautiful! She made three different-sized layers of her heavenly vanilla cream cake, but the butter cream icing and the sugar piping she used to decorate it made the cake the fanciest Melba had ever seen. She was simply stunned when Mama brought it out of the cupboard where she'd hidden it.

"Mama! How did you ever afford to make it?" Melba squealed. "I never dreamed I'd have a REAL wedding cake! It's…it's just the cat's meow!"

The remainder of the morning simply flew by, and suddenly it was time to get dressed for, as G.W. and Lindell joked, the "nuptials".

Janice, Betty and Nancy arrived a few minutes later, ready to help Melba with her hair and makeup. They were, of course, the bridesmaids.

Reverend Vermillion sat on the front porch with Papa, the two men sipping sweet tea while reminiscing about the past few years and Melba's "coming of age" during the craziness of Kilgore's oil boom.

Meanwhile, Aunt Dorleita, Mama, Aunt Elsie, Aunt Marie, Aunt Bertha and Aunt Fannie bustled about on the lawn, adding bows and flowers picked from the yard and contributed by neighbors to the simple arch Papa constructed out of twigs, vines and thin branches he gathered in the wooded areas near the house. The flowers and bows the women added looked lovely; they were pleased with their efforts.

"We couldn't have done better if we'd hired a fancy-schmancy decorator to do the honors!" Dorleita marveled. "This family just has what it takes to host a fine event, don't you agree?" The six women laughed and hugged one another; it was a truly happy moment.

In Melba and Jeannie's cramped little bedroom, the girls giggled nervously while they "oohed and aahed" over how pretty Melba looked.

"Wow! You're sure looking sweet, Melby!" Janice whispered. "You're such a looker!"

"She's right!" Jeannie said wistfully. "I know Clarence is gonna just DIE when he sees you!"

"Oh, come on, girls! I'm just the same old ME. If you don't stop all the nonsense, I'll be walking to the altar with a blood-red face; you make me feel…weird!" groaned Melba.

At exactly 5:00, everyone was seated in front of the altar on the benches Papa made of pine logs. Uncle Max picked up his fiddle and started strumming "Mari's Wedding".

As he played, Clarence walked up to the altar and stood looking back at the bridesmaids and their escorts. Janice walked to the altar on the arm of G.W.. They were followed by Betty on the arm of Lindell and Nancy on the arm of Elsie's son, Kelly Jr. When they reached the altar, they separated; the girls stood on the left, the boys on the right. Next was Bobby, carrying Melba's wedding ring on a satin pillow. He looked so cute! As usual, though, Bobby was a bit "active", running most of the way to the altar as guests whispered and giggled, finding it impossible to hide the fact that it was hard to keep from exploding with raucous laughter. So much for a solemn ceremony, mused Melba from her vantage point behind the screen door.

Uncle Max increased the volume as he strummed the upbeat wedding song, and Oscar appeared on the porch with Melba. She looked gorgeous in her pale pink tea-length pencil-style dress with a peplum hem. It accentuated her slim figure and brought out her curves; she was simply a "babe"! There was a hushed "Oooh!" from the guests, most of whom were relatives.

The rest of the ceremony was lost on both Melba and Clarence. They simply went through the motions as Reverend Vermillion pronounced them "husband and wife". It had actually happened! They were a married couple!

CHAPTER 32

Much sooner than Melba anticipated, Clarence left for Tulsa. He was determined to get the job he'd talked about, working for Greyhound, and he knew he had to go in person to cement his employment.

Before leaving his new bride, they talked long and hard about what this change would mean for them both. Clarence knew how lucky he was to have found Melba; she was amazingly supportive and encouraging, telling him she'd follow him anywhere.

"You know how I feel about leaving Kilgore. It's hard to know I'll be so far from the rest of the family. Leaving Jeannie breaks my heart. That said, what you need to do is what I want to do. Everything else will fall into place. So, Oklahoma, here we come!" Melba said with conviction and determination.

All Clarence could do was smile that lopsided grin that Melba found irresistible. Two weeks later, on April 10th, he boarded a bus bound for Tulsa. He also promised his "Melby" that when he got back to Kilgore it would be to pack up their few belongings, have a farewell dinner with Oscar and Annie, and head north.

"You're going to like Oklahoma", Clarence assured her. "It's not as hot as East Texas, and Tulsa's a big city. There's a lot to see and do. Besides, Mama's really looking forward to having us at home. She's been awful lonely!"

"I know", Melba stated. "It's just hard to leave what I'm used to. Jeannie and Bobby will be lonely, too, but at least they have each other."

That night it was hard to sleep. Both newly-weds felt as if the world would stop turning when they were separated, if only for a few weeks. At dawn, Clarence was out of bed and dressed, ready to hitch a ride to town and get on the Greyhound bus that would take him north to Tulsa.

"I love you, Melby" was all he could say as he walked away.

"Love you more!" she managed as the tears ran down her cheeks. Both of them knew it would be a very long two weeks, and then they'd be faced with the actual move. All the hardships both had endured before this moment seemed trivial compared to the intensity of their emotions NOW.

The tearful departure made Melba go back to her usual "whatever" mode of escaping the most upsetting things in her life. She simply would not allow missing Clarence to take over her life! Since Mama had never been a good housekeeper, Melba decided to give the place a "spring cleaning". All that work, she reasoned, would keep her too busy to be upset about either missing Clarence or about the upcoming move to Oklahoma.

Over the next days, the entire house was turned upside down as Melba scrubbed floors, washed windows, took down all the curtains to be washed and ironed, aired out all the bedding, scoured the bathroom and kitchen, organized the small closets, and made everything look its best. Of course, Mama just complained about the inconveniences of moving furniture and making the messes that are simply part of really cleaning. As always, it seemed to Melba, Mama did not appreciate her efforts. Despite getting no sign of gratitude, Melba was pleased with the results.

On April 21, Clarence's arrival back in Kilgore was absolutely thrilling! He walked into the house carrying a bouquet of flowers, grabbed Melba and lifted her off the ground, looked her in the eyes and said, "It's official! I'm employed by Greyhound, and I'm promised 60 cents per hour! I start work next Monday!"

Tulsa was a big city as compared to Kilgore, and Melba's first view of it when they drove into town in Estel's Model B Ford was breathtaking.

"Oh, my!" she whispered. "Look at the BUILDINGS! I knew they were here, but seeing them is simply sweet!"

Even though the years of Depression had really slowed population growth in Tulsa, the local economy was fairly healthy. Stores still provided plenty of merchandise, many people still had jobs, and in the past months a small but noticeable increase in average income was helping boost retail sales.

The remainder of the drive to Ina Belle's house was filled with exclamations about some of the "mansions" they passed and the size of the town. Estel drove them through downtown, and seeing the 15-story red brick Thompson Building, the snazzy art deco-style Philcade Building and the gorgeous Uptown Theater was simply too amazing! The most breathtaking architecture, in Melba's opinion, was the Boston

Avenue Methodist Church. Estel stopped to let Melba and Clarence walk inside. They learned the church was designed from a sketch done by a female art teacher at the University of Tulsa, Miss Ada Robinson. To Melba's way of thinking, knowing a WOMAN designed such an interesting building combining Gothic architecture and the newest art deco style simply affirmed her conviction that gender could not hold her back. She silently mused about the way she imagined her life might change with education as they drove toward Clarence's mother's house. Then, arriving at 4837 South 32th West Avenue late that afternoon, Melba was to FINALLY meet her mother-in-law.

Clarence took Melba's hand and squeezed it as they walked to the front door of the small, wood-framed house. Its dark green shutters and pretty flower garden made the house feel welcoming, and Melba said, "I'm not SO edgy now that we're here. Everything you've told me about your mom makes me know I'll love her!"

At that, the door was flung open and a smiling short-statured, somewhat plump woman with wavy light-colored hair held out her arms and said, "Welcome, Melba! You are just as pretty as he claimed!" With that, she enveloped Melba in a warm hug and ushered her inside. Then she hugged both Clarence and Estel and exclaimed, "You're right on time for supper! Nellie's home and the kids are starving! Ruby's here, too, so you get to join us tonight, Estel. Let's eat!"

Mom, as Melba would call Ina, had the food ready. She'd made fried chicken, as well as corn on the cob and fresh green beans from the garden. She'd even baked homemade yeast bread! As they ate, Melba realized she really did find this woman likeable. It was clear that her three years as a widow had been hard, but her inner strength was equally clear. It was obvious that she doted on her grandkids, Mary and Wesley, who quite plainly were in love with her, too. At least this woman seemed willing to work without whining and complaining, a welcome difference when compared to MAMA.

As Melba thought these thoughts, she felt her face flush; she knew her attitude about Mama was, at the very least, unchristian. She vowed, inwardly, to try to be less hateful, to be a better person.

Over the next two days, Melba would get to know her sister-in-laws, Nellie and Ruby. Although Ruby and Estel had no children at this point, they were all older than Melba and a bit hard boiled for her taste. Since both Nellie and Ruby had jobs, they tended to want to discuss things that happened at work or, in Nellie's case, the kids. Nellie and Mom had a lot to discuss when it came to Wesley and Mary, and when Ruby was around she and Nellie seemed to want to share a bunch of "inside" jokes regarding work. Melba felt left out and it reminded her of her younger days at school. She began to realize she was homesick.

In spite of how Melba felt, within the first two months, Clarence had earned the respect of his bosses. His attendance record and ability to work with the schedules and get his passengers to their destinations with few delays ensured the appreciation of both the local managers and the "big boys" headquartered in Chicago. Clarence was always courteous to his employers, but he still had an attitude, one that said, "I'm able to make the right decisions on my own. I can take care of myself." After all, he was the same person as the 13 year old boy who handled a large paper route for the *Tulsa Tribune* for four years, riding his pony many miles every day to make his deliveries and bringing home all his pay to help out at home after his dad got sick. The cockiness that had always been part of the kid who caddied for wealthy golfers at Tulsa's Oakhurst Country Club and brought home enough in tips to feed his mother and siblings knew, early on, that a bit of "swagger" could carry him a long way.

Melba was learning to fit in at Ina Belle's house. She took on much of the work, including cleaning and cooking, washing and ironing the clothes, and helping with Nellie's children. Most of the time she was too busy to think about herself, but she couldn't keep the occasional thoughts about "bettering herself" from secretly entering her mind.

Even though Mom was usually sweet and caring, she could be short-tempered about making ends meet. Clarence was certainly contributing a high percentage of the monthly income, and his job at Greyhound was important to the entire family. Nevertheless, his mother fussed about things needing repairs and she was constantly anxious about not having enough food.

Ina had lost trust in the government during the long years of the Great Depression, and even with the current recovery so promising, she believed "good times" might be short-lived. Unfortunately, her worries would turn out to be valid.

Melba faithfully wrote letters to her brothers and Anna Jean, and she always wrote separate ones to Mama and Papa. Once a week, Clarence took her long, informative letters to the downtown post office on South Boulder Avenue by the courthouse and mailed them. It was the one thing that kept Melba "connected" to her family and writing her letters was cathartic. Telling Jeannie and Bobby about her life in Tulsa helped the homesickness and gave her a reason to be positive.

"I'm not one hundred percent honest about everything", Melba confided to Clarence.. "I don't want them to worry about me. They need to believe we're doing swell and I want them to be happy when they get my letters."

Kilgore was 293 miles away, but it might as well have been 2,000! No matter what happened, Melba knew she would not be returning to Kilgore anytime soon. She was certainly correct about that since it would be another three years before she'd go back to her parent's home for a real visit.

Although Clarence was making good money for the harsh economic times, it was hard to pay for everything with his salary. Nellie contributed a little to her mother for rent and watching Wesley and Mary, and she bought some of the groceries each week. Harvey's pay helped with the expenses, too. Even so, the combined incomes could not cover everything; their pay was less than 50 cents an hour.

One morning, Ina told Melba she needed to discuss something with her. "You know I've been checking on the neighbor lady three houses down. Iris isn't doing well; her "consumption" is getting worse. She's having bad night sweats, running a fever almost all the time and feeling really bad.   I know she barely eats anything and can hardly get out of bed. You're young and healthy, so you likely won't get sick. She has a little extra money her husband left her when he died last year and she asked me if you'd come over each day and care for her by helping with bathing, washing her linens and nightgowns, fixing foods like soup that she can tolerate, and the like. We can use the additional cash for our needs."

Melba noted that her mother-in-law had trouble looking at her as she explained what she wanted her to do. No wonder, thought Melba! She's sending me to tend to Iris, knowing that I may come down with TB.

Instead of saying what she was thinking, though, Melba said, "Yes, I'll do it." The next day, she entered Iris' "sick house". Melba would tend to the dying woman for the next six months.

CHAPTER 33

Iris' death devastated Melba. Their relationship had grown from just a job to real friendship, despite the age difference. Iris was sweet and appreciative to the very end, and her passing was hard to take.

"It's awful to see someone so kind and good suffer such a terrible death", Melba lamented as tears rolled down her cheeks. "Iris deserved better. She lived a good life and I think she got sick because she helped out at the hospital and down at the Red Cross. Even when she was so thin and frail she could no longer hold her own cup, she never blamed anyone else for her illness. God bless her!"

Little did Melba know that her prolonged contact with Iris had infected her with the tuberculosis virus. The disease would lay dormant in her body for the next thirty years before almost claiming HER life...

Following Iris' death, Melba tried to stay busy at Ina Belle's, taking on more and more of the work for Clarence's mother. Although Clarence was unaware of just how much of the household management was handled by his wife, he did know she sometimes seemed tired and a bit withdrawn. He worried that keeping her from seeing her family for such a long time was taking a toll.

It seemed impossible that they had lived with his mom and his sister's family for a whole year. Clarence was pleased to have earned another raise from Greyhound; he was now making 75 cents per hour, and he was happy with his job. Clarence liked driving his routes, liked his employers, and enjoyed meeting the many passengers who traveled with him.

Around this time, Clarence determined it was time for him and Melba to find their own place to live. After all, he reasoned, he would still help supplement Mom's household.

The next few weeks were exciting as Melba and Clarence searched through ads in the *Tulsa Tribune* looking at houses for rent. They finally decided on a one-bedroom bungalow that would cost them $19.50 per month.

"It's a little more than we should be paying", Clarence stated, "but it's worth every penny!"

Melba laughed and agreed, saying "Oh, sweetheart! It's SO perfect! I love it!"

Within a few days, the move was done. After all, there was very little to transfer from Ina Belle's to the apartment. Ina seemed okay with the changes; the little house on 32nd was really crowded with the extended family. She reckoned she'd see Clarence and Melba often enough.

Actually setting up a home for the first time was one of the most exciting events of Melba's life. She was so involved in finding furniture in yard sales and newspaper ads that the days flew by. Even though the budget kept her from buying the new and luxurious trappings of her childhood dreams, just getting to look at bedroom and living room pieces made her giddy.

While making discoveries for the apartment, the couple slept on the twin bed mattress with a metal frame they'd brought from Kilgore. The tiny pine kitchen table and two ladder-back chairs plus an old beat-up rocking chair completed their furnishings.

"You know, Clarence, I don't even mind living with our old stuff; it's so keen having our own place and real privacy for the first time," Melba stated a few days after the move. "Don't you agree it's beyond comparison?"

"Whatever you like is good for me, Melby, but you WILL have the beautiful things you've told me you saw in Mr. Robinowitz' store back in Damon. I promise you that!" As he spoke, Clarence swept Melba off her feet and swung her around in a circle. They collapsed on the floor, laughing. Life was good.

Having moved to the bungalow in early June, 1937, Melba and Clarence celebrated living in Tulsa just over a year. Within a month, the couple had managed to purchase, paint and repair a round kitchen table and two extra ladder-back chairs. Melba used her sewing skills to make seat cushions and matching curtains for the kitchen area in a deep rose color. Next, they found a small sofa that was in terrible shape with worn and dirty upholstery, sagging seat and back and drooping armrests. With determination, Melba taught herself how to strip off the worn fabric, remove the nasty inner cushioning that was almost mushy from wear and tear, and take out the tacks holding everything in place. Next, she had to figure out how much fabric she needed to recover the couch, something she didn't learn while making clothes!

Clarence helped her locate a store selling heavy-duty upholstery fabric called barkcloth, where they found the PERFECT color to accent the apartment and carry out the colors in the kitchen. The fabric was a floral design of peony bouquets in rose and yellow on a background of forest green and ivory. Melba, curious as always, wanted to know how "barkcloth" was made and she discovered the fabric she purchased was a mixture of cotton and rayon woven with a nubby texture similar to tree bark and having a very dense weave.

"I know the couch will last forever!" Melba exclaimed as she told Clarence what she'd learned.

With Clarence's help, she learned how to use latex as the padding and how to attach the fabric to the wooden frame of the couch using tacks to hold the fabric tightly in place. Melba even figured out how to use welting along the arms and base of the sofa. She decided to stitch the cushions by hand using heavy-duty thread and large upholstery needles. Despite the time the upholstery people told Melba refinishing the couch by herself would take, it was completely done in less than two weeks! Especially rewarding to Melba, the finished product was truly "snazzy".

"I'm blown away by what we've done with our place!" Melba practically crooned. "It's just perfect!"

"You've turned our apartment into a real home, honey!" Clarence declared. "What would I do without you? No one will believe how sweet you've made our place, and on a tight budget, too! I adore you, Melby!" With that, they collapsed on the newly renovated sofa, smiles on both their faces, and smooching like brand new lovers. It was a heavenly time…

CHAPTER 34

For the remainder of 1937, optimism about the Depression being over ended as the United States was plunged into another major economic recession. Loss of jobs across the country was frightening as unemployment rose to 19 percent, almost as high as it was in 1933. Fears that the economy would never recover created widespread distrust of the government and, significantly, wariness toward President Roosevelt.

Once again, Clarence's job was not affected by lay-offs; he felt relatively secure at Greyhound. As he told Melba one evening, though, his mind was more on the problems in Europe and Asia than work issues: "I'm hearing rumors down at the terminal about another war and it sounds bad. The things I hear include some sort of alliance between Germany, Italy and Japan, and it sounds like the new leader in Germany, Adolf Hitler, is making big changes. There are rumors that Germany is planning to wage a war on France and England to take over their land and increase Germany's power. It's also rumored that Hitler wants to get rid of "problem Jews". He and his supporters believe Jewish people are inferior, evil and cowardly. Apparently, it's a big mess." Clarence's tone of voice belied his attempt at sounding calm. It was obvious to Melba that, once again, this new life they were trying to build might suffer because of politics, war, or both!

"What does it mean for US?" Melba asked in a tremulous voice. You know as well as me that everyone in Europe is still reeling from the horrible after-effects of the   Big

War; how can anyone want more hostilities? Over here, we're still trying to recuperate from the Depression! What does President Roosevelt say about the Germans?" Melba was fighting tears as she asked these questions.

Clarence tried to soothe her, but he was just as concerned and upset. "Our president is against getting into a conflict with them. He wants the United States to stay out of all the things going on in other countries. I know we've talked about his 'Isolationist' ideas, and we've always agreed with him. We need to take care of America and all the people HERE. Who cares what happens 'over there'! After all, look at what happened the last time we got involved in foreign conflict!"

What Clarence said was, basically, true. Most Americans failed to be overly concerned about the rumored "War in Europe", saying it was a "phony war" because there weren't any significant military engagements reported in the news. Much later, Americans would come to understand that the reason no one knew about most of the horrible things happening in Europe was due to the Nazi tactic of quietly arresting and killing Polish and Jewish citizens while keeping reporters at bay and uninformed. Hitler wanted to infiltrate and take over silently, and the less those outside his "inner circle" knew, the better his chances of carrying out his cruel plans. Americans, in general, knew nothing about the unspeakable atrocities happening "over there".

Clarence and most of their friends said things like, "The United States should be concerned about what happens inside ITS borders. We should have learned during the first war to stay out of European politics!"

Melba wasn't sure what was best but she wanted to believe staying out of the problems in Europe was truly best for America. Even so, she was unable to dismiss thoughts about what could happen if more fighting started between the already troubled European countries like Italy, Germany, France and even Great Britain. Japan was already involved, and there was rumor that the Soviet Union might join sides with Germany. It was definitely worrisome.

President Roosevelt's "fireside chats" certainly underscored the nation's firm belief in staying isolated from all the unrest in Europe. On September 3, 1939, the day that Nazi Germany invaded Poland and issued a declaration of war, Roosevelt gave his 14th Fireside Chat, saying:

> *"My fellow Americans and my friends:*
> *Tonight my single duty is to speak to the whole of America. Until four-thirty this morning I had hoped against hope that some miracle would prevent a devastating war in Europe and bring to an end the invasion of Poland by Germany.*
> *For four long years a succession of actual wars and constant crises have shaken the entire world and have threatened in each case to bring on the gigantic conflict which is today unhappily a fact.*
>
> *It is right that I should recall to your minds the consistent and at times successful efforts of your Government in these crises to throw the full weight of the United States into the cause of peace. In spite of spreading wars I think that we have every right and every reason to maintain as a national policy the fundamental moralities, the teachings of religion and the continuation of efforts to restore peace because some day, though the time may be distant, we can be of even greater help to a crippled humanity.*

It is right, too, to point out that the unfortunate events of these recent years have, without question, been based on the use of force and the threat of force. And it seems to me clear, even at the outbreak of this great war, that the influence of America should be consistent in seeking for humanity a final peace which will eliminate, as far as it is possible to do so, the continued use of force between nations. It is, of course, impossible to predict the future. I have my constant stream of information from American representatives and other sources throughout the world. You, the people of this country, are receiving news through your radios and your newspapers at every hour of the day.

You are, I believe, the most enlightened and the best informed people in all the world at this moment. You are subjected to no censorship of news, and I want to add that your Government has no information which it withholds or which it has any thought of withholding from you.

At the same time, as I told my Press Conference on Friday, it is of the highest importance that the press and the radio use the utmost caution to discriminate between actual verified fact on the one hand, and mere rumor on the other.

I can add to that by saying that I hope the people of this country will also discriminate most carefully between news and rumor. Do not believe of necessity everything you hear or read. Check up on it first.

You must master at the outset a simple but unalterable fact in modern foreign relations between nations. When peace has been broken anywhere, the peace of all countries everywhere is in danger.

It is easy for you and for me to shrug our shoulders and to say that conflicts taking place thousands of miles from the continental United States, and, indeed, thousands of miles from the whole American Hemisphere, do not seriously affect the Americas -- and that all the United States has to do is to ignore them and go about its own business. Passionately though we may desire detachment, we are forced to realize that every word that comes through the air, every ship that sails the sea, every battle that is fought does affect the American future.

Let no man or woman thoughtlessly or falsely talk of America sending its armies to European fields. At this moment there is being prepared a proclamation of American neutrality. This would have been done even if there had been no neutrality statute on the books, for this proclamation is in accordanc with international law and in accordance with American policy.

This will be followed by a Proclamation required by the existing Neutrality Act. And I trust that in the days to come our neutrality can be made a true neutrality.

It is of the utmost importance that the people of this country, with the best information in the world, think things through. The most dangerous enemies of American peace are those who, without well-rounded information on the whole broad subject of the past, the present and the future, undertake to speak with assumed authority, to talk in terms of glittering generalities, to give to the nation assurances or prophecies which are of little present or future value.

I myself cannot and do not prophesy the course of events abroad -- and the reason is that because I have of necessity such a complete picture of what is going on in every part of the world, that I do not dare to do so. And the other reason is that I think it is honest for me to be honest with the people of the United States.

I cannot prophesy the immediate economic effect of this new war on our nation but I do say that no American has the moral right to profiteer at the expense either of his fellow citizens or of the men, the women and the children who are living and dying in the midst of war in Europe.

Some things we do know. Most of us in the United States believe in spiritual values. Most of us, regardless of what church we belong to, believe in the spirit of the New Testament -- a great teaching which opposes itself to the use of force, of armed force, of marching armies and falling bombs. The overwhelming masses of our people seek peace -- peace at home, and the kind of peace in other lands which will not jeopardize our peace at home.

We have certain ideas and certain ideals of national safety and we must act to preserve that safety today and to preserve the safety of our children in future years.

That safety is and will be bound up with the safety of the Western Hemisphere and of the seas adjacent thereto. We seek to keep war from our own firesides by keeping war from coming to the Americas. For that we have historic precedent that goes back to the days of the Administration of President George Washington. It is serious enough and tragic enough to every American family in every state in the Union to live in a world that is torn by wars on other Continents. And those wars today affect every American home. It is our national duty to use every effort to keep those wars out of the Americas.

And at this time let me make the simple plea that partisanship and selfishness be adjourned; and that national unity be the thought that underlies all others.

This nation will remain a neutral nation, but I cannot ask that every American remain neutral in thought as well. Even a neutral has a right to take account of facts. Even a neutral cannot be asked to close his mind or close his conscience.

I have said not once but many times that I have seen war and that I hate war. I say that again and again.

I hope the United States will keep out of this war. I believe that it will. And I give you assurance and reassurance that every effort of your Government will be directed toward that end. As long as it remains within my power to prevent, there will be no blackout of peace in the United States."

After hearing Roosevelt speak on the evening of September 3, both Melba and Clarence looked at one another and, almost simultaneously, sighed with the relief brought by his words.

"I'm really glad the President is doing his 'chats'", Melba stated. "At least, like he said, he's not trying to keep the American people from knowing what's going on. I like that about him!"

Clarence agreed. On that particular evening, the couple felt reassured about the immediate future.

Roosevelt's advocacy for neutrality was understandable. It was even applauded by the majority of American citizens, many of whom had lost loved ones in World War I and could not fathom facing another conflict that could be even worse. The American people were at a difficult crossroads.

CHAPTER 35

Regardless of how much Melba and Clarence talked about the way things were going in Europe while trying to keep things "normal" at home, neither of them could stop worrying about the "what ifs".

As the days came and went, Clarence continued to drive his long bus routes and Melba continued to walk to Ina Belle's most mornings to help with Nellie's kids and do as much as she could for her mother-in-law.

Six weeks later, all the stresses about impending WAR and the things broadcast over the radio caused Melba to insist on going back to Kilgore for a visit. It was October, 1939, three and a half years since they'd moved to Tulsa. Clarence hated the idea of her being so far away, but he understood her need to see family.

There had been lots of changes at home since they'd left for Tulsa. G.W. had married Ozelle Timme, a girl who was one of his best friend's cousins, over a year ago. Melba felt terrible that she had only met her new sis-in-law in June during her quick trip home for Jeannie's wedding ten months ago, but really hadn't had time to get acquainted. Worse, G.W. and Ozelle had a four month old baby boy, Larry Lynn, who was Melba's first nephew; she was DESPERATE to meet him!

And the fact that Anna Jean was married still left Melba in shock! That Buron and Jeannie met while he was her Kilgore High School band director had something to do with her incredulity...

"Holy mackerel, Clarence! I just have to get back home and see G.W. and his new baby, not to mention spending time with Ozelle! And, good grief! Seeing Jeannie and catching up on all the details about her married life with Buron is beyond important! Thinking about my baby sister as a MARRIED woman is just crazy," Melba stated.

"Even though I was home last June so I could be her matron of honor, it was a very short three-day visit! As you know, I had to rush back here to help Mom with Nellie's kids and, besides, Buron and Jean left for their honeymoon. We've all managed to stay in touch with our letters, but it's just not the same as really being together, talking and hugging!

"I'm dying to hear Papa give his rendition of the day Buron and Jean went to the courthouse to get a marriage license. I'm sure the 'embellishments' will have me rolling on the floor with laughter! It's hard to believe both Jeannie and I married before we were 'legal'! I guess things were a bit different for them; we got lucky because Papa knew the judge in Kilgore and managed to give his blessings BEFORE we showed up to purchase our license. Of course, I heard about Jeannie and Buron's 'courthouse experience' when I came home for the wedding, but the telling is always better after time has passed! Going home is SO important to me!" Melba exhaled sharply after such a long expose' about why she needed to go home.

Thankfully, Clarence both understood and agreed, and within a few days he had Melba's bus tickets to Texas. Her trip home became a reality.

The day she arrived at the bus station in Kilgore was beyond good; it was without a doubt the best day in a very long time! Anna Jean met her at the bus station, accompanied by her tall, handsome husband, Buron.

Jeannie ran across the room, arms outstretched. "Oh, Sister! It's SO good to see you!" Both women hugged, laughed and cried over the next few minutes. Buron smiled as he watched the sisters' reunion, then he, too, hugged Melba and welcomed her home.

Buron got Melba's suitcase from the bus driver and they headed out to the street where his black 1926 Ford Model T sedan was parked. Melba was astonished! "Wow, Buron! What a keen car!"

"Well, it's nothing special, but I know I'm lucky to have it. It belonged to my Dad."

Buron was not one to brag, as Melba would learn and respect. Her overall impression of him was good. It was nice to know Buron was just two years younger than Clarence. Maybe, thought Melba, they could all become good friends despite the fact that Buron was a teacher who had earned his college degree. After all, she knew, Clarence was very smart even though he hadn't been as privileged as Buron.

Secretly, Melba always felt insecure about herself, and knowing Buron was well-educated while Clarence was not added to her paranoia. It was a problem she always tried to ignore. "I'll accomplish something special someday", she thought to herself, making a conscious effort to hide her insecurity.

Everyone was home for the family reunion!

Mama and Papa ran outside as soon as they heard the car drive up, and Bobby was the first one to greet the trio. "Sis! You look grand! Welcome home!" declared seven year old Bobby.

"Lands, I'm glad to see you, Sister!" Mama exclaimed, grabbing Melba in a tight "bear hug".

"Glad you're home, daughter! We've missed you." Papa said as he, too, hugged Melba.

G.W., with unusual seriousness, ushered his cute, tiny wife toward Melba. "Welcome home, Sissy! I know you and Ozelle will be best friends soon!"

Melba reached out and embraced Ozelle, saying with a smile, "Since G.W. is always right, I'm sure we're destined to become soul mates! Now where's my NEPHEW?"

"Larry's asleep in the house," G.W. said, "and you'll get to wake him up if he's still snoozing when we get inside!"

While everyone was still standing outside laughing and talking, another car, a brown Model B Ford, stopped in front of the house. Melba nearly flipped her wig when LINDELL opened the door and hollered, "Sis! Aren't you a sight for sore eyes!" In seconds, the two were hugging as Lindell grabbed his sister in a warm embrace. "We have some catching up to do, Mel!" he stated, unable to stop smiling.

It was so wonderful to actually be HOME! The next hours were spent talking about so much that the time simply flew. Buron turned out to have a zany sense of humor. His stories about his and Jeannie's wedding had everyone guffawing! The first part of Buron's wedding story recounted how G.W., Lindell and even little Bobby "fixed" his car.

127

Buron, in a very somber voice, declared: "When we came out of the chapel, Jean's brothers had painted a large JUST MARRIED sign on the back window of our car, BUT, they had also padlocked a heavy duty chain to the rear of the car and wired a bunch of tin cans to the links of the chain which was dragging five or six feet behind the car. We drove through town with tin cans clattering along the street and everybody following us and blowing their car horns!" He continued to explain what happened after the reception at Mama and Papa's house, declaring the 'best' was yet to come.

Buron looked at G.W., Lindell and Bobby, saying with deadpan solemnity, "You informed us 'your group' would follow us as far as Gladewater, and if I would treat all of you to a milkshake at the local drugstore, you would give me the key to the padlock on the chain."

Buron, hands held up in mock defeat, grinned and admitted milkshakes seemed like a bargain at the time. He said the whole noisy entourage left Kilgore for Gladewater, a distance of 14 miles. He admitted the group paid for its own milkshakes, there was a bit more teasing and fun, the key was produced, and he FINALLY hit the highway heading for Dallas with Jeannie urging him to hurry just in case the "boys" decided to follow!

It was the next thing that happened that had the whole family laughing. Jeannie was blushing before Buron finished the hotel tale, but she was good-natured about the teasing dished out by her brothers.

Here's the way Buron told the story of their first night together as husband and wife at the swanky Baker Hotel in downtown Dallas:

"We arrived in Dallas and went into the hotel lobby to check in. I told the room clerk that I wanted a room for two. He could see my lovely bride standing next to me, so imagine my chagrin when the bell hop took us up to our room and I discovered that the room had twin beds! After the bell hop left, Jeannie started laughing (I didn't laugh!). I started to go down to the lobby and tell the room clerk I wanted a room with a double bed, but then I thought...who needs it, anyway? The next morning we ruffled the covers on the other twin bed so the maid would think we'd used both beds...HAH!"

Jeannie, still blushing, giggled and said, "Well, it WAS funny! We were both too embarrassed to do anything about the situation except deal with it by doing nothing. As it turned out, it's one of the highlights of our honeymoon, and I'm sure it will just get funnier as time goes by!"

Of course, the brothers all had a lot to say about the pranks they played both before and after their "baby" sister's wedding. Melba joined in, promising Lindell and Bobby that their come-uppance would be a killer-diller when they were grooms.

Bobby, voice filled with glee, shouted, "Says you, Sister! We'll know what to look for and we won't let you near us!"

"Just try to stop us!" laughed Melba.   "We'll all be in cahoots, so you won't stand a chance!"

"Just wait and see, you guys", Lindell said in an ornery tone of voice. "I think MY girl will help me plan a tricky escape that you'll never figure out. She's clever that way, just ask Jeannie!"

Jeannie smiled sweetly, saying, "Well, Nedra IS a clever little thing. Even though we're great friends, she might decide it would behoove her to help Lindell escape the premises after their nuptials. Thing is, Lindell, are you planning something we haven't heard about? Are nuptials in the works?"

"Whoa, whoa, whoa! We aren't ready to go to the altar just yet; give it a rest!" Lindell said in protest. His tone of voice, however, was far from convincing!

The next days gave the sisters time for each other, and they enjoyed daily walks around town. Melba's surprise over the many changes in Kilgore since her move to Tulsa was genuine; there were so many new businesses, so many new oil derricks, and so many new people, taking it all in seemed impossible.

"When did the Kilgore Hotel open? It's magnificent!" Melba exclaimed on one of the many walks she took with Jeannie through downtown. "And, oh my! Just look at the new Crim Theater and the Texan! I hope we can take in at least one movie while I'm home!"

"I know Buron will bring us to the Texan to see one of the new movies. Next week, they're showing *Babes in Arms*, the new musical starring Judy Garland and Mickey Rooney. Buron's always interested in musical productions, and he adores Judy Garland! So, hot diggity dog! Let's hit him up for a 'date' when we get back home!" Jeannie giggled with glee.

"I'm with you! It's a grand plan, Sis!" Melba agreed.

. "Oh, look across the street!" Melba cried out. "The Jordan Dress Shop has always been simply snazzy; I'm sure you remember how Lydia and her bunch of bullies taunted me about going there with them. That was a terrible day! Now I just have to know whether YOU'VE bought any hot new threads in there since you became a married woman? Come on, tell the truth...!"

As the sisters continued their walk through the downtown area, Melba said, "I'm really surprised that most of the run-down stores and bars that used to be all over Main Street and Kilgore Avenue are actually gone. It looks more like a city now, and it's so PRETTY! It really makes me happy to see everything looking so much better. Kilgore's actually changing from an ugly "boom town" to a nice place to live. Maybe Clarence and I will get to move back here one of these days."

A few days later, Bobby was thrilled to get to take his "big sister" to his school. Kilgore Heights Elementary was growing. They'd added a new wing and 12 new classrooms since Melba left, and she had fun going to lunch with him and talking to two teachers she'd met when Anna Jean started at Kilgore Heights in fifth grade eight years ago, Miss Couch and Miss Bonham. They discussed Bobby and told Melba, "He's a good boy, but he does have a lot of energy! He's really excited to have you here, and we're both worried that he'll be upset when you leave."

"I'll be here for awhile", Melba told both teachers. "Bobby's spoiled because he's 'the baby', but I'm hoping he'll be okay when I go back to Tulsa. He knows Clarence and I intend to return to Kilgore as soon as we can and I think he's old enough to understand what that means."

Three weeks later, Melba got on the bus for her return trip to Tulsa. Little did she know, her Tulsa life was about to come to an end. New adventures and new challenges were on the horizon.

CHAPTER 36

Clarence met Melba's bus.

"Melba!" he yelled when he saw her descending the bus steps. "Come here, baby! I've missed you more than words can say!"

With that, they embraced and just stood there for a few minutes, holding each other. "I've been so lonely without you, Melby!" Clarence pronounced. "I'm SO glad you're home!"

Melba, too, had felt lost without her hubby. Although leaving Kilgore had been difficult, she knew her heart was wherever Clarence happened to be. It was good to be back in Tulsa.

That night, Clarence told her he had something serious to discuss. The threats of war were still rumbling, now more loudly than ever, and the underlying panic about what might happen was real. Clarence and Melba sat at the kitchen table, cups of coffee steaming in front of them.

"I'm considering taking a promotion with Greyhound. It would mean we'd have to relocate to Oklahoma City." As Clarence said these words, he studied Melba's face for her reaction.

"I've been offered a longer route, but I'd still be home almost as much. It's a good opportunity…"

"Oklahoma City, here we come!" Melba whooped, and her enthusiastic acceptance of his anxiously-made proposal surprised Clarence. He couldn't believe how easy Melba had made his decision.

"You're the best, Melby!" Clarence managed to say. The two sat in silence for more than a few minutes, just gazing at each other. Their eyes were twinkling, and they were smiling.

Two weeks later, Melba sat in the passenger seat of their new (to them, but pre-owned) 1937 Chevy pickup. In the back, carefully stacked and packed, rested all the furniture and household goods the couple had purchased in Tulsa. Clarence had found a new apartment in Oklahoma City that was similar to the one they vacated in Tulsa. Thankfully, the rent was almost identical.

Ina Belle, Nellie, Estel and the rest of the Tulsa family, though sad about the move, were supportive and sweet, wishing Clarence and Melba the best in their new venture. After all, Mom said, "Oklahoma City's only 100 miles away. We'll see you every now and then."

Clarence's job started with a bang! He was given the route between Oklahoma City and Tulsa for the first three weeks, after which they added a connecting route to Topeka, Kansas. He always loved the driving and scenery. No matter how many times he passed the same lakes, rivers, forested areas and towns, he never failed to notice something new.

Besides liking to drive, Clarence had always been fiercely competitive. He liked nothing more than having a stellar record for being on time, and he liked to challenge other drivers to "beat" his performance. It was of true importance to him to be THE best driver for Greyhound. He soon earned the respect of his employers and fellow drivers, and was driving longer, more important routes. Clarence was feeling good about life!

The first year in Oklahoma City was a joyful time for the young couple, and they even started talking about the possibility of having a baby... Actually, it was hard NOT to think about expanding their family. G.W. and Ozelle were expecting their SECOND child in June! It was certainly not too soon to start thinking about their plans for a child, or children!

At the same time, Melba and Clarence talked incessantly about the war in Europe and tried to understand what was really going on in those faraway places. They tuned in to all the fireside chats produced by President Roosevelt, listened to the daily news on the radio and voraciously read articles published in *The Daily Oklahoman*. It seemed impossible to form a lasting opinion about what the United States SHOULD do; the ensuing weeks and months were a time of confusion and fear about what could be coming, even during the happy days of their life in Oklahoma City.

Although Britain and France were at war with Germany following Germany's invasion of Poland, President Roosevelt continued to remain stoically determined to keep the United States out of a new war. Constant newspaper headlines gave American citizens at least some information about the unforgiveable atrocities Hitler was inflicting on most of Europe and even on parts of North Africa. Still, for almost two more years, American neutrality was upheld by Roosevelt. The fact that Britain was fighting the Germans without much outside support while managing to keep the Nazi nightmare at bay was troubling to many Americans who believed they should be helping the Brits. Meanwhile, the Nazi swastika symbol flew in more and more places. Then, on June 22, 1941, Hitler invaded the Soviet Union and the fighting escalated exponentially.

Tragically, the unspeakable horrors of Nazi rule meant the continuation of the systematic, yet carefully concealed, murders of what would eventually be more than six million Jews and another five million others of non-German origin, all at the hands of Hitler's minions. With all the nightmarish events going on overseas, life in Oklahoma seemed to be hovering in limbo. Plans for the future were definitely unsure, and life, in general, was on hold.

CHAPTER 37

A few weeks after Germany's invasion of the Soviet Union, Clarence entered the apartment looking very serious. He gave Melba a cursory kiss and said, "I have something to tell you. Greyhound has been good to us, so I guess my conscience is bothering me, especially since Lindell has been enlisted for almost a year! I know at my age I'll be called to active duty in the military if America ends up at war in Europe. The fact is, it's not IF we go to war, but WHEN. I don't want to wind up overseas, leaving you here alone. I've heard good things about the Border Patrol on the Texas-Mexico border. Maybe signing up with them would be a good thing. I know families are provided housing near the patrol stations and, hopefully, you could be with me."

Melba's expression was unreadable. She just looked at Clarence, apparently waiting for more of his thoughts.

Clarence continued, "If the war escalates in Europe, I'm afraid it may come to the United States through our unprotected borders in Mexico and Canada. The Border Patrol is a strong organization and working for them appeals to me. I can see the need for men on the Mexican border because it's not secure right now."

"How do you get trained if they select you as a recruit?" was the first question Melba had. "Will you get paid?"

"That's part of the good news, Melby," Clarence told her. "The pay is sweet! I'd be making more than I make right now with Greyhound just during training, and the annual salary for full-fledged Patrols is $2,000!"

"Wow! That sounds awesome, babe! Have you talked to anyone about signing up?" Melba, always the planner, just had to get some specific answers.

"There was an advertisement in *The Daily Oklahoman* last week," Clarence told her. I saved it to show you." With that, he went into the kitchen and returned with the paper.

<u>President Roosevelt's Call to Arms!</u>
United States Border Patrol Academy at Camp Chigas, El Paso, Texas
RECRUITING
Able-bodied, honorable, sound minded MEN.
THE JOB: Patrol & Control Texas/Mexican Border, Man Alien Detention Camps, Guard Diplomats, Assist Coast Guard in Searches for Axis Sabotaurs. **Apply TODAY! (contact # 3740)**

Melba read the advertisement, thought about it for a few minutes, smiled at Clarence and said, "Looks like I'll soon be the proud wife of a Border Patrolman!"

For the next two weeks, Clarence doggedly pursued the recruitment offices of the Border Patrol, gathering his personal information and going to the Oklahoma City   recruitment offices to complete the required paperwork. Of course, he never missed a day of work at Greyhound. After taking and passing the Civil Service Examination for Border Patrol duty, he waited for communication from the government. It seemed likely he'd be selected for training and Clarence hoped to be enrolled in the next patrol class scheduled to begin on November 3, 1941, two months away. As it turned out, the November class would begin without him. Clarence was learning about the "snail" pace inherent in governmental dealings!

Despite the disappointment of waiting an indefinite time before hearing back from the Border Patrol, some entirely different and amazing news was coming Clarence's way…

Melba met him at the door to their apartment on one of his returns from a "haul" to Kansas City. The look on her face confirmed she had something special to tell him. He guessed before she got the words out of her mouth.

"You're pregnant!!!" Clarence whooped.

Melba just beamed at the love of her life. "Yes, I am!" was all she said.

CHAPTER 38

"Oh, my God!" Clarence whispered as he wrapped his arms around Melba and gently hugged her. "This is the most fantastic news I've ever had; I'm speechless!"

Melba pulled away and looked into his eyes. Then she said, "You'll be the very best father, that much I know for certain. And you don't need to be speechless; we have a lot to discuss!" With that, she planted a big kiss on Clarence's cheek, gave him another hug and chuckled. "Have you ever changed a diaper, Mr. Winters?"

At that point, both of them were on "cloud 9" and lost in thoughts about bringing a new human being into the world. It was definitely exciting, but also overwhelming. With the probability of a second world war looming in the background, and with Clarence's decision to join the United States Border Patrol, the knowledge that a BABY was growing in Melba was almost too much to take in. Both partners knew life as they knew it was about to change forever, and it was both a beautiful truth and a frightening fact. Eventually, they settled down and began to discuss their options.

"I'm only a month along, baby." Melba stated in a low voice. "My due date won't be before next April, so we have plenty of time to plan the best way to handle where the baby will be born and what we'll do when you get recruited."

"I know, Hon. And I don't want to make any crazy decisions. After all, this is our CHILD and we have to consider EVERYTHING." Clarence made these comments in a serious tone of voice. He was obviously already filled with the sense of responsibility the birth of his child would give him. Clearly, he wanted to do the right thing.

Melba was comforted by the fact that Clarence was taking her pregnancy so seriously. She hadn't doubted how he'd react, but hearing him talk about things really made her feel safe. She knew he'd take care of her AND their child.

Melba, blessedly, had minimal morning sickness and Clarence's work schedule continued without interruption. During his days on the road, Melba busied herself with plans for leaving Oklahoma and began packing non-essential items.

Knowing she'd need larger clothes soon, and determined to conceal her condition as long as possible, Melba ordered a free maternity catalog from Lane Bryant. The pictures and comments in the catalog confirmed what Melba already knew about all things dealing with having a baby: well-bred women kept their impending motherhood to themselves! The goal of maternity clothing was to cover up and hide an expanding tummy during pregnancy for as long as possible.

"I know you're happy about my pregnancy, and so am I," she told Clarence, "but it's not appropriate for others to know about it yet. We'll have to wait awhile before telling the family, and I can't let the neighbors think I'm expecting."

"I just don't understand why people are such fuddy duddies about a married woman who's expecting! It makes me worse than angry; I want to shout our good news so the world will hear it!" Clarence spat these words and appeared to Melba like he might start a fight with the first person who looked his way.

"Oh, honey," Melba soothed, "we'll be showing off our new baby before you know it. As soon as I'm really 'showing', we'll tell the family. It's just considered poor taste to openly discuss such a private matter, especially at first."

"Well, you know I don't agree, but I promise not to 'grand stand' about our little secret. But my promise won't hold up much longer; I'm dying to tell everyone we know!" With those words still hanging in the air, Clarence left the apartment and headed to work.

In a blink, it was early October, 1940, and Melba was in the last month of her first trimester. She was still wearing her regular clothes, but they were beginning to be a bit tight around the waist. She had made a few maternity dresses but wasn't yet wearing them.

"I'll be wearing my 'big' clothes soon enough", Melba thought as she tried to imagine how her belly would look when the baby grew larger. There were so many things to consider, Melba thought with a mixture of happy anticipation and dread.

As it turned out, the days of autumn came and went relentlessly fast, and it soon became reasonable to inform the family and a few close friends about the pregnancy. When Thanksgiving arrived, Clarence had the day off and they drove to Tulsa to celebrate with the family. Melba was close to the end of her fourth month, and she had a definite "baby bump". She and Clarence decided to let Mom, Nellie, Harvey, Estel and Ruby be surprised, so they arrived at 4837 South 32 West Avenue, honked the horn on the truck, and got out to greet everyone.

"Hi-de-ho, everyone!" Clarence yelled as they walked across the lawn. "It's grand to see you!"

"Oh, my gosh, you guys!" Nellie gasped with a huge smile on her face. "Melba, why didn't you tell us? You're expecting!"

"So I am!" Melba laughed. "We wanted to let you know in person, so we waited until now. I'm due sometime in the spring, probably about mid-April. We're really excited!"

Mom was thrilled! She gave both of them crushing hugs and exclaimed, "It's about time you provided me with a grandchild! Wonder of wonders, it's simply KEEN!"

With that, everyone started talking at once. The next hour was spent catching up and, of course, discussing BABIES!

Nellie told Melba she had lots of "baby things" to pass her way and the two simply could not stop talking. "Melba, you know I had a pretty good job when the kids were little. I was able to buy plenty of baby clothes, and I have a cool stroller, a cradle and even a crib for later. I want you to have everything!"

Melba was taken aback with this offer; Nellie had never been overly friendly toward her and it was hard to believe she'd give her all her baby stuff! "Gosh, Nellie! That's really swell of you! Are you sure Harvey won't mind?"

"Course not! We're not having anymore kids unless God plays a trick on us! You and Clarence will need all you can get, especially with this war coming our way. Things are tight with the rationing; my nephew or niece should inherit our 'collection'!" Nellie said all this with a conviction that surprised Melba. Her sister-in-law wasn't usually like this…

The day was unseasonably warm for late November, reaching a high in the mid-seventies by late afternoon. After the turkey and dressing (yes, Mom managed to get the bird and the rest of the ingredients!), followed by pumpkin and mincemeat pies, the family sat outside and enjoyed the afternoon. It seemed impossible that war was in full swing across the Atlantic, and everyone tried to avoid any mention of "it".

They made turkey sandwiches late in the day, ate some more pie, and said their farewells. It was agreed that they'd get together before the baby was due and exchange the layette items.

Clarence explained his situation, saying, "I'm waiting for confirmation that I've been accepted as a trainee for the Texas Border Patrol. When that comes, I'll be sent to El Paso for six weeks at their Academy, and Melba and I have agreed I'll take her to Kilgore to her Mom and Dad's. Depending on when I'm called, the baby may have already arrived, but, chances are good Melba will still be awaiting the birth. I'm praying I can be with her when her time comes."

"Whatever the scenario, babe, it will be okay!" Melba stated this with passion. "You know how I feel about your training and induction; it's just as important to me as it is to you. My family in Kilgore will take good care of me and our baby, regardless."

Following nods of understanding and a few more questions from Nellie, hugs were shared. They said goodbye to their Tulsa family and headed back to Oklahoma City.

CHAPTER 39

Little did they know what was coming in just a few days. America would be thrust into World War II following the hellish, devastating attack by Japanese bombers on Pearl Harbor, Hawaii. It would happen on December 7, 1941, followed by Germany's declaration of war on America just one day later. The reality of war would change everything.

The surprise attack on an American military base was shockingly brutal; more than 2,400 servicemen and civilians lost their lives within a two-hour period of time.

President Roosevelt's isolationist policy came to a screeching halt on December 8, 1941 when he made the following announcement to the world: "No matter how long it may take us to overcome this premeditated invasion, the American people in their righteous might will win through to absolute victory."

On the same day, President Roosevelt asked Congress to declare war against Japan. The declaration passed with just one dissenting vote. Three days later, Germany and Italy sided with their Japanese allies and declared war on the United States. America was suddenly deeply invested in a global war that would have a formidable effect on the entire civilized world.

Two days after Pearl Harbor, Melba received a frantic call from Mama.

"We got an urgent telegraph from the Philippines this morning. Lindell has been injured! He's in a hospital at Fort Stotsenberg, near Clark Field, in critical condition! His squadron, you know, has been at Clark Field for the past two months, awaiting orders. The Japs attacked them during a three-hour air raid, blowing up planes, barracks, field shops, everything. Our men were killed running to their planes; they were unable to defend themselves. We don't know when we'll hear anything more since all the Philippine Islands are being attacked by the Japs. It doesn't look good..." Mama was sobbing and Papa was just as upset, saying "Lindell has to make it, Sister! I know he'll be alright. You just have to pray...!"

Melba was in shock. How could this have happened? Back in October, Lindell had written letters from California and then from Guam, talking about his deployment to the South Pacific. He'd talked about how bored the men were with the slow journey to the Philippines. After they'd arrived, he'd written about having little to do as he waited for flight instructions.

It just wasn't possible! Why, just two weeks ago she got a letter from Lindell. In it, he'd said, "This is some place! Palm trees, papayas, mangos, bamboo, and even orchids growing everywhere. In fact, most of the trees here on the post have orchids growing on them. They are not very big, but they are the real thing!" He'd continued the letter, telling her about his hoped-for assignment to the 28th Bombardment Squadron, saying, "The 28th is a medium bombardment outfit with B-18s. I hope to find out where I'll be soon."

All Melba could do was share the awful news with Clarence and pray for her brother. How could the world be such a hateful place? It just wasn't fair, she mused.

CHAPTER 40

As it turned out, Clarence did not get any communication from the Border Patrol for another three months, despite America's deepening involvement in the War. He checked back with the recruitment office repeatedly, but they stated they were overwhelmed with the need to recruit and train over 100 men per month. Clarence was told he would hear from them as soon as possible, and encouraged not to worry.

In the meantime, work at Greyhound had become more intensive with America's involvement in the war; the government was shipping recruits for the military to training bases throughout the United States. Greyhound drivers were in demand, and overtime pay was available. Because Clarence was a top-ranked driver, he was able to secure a good measure of overtime. With the impending birth of their child, he was more than happy to put in the extra hours. Melba was supportive; she recognized that the overtime pay would help them during the transition to new work for the government via the Border Patrol.

Regardless of her understanding, she was desperately lonely when Clarence was away more than a few days. She called and sent letters to Kilgore and told her parents and siblings what was going on. She told them she was expecting their first baby, told them about Clarence's decision to join the Border Patrol, told them about the "double" waiting game they were enduring, and asked for prayers and understanding, even as they continued to ask HER for prayers for Lindell.

Melba let her parents know their tentative plans for having her come to Kilgore while Clarence went through training in El Paso. The big question was when this would happen, and whether their baby would be born before Clarence was deployed.

All the questions about their future weighed heavily on both of them, but Melba was left to worry and stress over the possibilities all alone when Clarence was on a "run". Her worries about Lindell were almost overwhelming, but she knew her own situation deserved her attention and commitment.

She truly tried to keep busy. Preparing the baby's layette, taking care of her health by going on long daily walks and eating as wholesomely as possible, making sure she got enough rest, and keeping up with letter-writing to ensure the family knew what was going on did add up to "busy". All that coupled with trying to find out about any news from Lindell gave Melba a lot to do. Still, Melba couldn't help thinking, at least occasionally, about the REAL future. After all, she reasoned, at some point she knew she would do something truly special with her life, something more than being a wife and mother, a sister, a child. It wasn't that these things were unimportant to her, but she knew there had to be more to her life than motherhood and homemaking. She never forgot Papa's words to Mama years ago in Damon when he was telling her about the oil boom in Kilgore and planning the move. She knew she HAD to "hitch her wagon to a star" and make some kind of real difference in the world. What would happen with the war? What would happen with Lindell? Would she be needed to work in the military? She couldn't help wondering when all the events taking place both in and around her would allow time for "making a difference."

It was Wednesday, February 18, 1942. Clarence was working and on the road to Kansas City. That very afternoon, a letter was in the mail that took Melba's breath away. It was the acceptance letter from the United States Border Patrol Agency, and it detailed Clarence's assignment for training. He was told to report for duty in El Paso on Sunday, March 15th. That meant he must give his "two week notice" on Monday! His last day of work for Greyhound would be Friday, March 6, Melba calculated. The sudden knowledge they'd be on the road to Kilgore the very next week and Clarence would be leaving her right at the end of her pregnancy seemed crazy! She would be having the baby ALONE! Sudden terror hit her like a brick!

Slumping on the sofa, Melba held the letter, nearly tearing it apart as she gripped it as if the paper was ALIVE! As she tried to calm down and come to grips with the actual facts regarding the near future, she realized things would not be as she had imagined. Now all she wanted was the instant return of her HUSBAND, but she knew Clarence wouldn't be home for another day.

"Damn it!" Melba moaned. "Damn it, damn it, damn it!!" After a few (admittedly self-pitying!) tears, she inhaled deeply, sighed, and got up. What good will a "pity party" accomplish, she thought. I just have to do what Papa always said when any of us got upset or moody: "You have to pull yourself up by your bootstraps and get on with your life!"

Melba grabbed a sweater from the closet and set out for a long walk. She decided to go to the Carnegie Library   on

NW Third and Robinson, about a 2.5 mile walk each way. Maybe it was because she was upset about having to be in Kilgore for the birth of their baby, but Melba was feeling a little reckless. So what if the walk was a little too long, she fumed.

Walking at a brisk pace, she arrived at the sandstone and brick two-story library building in 55 minutes. Although somewhat winded, she managed to sit on one of the many wrought iron benches adorning the lawn to regain her composure. When she entered the building, her first stop was the librarian's desk to request books about labor and delivery. The librarian was very helpful, and the most recently publicized book about childbirth was the one she advised Melba to read. She checked it out and started the walk back home.

Later, Melba told everyone in the family (the women, at least!) about the amazing book by Grantley Dick-Read called *Childbirth Without Fear.* From the minute she started reading after finally getting home from her "marathon" walk, the gripping fear that had been haunting her simply vanished! Dr. Read's explanations about everything that would happen during the baby's birth just made SENSE, and the fears Melba had tried to hold at bay for the past six months truly did melt away.

"Well!" she thought. "I've been rather silly about my situation! Just wait 'til I explain all the birthing stuff to Clarence! I know he's just as worried as me, but we've pretended we're fine. What a laugh! I know I'll be SO much better off after we've talked!" With those things flitting about in her much more relaxed mind, Melba got into bed and fell into a deep, healing sleep.

The next day, she continued to read and reread *Childbirth Without Fear*, taking notes when she was afraid she'd forget something important. After witnessing the birth of Bobby back in Damon, Melba had every reason to face the birth of her own child with a great deal of trepidation! Mama was no role model for "pleasant" childbirth! Good grief! Her entire pregnancy had been a nightmare for the family, not to mention how it had affected poor Papa. Melba just prayed HER experience would be less dreadful. She still remembered with great clarity the long and frightening night Bobby was born!

One of the reportedly positive techniques advocated by Dr. Read was relaxation aided by deep breathing. Melba thought it sounded, basically, good; she just had difficulty imaging RELAXING during labor! Maybe the doctor in Kilgore (whoever he turned out to be!) would be able to help her understand how to make it work. Melba determined to ask Ozelle what she knew about the birthing process Dr. Read called "natural".

It was simply weird to her that she and Ozelle were expecting their babies at the same time! In Jeannie's letters, she told Melba Ozelle's due date was in June! How truly awesome was that? Jeannie told Melba the doctor Ozelle was using, Dr. Allums, had been Mama's "attending" physician back when Bobby was born, but that Mama had opted to use a midwife. (Apparently, Jeannie never realized Papa could not afford to let Mama have Bobby in the hospital! Apparently, too, Jeannie had forgotten that Melba knew the doctor!) Dr. Allums, according to Jeannie, used all the "newest" medical knowledge in his practice, and both Jeannie and Ozelle were SURE Melba would find him more than acceptable.

CHAPTER 41

Late that night, Clarence got home. Melba tried not to show too much excitement as she welcomed him home and said, "Something came in the mail yesterday that I know you'll want to see!" With that, she held out the letter from the Border Patrol.

Clarence looked at it, and his expression said it all. His eyes grew wide, a big grin appeared, and he actually WHOOPED in delight. "I made it!! I thought I'd NEVER hear from them! I'm gonna flip my wig! This is SWEET!" With that, he grabbed Melba's hands and pulled her to him for a crushing hug.

"When do I report for duty?" Clarence finally managed to ask. "How long do we have?"

"Not long, babe", Melba said. "Not long at all! You have to be in El Paso on March 15th! That means we'll be going to Kilgore in just over two weeks if you turn in your resignation and give Greyhound your two week notice on Monday. We should be leaving for Kilgore around March 10. We don't have much time!"

Clarence looked stunned, but elated. "It's hard to take all this in after such a long wait! I'd about given up on being selected as a recruit, and now it's REAL. Part of me hates leaving Greyhound, but I know it's for the best. I have to do whatever I can to help the United States. This war continues to escalate and things look grim. I just hope my decision to go with the Border Patrol turns out to be right for our family!"

For the next few minutes both were silent, thinking their own thoughts and coming to grips with the suddenly urgent time-frame; both Clarence and Melba were attempting to deal with the immediacy of their situation.

As always after a three-day haul for Greyhound, Clarence was tired. But with this stunning news, he was wide awake and beginning to feel the effects of such long-awaited, expected but not yet "real" news. It was to be a late-to-bed night, with lots of discussion still to come.

Melba, too, was wide-eyed. She desperately wanted to talk! In fact, she was so keen to tell him all about Dr. Read's book and her new thoughts about childbirth that she could hardly stand having to "wait in line". After all, the birth of their child WAS important...maybe even more important, thought Melba, than the Border Patrol!

"You won't believe what I've been reading!" Melba finally blurted. "I waked to the library the other day; your letter from the Border Patrol came and I was upset with the timing. It was frightening to know I'll probably be having the baby without YOU. So I determined to get as much information about childbirth as I could find. You know I've only seen Dr. Donaldson, and he's not even an obstetrician. He really hasn't had much to say other than that I need to eat "right" and get plenty of rest. I've been left to wonder about the actual BIRTH! All Dr. Donaldson says is, "Don't worry your pretty little head about that. I'll take care of you; after all, you and Clarence told me you want the baby to be born in the hospital."

"Anyway, honey, I finally decided it was up to ME to find every bit of 'birthing' information that's available. The library seemed like a good place to start!" With these words, Melba looked at her husband to see if he understood her mood. Clarence just nodded and asked, "What did you learn?"

"The librarian at Carnegie was helpful. She suggested I check out a new book written by Dr. Grantley Dick-Read called *Childbirth Without Fear*. I've read it, honey. I like what Dr. Read says! You know I was only 13 years old when Mama birthed Bobby at home. I really didn't know the midwife, Mrs. Cooper. She seemed nice enough, but I wondered if she knew enough to help Mama. It was a horrible experience for me; no one explained anything and all I knew was Mama was screaming in pain for hours, Papa was outside the house, and I was SURE Mama was going to die! It was the worst thing I've ever experienced, and no one ever talked to me about the facts of childbirth. Mama never even MENTIONED the delivery after Bobby arrived. It left a lot of emotional scars..."

Clarence pulled Melba close to him and whispered, "It will be okay, baby. Tell me more about this Dr. Read's birthing techniques."

They talked for another two hours, sometimes dwelling on the baby's birth and all the preparations for the temporary move to Kilgore, and sometimes taking a "detour" to discuss Clarence's impending "boot camp" in El Paso. There was SO much to handle! But, eventually, both partners were worn out and ready to sleep. The next weeks would be busy, to say the least, but both knew they had each other.

CHAPTER 42

Clarence turned in his resignation, as planned, on the next workday. Giving two weeks notice, his last day with Greyhound would be March 6, 1942. They made several long-distance calls to Kilgore, using a pay phone. Papa had installed their own telephone (on a "party line" with 5 neighboring families), and actually getting to talk to the family was comforting! Plans were made for the move. Clarence still had to make the drive to Tulsa to get the baby furniture and all the other "stuff" Nellie was donating.

After getting the crib, highchair, stroller and changing table from Nellie, Clarence knew he could not get all their things in the back of his pickup. Estel, thankfully, agreed to pitch in and haul the rest in HIS pickup. They really didn't have a lot, but the pickup beds weren't that big, either. On moving day, March 10, everything was loaded and covered with waterproof tarps. The now "homeless" couple and Estel set off for Kilgore, a 323 mile, five hour drive in the best of conditions. Fortunately, the weather was good with clear skies and a spring-like temperature hovering in the sixties.

Just before dusk, the two-vehicle caravan pulled into Buster's driveway. Melba felt strange; coming home eight months pregnant seemed bizarre despite her six years of marriage!

"Over two years have flown by since I was last here and it sometimes seems even longer", Melba said in a soft voice.

"I can't think how I'll feel giving birth in KILGORE! I'm a scaredy cat; afraid of my shadow!"

Clarence helped her out of the truck and they walked to the door. No one had heard them arrive and Melba tapped on the door, saying, "Hello! Anybody home?"

She heard Bobby yell, "It's Sister!!"

The door was flung open and Bobby almost knocked them down as he hugged Melba and high-fived the men. "You're lookin' swell, Sis! Just wait 'til all the women see you!"

At that, Mama came to greet them. "Lands, Sister! It sure is good that I'm about to be blessed with another grandchild! Jean Ann's not a baby anymore! Just lookin' at the way your baby's situated, I'll be real surprised if it's not a girl!"

Melba felt herself blushing. Why did Mama have to be so quick to talk about her "condition" in front of the men and Bobby? The unexpected giggle that escaped her throat was followed by cathartic laughter. "Oh, Mama! I'd love to have a girl! Thanks for being YOU; I needed to laugh!" With that, the two women embraced and Mama, always a "hands-on" woman, patted Melba's belly and said, "Welcome to Kilgore, little one!"

"Where's Papa?" Melba asked.

"He's down at Laird Hill checking a pump. He wanted to be here, but said he'll be back for supper. And Jeannie and Buron are coming for supper tonight; she can't wait to see you and your baby bump! As soon as Buron gets home from work they'll be on the way. Let's go inside and finish up with the cooking!" Mama said all this so fast that it was hard to hear her; she was just as excited as Melba!

Following Mama into the kitchen, Melba suddenly felt faint. She stood at the counter, both hands gripping the top. Mama noticed, saying, "Oh, my, honey! You've exhausted yourself with this long trip! Come on back to the parlor and rest on the sofa while I finish up dinner."

As Melba rested, her mind was whirling. She couldn't help thinking about Lindell. Just being in this house brought memories front and center. She remembered Lindell when he completed his flight training at Stockton Field Air Corps Advanced Flying School in California. He was so proud, and so was the entire family! Papa had a framed photo of him in his aviator's uniform sitting on a table in the parlor. He was amazingly handsome, Melba mused. Of course, immediately after he earned his pilot's license, he was deployed to U.S. held Clark Field near Manila, Philippines. Not long afterward, America entered the war. Part of her hated that he was so smart and so dedicated; he was placed in harm's way because of his training. Even so, she was fiercely proud of Lindell! Now he was injured and, Melba knew, in critical condition. She would always respect and love him, but not having the chance to tell him face to face was upsetting. Not being able to comfort him and assist with his recovery was equally upsetting!

G.W. and Ozelle would soon be here, Melba knew, and she could hardly wait to see both her nephew, Larry, and her baby niece, Jean Ann. Since Jean Ann was only 20 months old, she was just a toddler, and Melba knew she would be adorable! It did not seem possible that G.W. and Ozelle had another child! The time away from her family was beginning to be more than a "blip"; the birth of the next generation was happening, and she knew she had missed some of it! Maybe, with the fact that she had to come home to have HER baby, things would change and become more the way she always envisioned. There's no doubt that we are close. There's no doubt that sharing our lives is important. There's no doubt that, despite distances and war, we all want to keep our family at the forefront! These were Melba's thoughts as her things were unpacked and the upcoming events of the next six weeks became her reality.

Estel and Clarence unloaded everything. Mama and Papa had cleared the bedroom that used to be shared by Melba and Jeannie, making room for Melba's bed, the rocking chair and the baby's crib. The rest of their things would be stored in the one-car garage. Clarence would only be here with Melba for four more days and then he'd be gone. She was already upset.

CHAPTER 43

As it turned out, Melba had almost no time to worry about ANYTHING, not even about being in Kilgore without Clarence when the baby came. It seemed the world moved at its own pace, as indeed it tends to do. The day of Clarence's departure for training came and went, and both of them survived the ordeal of saying goodbye. March 15 was probably harder on Clarence than on Melba. He was distraught about not being with her when the baby arrived.

"Melby, you know not being here is going to kill me!" he mourned. "I don't care what the 'rules' are about phone calls. When you go into labor, I have to talk to you! If there's any way at all to get back here, I'll do it!"

"I know you will, honey!" Melba said much more calmly than she imagined possible. "I'll be okay! You know Dr. Allums will take good care of me AND our baby! I really trust him; he has been good to our family, and he knows what he's doing."

Clarence did not look convinced, but he reached out and took Melba's hand, saying, "Baby, you just have to be okay! You are my life; I could not live without you!"

"You know I feel the same! Me and the baby will be waiting for your return, no matter WHEN it happens. Try not to worry about us and take care of yourself! I want you to be the very best cadet the Border Patrol has ever seen! You are going to 'wow' them, Clarence! Just make me proud, and I will do the same for you! Having our baby is the best thing   that's ever happened to me; I want you to be the happiest, proudest new dad that anyone has ever seen! Won't it be just glorious to return to us with your training DONE and your new baby HERE, just waiting to meet her daddy?"

Melba said the last words laughingly since they really did not know whether the baby would be male or female. Melba had joked all along, though, that their baby GIRL would be the "apple of her daddy's eyes". Now they would just have to wait and see…

Then it was time for Clarence to leave.

Buron came by to drive his brother-in-law to the bus station for the trip to El Paso, and Melba gave Clarence one last hug. He was on his way, and Melba held back the tears; she refused to send him to training with anything except smiles and positive well-wishes.

The next week was harder than either Melba or Clarence had anticipated, but in completely different ways.

Clarence arrived at camp late Sunday evening, was greeted by one of the officers in charge of recruits, and was introduced to a group of trainees. Following a brief review of the next day's events, a light dinner was served and the men were taken to their dormitory for the night.

The night seemed short, and the early-morning bugle call was startling! Clarence jumped up, quickly made up his cot, pulled on his training clothes, and raced through his morning ritual to arrive at "all call" just on time: a quarter past 6:00. The sergeant in charge called roll, issued orders regarding the first event of the morning, and stood watch as the 15 recruits ran the required 2 miles. That was followed by a series of strenuous exercises…

Breakfast was appreciated following the morning workout. Then training began on use of weapons, handling obstacles in the field, working with partners to reduce chances of injury, and learning Spanish. The day's activities were nonstop; Clarence suddenly understood why so many recruits failed to make the "cut". He made a personal vow to do whatever it took to succeed, and he realized he was paying more attention to his trainers than he'd ever paid to other superiors in the past. Although Clarence was confident about his ability to handle the physical rigors of training, he knew he had to recognize and work to overcome his own limitations in order to survive and excel.

The days of training went by quickly. There was so much to take in, and Clarence found himself completely caught up in every aspect of "boot camp". He thought about Melba, but mostly when the day's classes ended and he had a few hours to himself. Letters were written almost daily, but mostly Clarence had just enough energy to write a few lines about the grueling training and a few more lines about his worries for his "Melby" and their soon-to-be-born child.

Simultaneously, Clarence could not help thinking about the requirements for graduation from the Academy: Border Patrol Agent trainees must successfully pass the entire test during one class period and the test consisted of three timed events in addition to a long written exam. The events kept filtering through his mind, almost constantly: one and a half mile run (maximum time 13 minutes), confidence   course

(maximum time two and a half minutes), 220 yard dash
(maximum time 46 seconds)...

"Oh, bother!" thought Clarence as he drifted off to a dreamless sleep. He was simply too tired to dream!

Melba's first week back in Kilgore was filled with the excitement of seeing family, but her heart was sad since she could not be with Clarence. In between "good" things, she could not shake her worries about both Clarence and what he was going through and the fact that her "time" was just about to be reality! Going through the motions of living was okay, but she knew her life was changing at breakneck speed and felt like a rider on a roller coaster being pulled to the top of the "drop off". She was either euphoric with anticipation or melancholy with dread. What would the future hold? Would the baby be born healthy? Would they both survive the birth? Would they have to move to some dreadful place when Clarence was assigned a post? She felt physically weighted down by her pregnancy and mentally weighted down by fear and the unknown. What a mess...!

Trying to shake herself free of these oppressive thoughts, Melba decided to go for a long walk; after all, she reasoned, walking had always helped her cope with whatever was wrong!

"Mama?" she called. "I'm going out for a walk. I'll be back after while."

"Okay, Sister, but just don't go too far! Remember you could go into labor no matter what Doc Allums told you about it being a few weeks away. He sure wasn't right about ME when Bobby decided to arrive!"

"I know, Mama. I'll be careful. I just need to move around and try to shake my doldrums" Melba said as she went out the front door.

An hour later, she was walking down Main Street, window shopping and wondering if the next time she visited the shops in Kilgore might be AFTER the baby arrived. Her thoughts included how it would feel to go on walks with her new baby in the stroller Nellie had given her. It would be such fun, she mused.

By the time Melba arrived back at the house, she was feeling much better! The unhappy mood she'd been trying to get out of for the past few days was actually gone; she smiled and hummed "Chattanooga Choo Choo" as she walked into the kitchen to see what Mama was doing.

"Well, if you don't look like a ray of sunshine!" Mama exclaimed when she saw Sister. "What's got you looking so happy?"

"Oh, Mama", Sister said dreamily. "I've been thinking about our baby and how wonderful it will be to hold him or her and just look at each little finger and toe! It's finally feeling real, and I'm just a happy girl!"

"Well, you should be!" Mama pretended to scold. "After all, you and Clarence will soon be in your own house with your very own baby. What could be better?"

"I know, Mama", Melba said. "I just wish there was no war. I can't help worrying about Lindell and all the others who are already in the middle of the conflict…"

"There, there, Sis. Don't get yourself back in a funk. Just keep being positive for the sake of your baby." Mama said this with a tiny catch in her voice. Uncertainty about her second-born son made for lots of late-night tears, but she did not want to upset Sister.

As always, there was no time for "brooding". It was time to fix supper, do chores and get some letters written to Nellie and Mom as well as to Clarence. Thank goodness, Melba thought, the days were full of plenty to do; she knew staying busy was mandatory for her sanity!

CHAPTER 44

The next three weeks sped by in a whir of "baby preparations", helping Mama around the house, keeping up with Anna Jean and HER issues as a new bride whose husband might be conscripted into the service at any moment, writing letters and taking them to the post office, and staying active by walking just about everywhere.

Before long, there were only three weeks left until Clarence would graduate and come home! Melba was sure the baby would arrive before he got home, but she couldn't help hoping the baby's birth would be late! Then she had her scheduled appointment on April 8. Doc Allums told her that she was "dilating". Melba suddenly knew the birth was imminent. Jeannie had accompanied her that afternoon, and both of them were ecstatic and giggling like school girls as they left the clinic.

The very first thing Melba wanted to do was call Clarence, but she knew a call had to be "an emergency". With great effort, she refrained from going to the phone. Doctor Allums' instructions were to take it easy, stop walking long distances, and to call him immediately when she started having contractions. He told her she might not start labor for several days, or even longer. That seemed preposterous to Melba! "Good grief", she exclaimed when she and Jeannie

166

were alone, "how can I just sit around and WAIT?"

Jeannie laughed and reached out to hug her sister, saying, "Only you would say such a thing! After all, having a baby is nothing but a 'waiting game'!"

It was Wednesday. Melba wrote a letter to Clarence and told him she was dilating; the birth would be very soon! She would call, she assured him, when her contractions started and were a "sure thing". She expressed her undying love...

At 2:00 a.m. on Monday, April 13, Melba was awakened by the pain of a contraction. Buron was called to take her to the hospital where Dr. Allums said he would meet them. Upon arriving at Roy H. Laird Memorial Hospital, Melba told the man at the front desk that she HAD to call her husband! Even as she said this, a briskly-walking nurse appeared pushing a wheelchair. Before she could even move, the nurse pushed the wheelchair behind Melba and "encouraged" her to sit.

"Now, now, honey", the nurse said firmly, "just relax. I'll take good care of you and your baby!"

"But you don't understand!" Melba responded just as firmly. "I need a telephone! My husband is in El Paso training for the Border Patrol, and he HAS to be told I'm in labor!"

"We'll have to ask the doctor about making that phone call", the nurse replied with a bit less sweetness in her voice.

Buron tried to reassure her, saying he would call Clarence as soon as the doctor arrived. Tears of frustration streamed down Melba's cheeks as she tried to behave "appropriately" (whatever THAT means, she thought!). But the nurse continued pushing her down the hallway into the

168

maternity ward.

Buron was told to go to the designated "Waiting Room". It had a telephone he could use.

Then Dr. Allums arrived and everything happened so fast, it was impossible to react. Melba just did what she was told, hoping Buron could reach Clarence and something would be done about the unexpected decisions being made…

"Mrs. Winters! Wake up, dear! You have a beautiful baby girl!" A different nurse was standing next to Melba's hospital bed, and she was back in a regular room.

"Don't you want to hold her, honey?" the nurse soothed. "You've been 'out' for awhile, but everything is good! Your baby is healthy and doing well, and you are in good shape, too. Just look at her…" The nurse held out a tiny bundle wrapped in a pink blanket. Melba could see a bit of dark brown hair peeking out of the blanket. She felt disengaged from her body, and her brain refused to "tune in". But when the nurse placed Toby (yes, her name would be Toby!) in her arms, Melba was simply mesmerized. Toby was PERFECT! She had an adorable round face and dark wispy curls adorned her head. Her mouth was set in a precious pink pout, and her almost-black eyes stared at Melba with what seemed to be curiosity! Although Melba felt sure she was wrong about the look Toby seemed to be giving her, she could not help gazing back and mentally encouraging this newborn baby to acknowledge HER as important. After all, she'd just given birth to the infant! Surely some form of "thank you" was in order!

As quickly as these thoughts raced through Melba's mind, they vanished and she simply cradled Toby. There was instant bonding; this child was HERS. She would never allow anything to happen to Toby! Taking care of her became the only reality for Melba, and she was overpowered with a feeling so deep and so strong that it took her breath away. She was experiencing the ultimate joy that should, but doesn't always, accompany motherhood. It was exhilarating!

The nurse told Melba to enjoy her time with the baby. Feeding time would soon be over; new mothers must have plenty of rest! Melba was incensed!

"What do you mean? Are you telling me I can't keep my baby right here with me?" Melba demanded with fury in her voice.

"Calm down, honey", the nurse said sweetly. "We have to allow your body to heal, and your baby will be perfectly fine in the nursery. After all, we certainly know how to tend to these newborns, and your baby is healthy. She'll be brought back to you for her next feeding in four hours."

Although Melba was angry, she recognized the futility of trying to fight "the system". When Dr. Allums came to check on her, she'd let him know her opinion and how she wanted things to be done! Surely he would listen to her and ensure Toby was left in her room, not down the hall in the nursery with other babies! And then the tears started flowing. Melba suddenly felt so alone; she needed Clarence here to fight these battles and to take care of Toby and her. It just wasn't fair!

It seemed the time with Toby ended much too fast. Melba told the nurse, "I intend to speak to Dr. Allums about this! It's not right for you to make MY decision for me. I want to keep Toby right here!"

"That's just fine, Mrs. Winters. But until we get different orders from your doctor, all newborns are returned to the nursery after feedings." The nurse wasn't mean-sounding when she said this, but she seemed to be sure of her "rights".

Melba said nothing more, but this situation solidified her determination to use knowledge as leverage for change; women deserved better and she would not be a passive weakling! She would speak to the doctor even though it was clear that Dr. Allums was part of the problem. Melba instinctively knew the nurse's orders were not policies written by WOMEN!

CHAPTER 45

Melba was out of the hospital bed, showered, dressed and ready to receive Toby from the nursery long before her scheduled feeding time. She was ready for the scolding from Nurse Eugenia since post-delivery mothers were expected to stay in bed.

Melba had been informed she was risking severe consequences if she disobeyed the hospital's policies about post-partum care. The policies, Dr. Allums had informed her, were in place to prevent the many disastrous outcomes evidenced throughout history. Melba did not care; she was going home!

It was Sunday, April 19, 1942. Melba heard the crying babies before the clatter of hospital cribs rolling down the hallway alerted her to Toby's arrival. Nurse Eugenia pushed the crib into the room, and immediately demanded, "What are you doing out of bed, Mrs. Winters? You know the rules!"

"I'm going home today. My sister brought Toby's gown and blanket last night, and I intend to feed her, then get her ready for the ride home. I appreciate your concerns about my decision to travel home by automobile, but there is no reason to go by ambulance! I am perfectly okay! My mother had ALL her babies at home, all five of us. There were no complications and she never set foot in a hospital. My mind is made up!"

Melba's tone of voice gave no room for argument and Nurse Eugenia simply nodded disapprovingly and pushed   the mobile crib holding Toby inside the room. Then she left abruptly, never looking back.

Melba sighed, then smiled as she picked up her precious newborn. Cradling Toby carefully, she patted her back and crooned, "We're going home, baby girl! The world awaits you, and the world will never be the same…" She could not stop smiling as she sat in the rocking chair, picked up the bottle of formula (Women were encouraged to select bottle feeding over breast feeding at that time in U.S. history; breast feeding was looked upon as "low class") and began to feed her hungry daughter.

Twenty minutes later, Melba laid Toby on the bed and dressed her for her world "debut". The door opened and Dr. Allums entered, frowning and shaking his head.

"Good morning, Doctor", Melba said, smiling sweetly at the man who had (deliberately?) led her to believe he would allow "natural childbirth". "I hope you agree with my decision to go home in our family's vehicle, not an ambulance. Since I am doing nicely and Toby is, well…perfect, I see no reason to quibble over HOW we get home. Am I right?"

Dr. Allums seemed a bit surprised by Melba's candor, but he smiled back and stated, "Of course it's okay for you to ride in a car. I just want you to follow my instructions after you get home. You MUST stay in bed for the next few weeks. Let your family take care of you! We simply cannot allow too much activity; your female organs have to properly heal."

"That's understood, Doctor", Melba stated. "I'll just let Mama dote on me. After all, such attention will be a first!"

Dr. Allums gave Melba a nonplused glance coupled with a furtive grin and said, "I wish you the best, Melba. Having this child alone, without Clarence, was difficult. Your desire to deliver using natural birthing procedures was commendable, but my medical expertise just got in the way. I did not believe "natural" was in your best interests, and I did not believe it was best for little Toby. I have to live with my decisions, and I hope that, someday, you will understand and appreciate them. My best wishes to you and your family." With that, Loraine Louis Allums left the room.

Almost immediately, Jeannie ran into the room. She was clearly excited about getting to hold Toby for the first time, and her excitement was contagious! Melba hugged her, saying "Okay, Auntie Jean! Let's see your baby expertise!" With that, she lifted Toby off the bed and handed her to Jeannie.

Jeannie could do nothing but "oooh and aaah"; she exclaimed, "Oh, Sister! She is TOO beautiful!"

Buron finally arrived, after parking the car.

"Oh, my", he said. "I'm simply out of my element! She is…amazing!" Jeannie held Toby out for Buron to hold. He acquiesced, but not without trepidation.

"I'm not sure what to do", he stammered.

"Nothing, sweetie", soothed Jeannie. "Just hold her and be the best uncle a child could ever hope for! After all, YOU will be a daddy one day, so this is a nice bit of practice…"

Within ten minutes, Nurse Eugenia came in with the required paperwork for Melba to sign. Soon afterward, Melba was placed in the hated wheelchair, handed Toby, and rolled down the hallway to the elevator. Once again, Buron went

175

ahead to get the car. With almost no ceremony, Melba was helped into the back seat, handed the baby, and they were on their way to Buster's house.

Mama and Papa were both at the car before anyone could open a door.

"Just let me have my granddaughter!" Mama demanded, laughing. "Oh, you are even prettier than when I saw you in the hospital" she exclaimed, looking at Toby. Papa was equally delighted to have his daughter and granddaughter home, saying, "Well, now! I never thought I'd see such a living princess during my lifetime! You are quite the looker, Miss Toby! Welcome to your Granddaddy's house!"

Then, uncharacteristically, Papa held out his hands to help Melba get out of the car. "You look beautiful, daughter", he said. "I'm glad you're home!"

Mama held out her arms for Toby, and they went into the house, laughing and talking as Melba and Toby were showered with attention. Melba felt loved, but her heart ached when she thought about Clarence and how he was missing this important moment. She just had to keep reminding herself that he'd be home very soon. The fact that they had talked via telephone on two occasions since Toby's birth helped Melba handle being alone, but she was anxious for her hubby.

On April 27th, Clarence arrived at the train depot in Kilgore. It was 10:00 in the morning; he had traveled all night, leaving El Paso on Sunday evening. Clutching his newly-earned Border Patrol Agent badge and his paperwork detailing his first official appointment, he got off the train. Smiling at everyone he saw, it was evident he was happy about something. In reality, he was simply relieved to finally be back in Kilgore! He was to report to the commanding officer at Catoola, Texas on May 11, so he knew his time in Kilgore would be short.

When Buron met him at the depot that morning, the men embraced. They quickly loaded Clarence's one small bag into the car and sped away; the very idea of seeing Melba and his new baby girl had Clarence in a tailspin!

"Don't flip your wig, C.E.!" Buron implored his brother-in-law. "We'll be there in a jiffy! Melba's just as impatient as you, and I honestly think little Toby is excited, too! Matter of fact, we've ALL been waiting for today with a lot of restlessness! Melba has been amazing, but she longed for this day more I can say." Buron drove purposefully, and they DID arrive at Oscar's house in record time.

The minute Buron stopped the car, Clarence jumped out and ran to the door, pushing it open and then simply standing there, staring at his wife and Toby. Tears rolled down his cheeks, and he walked over to them, barely daring to touch Melba for fear of hurting her. She smiled at him, kissed him gently and held his daughter out to him. Clarence said nothing, but the look on his face spoke volumes; he was in love!

Sitting down on the couch beside Melba, he was, initially, speechless. It must have been ten minutes before he said or did anything except to touch a little hand or foot, exclaim things like, "Oh, just look at that sweet face!" and whisper for Melba's ears, "She is beautiful; she looks just like you!"

CHAPTER 46

The week at Oscar's passed far too fast and all kinds of decisions had to be made before Clarence reported to Catoola. Melba was not to travel before May 25th, and Dr. Allums was not pleased that she planned to embark on a MOVE on that date. After Melba's decisions in the hospital, though, he determined the best course of action was to say nothing negative.

Clarence learned that there was some "tolerable" housing available for newly assigned agents, and even received a photograph of a small bungalow that was ready for occupancy. After several phone calls to Catoola, he decided to accept the housing offer, and was told he would be able to move in upon his arrival in south Texas the following week. As for furniture, he and Melba decided to take what they had. It would fill up the small dwelling, but that was okay.

"Hon, what are your biggest worries about moving to this little town of Catoola? I know it's not the best spot in Texas, but it's close to the border and where I'm needed at the moment." Clarence asked this question while categorizing what he knew about Catoola. He was unsure of what support would be available. He worried about doctors, grocery stores, churches, the people living there, and whether Melba would be happy. He also worried about the war...

Melba surprised him by saying, "You know, baby, I'll be okay as long as you are doing what you need to do. Toby will be okay as long as we're together and giving her the love and attention she deserves. We'll handle all the inconveniences. Just think what other families are enduring. Lots of our peers are already in Europe or Africa or the Pacific Islands. They are torn apart; husbands and wives are not together, and children don't even know their daddies. I know how lucky we are, and I am so grateful you chose to sign up with the Border Patrol. It's allowing us to be with you!"

Clarence, once again, thanked his lucky stars for Melba. She was simply the best, and he knew it. They would be okay, no matter what happened, for the simple reason they would be together. "Bring it on!" he thought.

"Bring it on" turned out to be an understatement. The next weeks were filled with craziness: his arrival in Catoola, everything that happened when he arrived, including meeting his bosses and co-workers, getting involved in the work assignments, trying to arrange for Melba's move, dealing with the housing and finding a way to move their belongings to Catoola, and just adjusting to the real meaning of being an active Border Patrolman! It was mind-boggling, but Clarence felt invigorated and ready for whatever came his way. After all, he was finally fulfilling his dream of being a BPA, and loving his new role of "daddy". Life was good, even in the midst of war.

May 25th was a warm, sunny East Texas day, perfect for the long drive to Catoola. Estel had arrived from Tulsa on Friday, enjoying a visit with Buster and Annie, meeting his baby niece and spending time with the rest of the family. Clarence had asked Estel to pull a trailer to Catoola, transporting Melba and Toby at the same time. Fortunately, Estel was able to take a few days from his job in order to help his younger brother.

In truth, he was glad Clarence had asked for his assistance; it had been a long time since the move to Kilgore back in March! He knew Clarence had a lot to tell him about his training in El Paso. Estel was especially interested in something called the "autogiro" he'd read about in the *Tulsa Herald*.

The article stated, "The Rio Grande border patrol has put to use inventions and instruments that most folks figure are still laboratory playthings. Chief among these is a flying machine called the autogiro." Estel was mighty curious...

The pickup and small trailer had been loaded the previous evening, so the travelers only needed to eat a quick breakfast and say their goodbyes to Mama, Papa and Bobby. Everyone hugged. Melba got in the truck and Mama handed Toby to her. As Estel pulled away, they all waved and blew kisses; the new adventure was officially underway.

CHAPTER 47

Eight hours and three stops later, Estel pulled his pickup into the dirt driveway of Melba's new home. They had driven 420 miles! Toby proved to be a remarkable little traveler, sleeping much of the way and appearing to love the movement of their vehicle. Melba was tired, but did not complain. After all, she was ready for her new life as a Border Patrol officer's wife! Setting up house with Clarence and their baby girl was all she wanted!

Minutes after their arrival, Clarence pulled up. He waved and yelled out, "Welcome home, honey! Welcome home, Toby!" He and Estel exchanged "knuckle punches", and Clarence grabbed Toby while pulling Melba into his arms.

"I'm SO glad you're here!" he murmured into her ear. Then he cradled Toby in his arms, talking to her and telling her all about Catoola as though she could understand every word!

Clarence said, "Come on, let's do a tour of our new home! Then we'll get the furniture unloaded and set up." The miniscule size of the tiny dwelling enabled a fast "tour" and the two brothers were ready to get busy.

Melba took Toby and said, "Okay, fellows, shake a leg! Let's get the stuff inside! I know you're hungry and I'll get this box of kitchen stuff unpacked so I can start on some bacon, eggs, biscuits and grits while you're bringing in our furniture. That's assuming you were able to get the list of food we talked about yesterday. Did you manage, honey?"

"Of course I did!" Clarence laughed. "You didn't think I'd let you and Toby get here and find nothing to eat, did you? Breakfast for supper sounds swell!"

Within an hour, everything was unloaded. Toby's cradle was the first thing set up and Clarence took over her feeding and diaper changing, then sat in the rocking chair and enjoyed some "daddy time".

Having arranged the kitchen utensils, dishes, pots and pans in the one cabinet above the stove, Melba was working on supper. It smelled delicious, and soon they were gobbling up their first meal together in Catoola.

Estel faced a very long drive back to Tulsa, and he planned to leave early the next morning. It was just over 600 miles, and Estel said he hoped to make it in under eleven hours. Everyone was tired, and Clarence had to report for duty at 7:00 a.m. the next day. Even so, Estel quizzed him about the autogiro "gizmos" and the brothers shared a few chuckles as Clarence tried to explain how the things worked. It was nice to have a little time to talk and reminisce, but, all too soon, they had to call it a night. Turning in early, Estel bunking on the couch, the men slept soundly.

Melba got up twice with Toby, but she did not mind; being HOME was like a piece of Heaven, and she had no reason to complain. A new segment of her life was beginning.

Estel was on the road by 5:30 a.m. and Melba fixed oatmeal for Clarence while he got ready for work. By 6:30, he was gone, too, and Melba had the day to put things away and try to get the house organized. Of course, things like organizing would be done only in between taking care of baby Toby!

They had a small radio that sometimes picked up a Laredo station. Melba tuned it in and tried to listen to any news about the war. She was absolutely sick about Lindell, and she knew it was unlikely that Mama and Papa would learn anything about where he was being treated for his injuries. It was so hard to know NOTHING!

During a noontime broadcast that Melba was able to pick up, she heard several things that would impact their lives in Catoola. Rationing was in full swing, and it would be impossible to purchase tires. It was a lucky thing, thought Melba, Estel had been able to help them move! His truck's tires were old, but better than the ones on Clarence's truck. Now, it was announced, gasoline would be rationed. The kind of trip Estel was taking today would not be possible within a few days! Melba prayed Estel would make it back to Tulsa without incident.

Food was being rationed, too. Melba knew they would soon be issued coupon books and stamps. Then they would be allowed only a limited purchase of rationed items. Her main concern had to do with baby items, especially formula. Thankfully, there was no news about formula being added to the rationing list!

The news report was bad regarding the war in the Pacific Islands: the Bataan Death March, as a forced 60 mile walk for war prisoners was called, ended in the deaths of thousands of Filipino troops and hundreds of American soldiers. Three U.S. officers managed to escape and tell the story. Prisoners, they reported, were still being held in unthinkable conditions at Camp O'Donnell in Capas, Tarlac, Philippines.

Of course, Melba was keenly interested in this report since Lindell had been at Clark Field, Philippines. She was actually thankful that the news from Papa indicated Lindell had been injured and evacuated to a U.S. hospital ship. (Yes, she was glad about Lindell's injury, terrible though it was; at least he wasn't a prisoner of war!) It frightened her that the U.S. had been unable to contain Japan in the Islands. What did that mean for the war? Melba just hoped the news reports about a recent "Battle of the Coral Sea" were accurate since the reports were saying Japan lost to U.S. air forces. "It's about time!" Melba thought.

When Clarence got home that night, Melba told him what she'd heard on the radio earlier in the day.

"What do you think about the rationing, Melby?" Clarence questioned. "Is it likely to cause us a lot of problems?"

"I don't know what to think just yet", Melba stated, "but I know we have to support our troops the best way we can. What are they telling you at the station? Are they tightening things around here? I know you've been assigned mounted patrol duty out in the 'scrub-lands', and I'm worried about why the superior officers think more of our rangers need to be scouring the land between here and Laredo. What do you think is going on? Do you believe enemy forces will try to get to us from Mexico?" Melba queried with just a hint of fear in her voice.

"It's nothing to get upset over," Clarence answered. "I understand that Chief Kelly has sent orders for more coverage of the territory between here and Laredo since it's true the areas both east and west of there on the Rio Grande are used for crossing over here from Mexico. After that, the Nueces River is right there, and available for moving north. The Japs or even the Germans might do something unexpected; we can't be complacent since things have revved up in the Islands AND in Europe! We just have to be ready for anything, even out here in the middle of nowhere." Clarence said these things thoughtfully, weighing what he told Melba.

"I want you to keep my pistol with you when you're here by yourself. Don't answer the door unless you know who's there. Don't talk to strangers. Be careful what you say to ANYONE; we can't trust even the most innocent-looking people, not even here in Catoola!" These last words were spoken with harsh emphasis, and Melba definitely noted the tone he used. It made her feel more afraid than ever…but she refused to let Clarence know she was afraid. Fear would be another of her secrets, and it would simply add to her determination to handle life with ambition and purpose, to make a difference.

The "new chapter" in their lives was starting out less than positive. Melba realized Clarence's job was not as safe and secure as they had assumed, and the realities of adverse scenarios plagued her thoughts as she watched over Toby.

CHAPTER 48

The days and weeks in Catoola passed by more quickly than imagined with all the daily activities. Clarence honestly liked his work even though he was frequently called out before dawn to drive south of Catoola with a caravan of horse trailers. He and his patrol group would then mount up somewhere along the Nueces River and begin carefully scouting the riverbanks in search of evidence of "foreigners". Of course, the possibility of encountering fugitives was always present, but Clarence was sure of himself. He told Melba daily, "I can take care of myself! The 'bad guys' had better watch out if they see me coming!"

This bravado did little to assuage Melba's worries, but she just smiled at her husband, told him to be safe, and continued to manage the household without incidence. Of course, she had to admit the rationing was sometimes frustrating. She had lived in poverty all her life, though, and doing without things was her "norm". In fact, she was enjoying having more food and more belongings than at any other time in her life. The war was causing no more personal hardship than she'd known when living at home with Mama and Papa, thank the Lord! If not for her concerns for Clarence and some deeply buried fears that the war might come to the United States, life was good. Of course, she constantly thought about Lindell and what he must be enduring.

G.W. was involved in the war, too, but had remained a civilian. He worked with the Army and helped oversee the transporting of big equipment such as trucks and tankers to success, but at least he wasn't in the midst of battle!

News about the war trickled in, and Melba tried to listen to all updates each day. In early June, one month after the report about the Coral Sea victory, U.S. Naval forces were praised for stopping an invasion of Midway Island near Hawaii. The reporters practically screamed with excitement as they explained the attack. U.S. divebombers sank four Japanese aircraft carriers; one American carrier was lost. This victory was proclaimed "a turning point in the Pacific War". Touted as "the most stunning and decisive blow in the history of naval warfare" it was Japan's first naval defeat since the Battle of Shimonoseki Straits in 1863. Melba listened with pride as the news reporters broadcast this latest happening; maybe the war would soon be over!

The last news from Lindell, thank God, was really good! According to Mama, Lindell sent a letter from Australia where the hospital ship was currently docked. He had endured four surgeries on his leg, and although it was questionable that he would ever walk again without assistance he was positive about the future. Melba just prayed that ending the war would make the military bring Lindell back to the States for better medical treatment.

Things changed quickly. The battles of the war continued to rage, and the atrocities carried out by the German forces, led by Adolf Hitler, grew exponentially. Although there were reports of "bad things", the American people were kept from learning details about death camps.

In the states, Internment Camps, such as those set up to house Japanese Americans, were "accepted" as a necessary part of war. The camps involved the relocation and incarceration of between 120,000 to 130,000 people of Japanese ancestry who lived mostly in California. Sixty-two percent of the internees were U.S. citizens, and the decision to involuntarily move these families to "war camps" was made by President Roosevelt. Most Americans did not protest his decision. His Executive Order on February 19, 1942, to the Secretary of War did not specifically order confinement of Japanese Americans, but it gave authority for "restrictions":

"NOW, THEREFORE, by the virtue of the authority vested in me as President of the United States, and Commander-in-Chief of the Army and Navy, I hereby authorize and direct the Secretary of War, and the Military Commanders whom he may from time to time designate, whenever he or any designated Commander deems such action necessary or desirable, to prescribe military areas in such places and of such extent as he or the appropriate Military Commander may determine, from which any or all persons may be excluded, and with respect to which, the right of any person to enter, remain in, or leave shall be subject to whatever restrictions the Secretary of War or the appropriate Military Commanders may impose in his discretion . . ."

Melba and Clarence talked about the likely effect of Roosevelt's decree, the imprisonment of citizens. Melba struggled to make sense of it, saying, "Honey, you know many of those people were born here, and, for sure, their children were born in America! It seems unfair to me to throw them out of their homes into PRISON camps just because their ancestors were from Japan!"

Clarence had a different perspective, and he was quick to share his opinion. "Melba, we can't be too careful. We have to think about possible 'spies', those who could be used to send messages or help the enemy infiltrate into our country. You have to agree it's possible."

"I understand, Clarence, but I still feel bad for all those people! This war is making people do crazy things; I just want it to end! And I can't help but think your training and work cloud your feelings about Japanese-Americans…and about Mexican-Americans, too." Melba said all this without any venom; in fact, she said it in a soft voice that sounded more wistful than angry. "I care about people, and most everyone has had a rough time for the past fifteen years. Why, just making enough money to feed a family has been a stretch for most of us. Just when we thought things were getting better, we're thrown into a terrible war! And then we start treating our own citizens like the enemy! Where will all this end?" At this last comment, Melba's voice quavered as she fought back tears.

Clarence reached out for his wife and lovingly pulled her to him. "Shush, baby", he whispered. "I know what you mean, and I feel bad for the families sent to the camps. I feel like you do about the war, but it's important to bring it to an end by stopping the Axis powers before they can do more damage. We have to stand up for our American values! I know you want Toby to grow up in a better world." Clarence rubbed Melba's back and kissed her forehead. Then he kissed the tears that were trailing down her cheeks. "I love you, Melby. We have to be strong."

Melba pulled away and looked at Clarence with a solemn expression when she said, "I love this country, and I am VERY patriotic! You know how I feel about our men and women in uniform, and that includes YOU. But, regardless of my patriotism, I can't support being unjust to any of our people, whether they have been able to earn citizenship yet or are still in limbo. Most of the Japanese immigrants to America came for work and to build a new life. I think they wanted the freedom to buy land and decide how to conduct business, things they couldn't do in their homeland. And I've heard terrible things about abusive work conditions for the Japanese, especially out in California where most of them live. I've read about lots of bad things happening to those people. It just seems racist and wrong!"

"Yes, but don't forget the horrible things being done by Japan! Japan's the main reason we're involved in another World War! I know people are showing prejudice, but it's hard not to!" Clarence could not stop himself from saying these things, even if it DID make Melba mad. She couldn't deny the unconscionable actions Japan was taking in its determination to industrialize and expand. Human life was certainly not the resource they most wanted to preserve!

Toby's cries prompted an end to their discussion of war issues. Like Melba always said, "Life goes on, no matter what!"

CHAPTER 49

As it turned out, the months of July through December of 1942 were not as productive for the Allies as most Americans had hoped. Defensive moves were slow, according to reports, and Melba listened to the radio almost constantly. The Marines landed on Japanese-held Guadalcanal in the Solomon Islands in early August, beginning what was to become a six-month ordeal. News reports suggested American infiltration of the Solomons was an attempt to prevent the Japs from using the islands as bases. From Guadalcanal, Japan could easily threaten America's supply routes to Australia.

Melba felt frustrated, but she could only imagine how the troops were feeling! As always, she wondered where Lindell was and if he was getting better. For some reason, Melba never worried that Lindell would die; she simply "felt" he would come home.

Fortunately and unexpectedly, that very week she received a letter from Mama telling her that Lindell was ON AMERICAN SOIL! He was in Fort Dix, New Jersey at the Tilton General Hospital, a hospital on the army base that was busily taking in injured troops from both the Pacific Theatre and Europe. The situation with Japan trying to interfere with America's access to Australia was problematic, and Melba was grateful her brother was safe and not so far away!

When Clarence came home on the evening of December 11, 1942, he had news that made Melba instantly forget about "war worries". As they shared cups of coffee during what had become their after-work ritual, Clarence played with Toby and talked about the day's activities. "I have something important to tell you, honey", Clarence eventually said with a smile. "We're going to Laredo! I've been reassigned; Laredo is a real 'hot spot' and they need more of us at that location."

Melba didn't even hesitate before saying, "I'm not too surprised. You've been telling me Laredo's post is short-handed. When do we leave?"

"We'll stay here for Christmas, and move on December 28th, the Monday after Christmas", Clarence explained. "I'm just glad we don't have to move before the holiday; we'll be here two more weeks."

For the next few days, Melba contacted family to tell them about the relocation. She began to pack non-essentials and get things organized. Clarence let her know the housing would be very similar to their current residence, and that was a relief. Melba felt ready to get to a larger town; Catoola was very limited! She knew that even with rationing, finding necessities and utilizing their food coupons would be much easier in Laredo. With the preparation for both the move and Christmas, time flew by. Soon, it was Christmas day.

Their first Christmas with Toby was a joyful event! Toby was eight months old, and she liked all the festivities. They trimmed a small tree, setting it outside on the front porch and stringing cranberries and popcorn for decorations. Melba made a few paper ornaments and hung them, placing a paper star at the top of the tree. Santa visited, bringing Toby three new toys: a small bag of ABC wooden blocks, a sock monkey, and a Little Golden Book of nursery rhymes. What fun she had...not to mention the fun had by Melba and Clarence as they showed her the new "treasures"! The special day ended with an exhausted Toby, but a Toby who was sweetly contented and happy. Melba and Clarence just hoped future Christmases would be as perfect as this one.

CHAPTER 50

The move to Laredo was almost uneventful. Clarence was able to get two of his patrol buddies to pitch in and haul a pickup load of their things to Laredo. In exchange, Melba prepared a nice dinner for them and they enjoyed some time just visiting and sharing stories about their earlier lives.

When the men left to return to Catoola, Melba and Clarence spent the remainder of the weekend getting everything set back up. It really wasn't such a big job, they agreed, happily settling into their old bed in the new house late Sunday night. Clarence knew his new post would be stressful, but he admitted he was ready for the challenge. Catoola had been a bit too tranquil for him. He wanted to see some REAL action. Maybe in Laredo, some illegals would try to enter the U.S. and he would be able to thwart their plans! It would certainly make him feel more "needed" as a Border Patrolman! After all, his fellow countrymen were dying in Europe, Africa and the Pacific, fighting incredibly devastating battles. Clarence wanted to prove his worth and make some kind of difference.

Within a few weeks after arriving in Laredo, Clarence realized his "calling". He requested a transfer from the Justice Department to the War Department. The facility instructed recruits in aerial gunnery, and the 2nd Aerial Gunnery Training Squad had seven divisions. The training for new cadets was primarily for the B-17 "Flying Fortress" and the B-24 "Liberator". Cadets were trained how to use the .50 and .30 caliber Browning Machine Guns and their firing platforms.

Clarence's transfer came quickly; he was adept at learning about the automatic guns, and his abilities were soon in great demand...

The couple had been in Laredo for ten months, and Toby was now 19 months old. She was walking and talking, and Melba and Clarence thought she was the smartest and cutest baby in the world! With Clarence's work in the War Department, it was impossible to know just how many overtime hours might be necessary since the Border Patrol agents working in the War Department had to retrieve debris from the training flights to make sure no aviation secrets could be stolen and reported to Axis powers. Melba learned to deal with Clarence's off-the-wall schedule and she appreciated that Toby kept her busy while also helping her avoid the doldrums. Her mantra became, "I can do this! I KNOW I can do this!"

In truth, Toby was a really good baby. She loved to play and she was really attentive during "reading time" when Melba opened the few children's books they'd managed to accumulate. Toby's favorites were the nursery rhymes, and she knew them all! When Melba started reading "Georgie Porgie", for instance, Toby would chime in with the remaining words, laughing and clapping enthusiastically. When Melba was able to acquire a newspaper, she read the news stories out loud and Toby listened as if she understood every word.

Mixed with joys involving Toby, the ugly war news was never-ending. It was October, 1944. News headlines heralded the U.S. takeover of Aachen, Germany and the surrender of more than 5,000 German soldiers. Right after that victory, it was announced on the airways that U.S. Naval forces invaded

Leyte in the Philippines. What followed, news sources stated, was the Battle of Leyte Gulf and it was touted as the greatest naval victory of the war with near destruction of the Japanese Navy. Leyte Gulf was decisive in that it destroyed much of the remaining Japanese surface fleet while virtually ending Japan's ability to move resources from Southeast Asia to its home islands. Japanese losses included four aircraft carriers, three battleships, six heavy and four light cruisers, and eleven destroyers, along with several hundred aircraft and over 12,000 soldiers.

Over 2,800 Allied soldiers died in the battles at Leyte, and the United States lost one light carrier, two escort carriers, two destroyers and one destroyer-escort during the three-day conflict, but the victory helped make the terrible losses a bit less shattering.

"Hallelujah!" Melba yelled to no one but Toby. "This is great news!" She could hardly wait until Clarence got home to share the amazing story of victory on two fronts. Maybe, she thought (not for the first time), the war would really be over soon.

When Clarence drove up to the house that afternoon, Melba ran out to greet him. "You won't believe what's happened!" she shouted. "I know the war is going to be over soon; the news from both Europe and the Pacific is better than nifty! The *Laredo Daily Times* ran two featured stories today, one about a battle in Germany and another about a huge naval victory near the Philippines in the Pacific Islands. It sounds like our forces can't be beat!" Melba said all this so fast that Clarence had trouble taking it all in. He could see that   Melba

197

was simply over the top with excitement about the war news, and he was instantly on board, sharing the thrill of the moment with laughter and hugs. It was the best news they could remember in a long, long time!

They decided to call the family in Kilgore that night. Melba really wanted to see if Mama and Papa had any news from Lindell. She couldn't help but wonder how Lindell's girlfriend, Nedra Cook, was handling not knowing what he was enduring. Melba remembered Nedra from school days, but she was five years younger and her romance with Lindell started after she and Clarence were in Tulsa.

The phone was answered by Mama. "Hello?" she asked. To Melba's ear, Mama's voice sounded worried. Realizing Mama was probably frightened every time the phone rang, Melba quickly said, "Hi, Mama! It's just me calling. I hope you heard the good news from our front lines today!"

"Oh, yes, Sister, we are so happy to know our men are making progress against the Germans and Japs! Papa and I have been listening to the radio for the past hour." Mama's tone said it all; she was clearly feeling good about the war news.

"Mama, have you and Pa heard anything new about Lindell?" Melba asked somewhat gingerly. She did not want to upset them, but she was ALWAYS concerned about her brother. Not knowing how his injuries were being treated and whether he was even able to walk with aid escalated her worries.

"Yes, we sure have heard about Lindell! It's the best news of all!" Mama stated with real happiness in her voice. "We got a letter today from Lindell."

"What?" Melba almost shouted. "You heard from Lindell?"

"We did, Sister, and you won't believe what's going on! Lindell is actually back on active duty status, and is in flight training right here in Texas! He's at San Angelo and he says he can't really tell us more than where he is. The training will take about 12 weeks. Papa and I think he'll be moved after he graduates and that should be sometime in December. Papa and I had no idea he was doing well enough to be called back to active duty! He says he walks without any assistance and is gaining strength and stamina daily!"

"We just hope he'll get to come home on leave before he's deployed; he deserves to see his family!" Mama continued. "It just about kills me to know he's back in training after the past two awful years he spent in hospitals!" Mama's voice broke as she said these words. Even now, her son was not out of harm's way.

"We talked to Nedra while ago and she is elated that Lindell is so close. She plans to go see him; they are talking marriage!" As Mama spoke these words, the happiness she clearly felt for Lindell was clear. It made Melba's heart sing, too!

Melba tried to find out if Mama and Papa knew more about Lindell's "training", but she soon realized they didn't have more information. Both were simply grateful to know he was, for the next few weeks, on Texas soil. They talked for a few more minutes about the rest of the family, then said goodbye.

"I'm glad we talked to them", Melba said. "Mama's so worried about Lindell, and Papa's just as worried, but he's also trying to keep food on the table. I know they were glad to hear from us, even though it was only last week when I sent a letter. I try to keep them updated about Toby and what's going on here with your work. It scares me when you have to go into Mexico like you did a few days ago. There's no way to know if you'll return safely to us…"

"Stop worrying, Melby. You know I'll be okay", Clarence said with conviction. Melba could only hope he was right. So many bad things were happening, how could Clarence be so positive?

CHAPTER 51

Toby's illness was a complete surprise. Her growth and development had been miraculously unblemished. The only time she'd had anything wrong was at nine months when she'd run a low-grade temperature and had a runny nose. This time, it was different. It was three weeks since the phone call home, and no new war reports had come through. There was also no more news about Lindell. Clarence was at work, and Toby was down for a nap.

Her shrill cries made Melba's heart lurch as she ran into the bedroom to see what was wrong. Toby was standing in the crib and crying like she was in terrible pain. She held up her arms to Melba and said, "Toby hot!" Melba picked her up, realizing as she did that Toby was, indeed, very hot! Her skin felt like fire.

Melba immediately grabbed wash cloths, soaked them in cold water and applied them to Toby's forehead. She melted half of an aspirin tablet in water, added it to a few ounces of juice and got Toby to drink it, all the while praying it would bring the fever down. After getting a phone line, she dialed Toby's doctor and made an appointment for the following morning.

The next few days were frightening. After the first visit to a doctor at Mercy Hospital's pediatric clinic on November 13th where Toby was diagnosed with a "throat infection", Melba felt out of control and completely unnerved. The doctor, Sergio Garcia, prescribed medication which included

Disprin (aspirin that dissolves easily in water or juice) and Prontosil (a sulfa drug), and Melba and Clarence did everything they could to comfort Toby and help keep her fever down. Of course, she did not want to eat or drink because it hurt to swallow, so they coaxed her into taking fluids by warming her milk and juice, adding the aspirin every four hours to try to keep the fever at bay. They prepared warm meals with "soft" foods such as cream of rice cereal, mashed bananas, puddings and applesauce. Still, Toby languished. She tried to play, but usually ended up laying down on her "blankie" and resting. She was pitiful, and both Melba and Clarence were painfully worried about her progress.

A week later, the fever was still "spiking" at night even though Toby had some time each day without an elevated temperature. Unfortunately, those fever-free times were sporadic, at best.

Clarence went to work, but his heart was at home. He contacted others in Laredo, trying to determine if there was better health care somewhere else. Mercy Hospital seemed alright. They believed the doctor they were seeing was good; he was well-trained, having attended the Tulane University School of Medicine in New Orleans, Louisiana. But when Toby continued to be sick, both Melba and Clarence questioned whether Dr. Garcia was doing everything possible.

Finally, more than two weeks after becoming sick, Toby seemed better. Her fever stayed down, she was eating better, and she stopped complaining about her throat. Both Melba and Clarence felt like a giant weight had been lifted; they wanted to celebrate!

Within days, Toby was acting like herself. She babbled nonstop, played with her toys, wanted to hear her storybooks, and ran around as if she'd never been ill. It was such a relief! Melba called Kilgore to tell Mama about Toby's recovery, and it looked as if they were all "back on track". It was December 5, 1944.

CHAPTER 52

Clarence's job kept him moving, as the training school was moving hundreds of recruits through the gunnery program each month. During the month of December, the number of troops being trained for duty in Europe skyrocketed. Just following the training flights and keeping up with salvage operations kept Clarence away many more nights than he was able to be home with Melba and Toby.

He and Melba were grateful that Toby seemed healthy at this point, and they tried not to worry about any future illnesses. Dr. Garcia specifically warned them after her last visit at the clinic that some children "relapsed" after having strep throat and got sick again. He told them a relapse could be very bad, and stressed that any sign of illness should be reported immediately. Melba was shaken by this information, and she kept a vigilant watch over Toby. So far, there was no indication of any kind of malaise from the very active and happy Toby.

News from the war was less-than-hopeful, though. Back during the month of November, Japan sent pilots on "suicide missions" called Kamikaze attacks. One such attack by a series of Jap flyers heavily damaged one of the largest U.S. aircraft carriers, the U.S.S. Lexington, causing extensive loss of life and significantly slowing U.S. military operations. Then, in December, a second major loss for U.S. forces devastated ground troops in France. Hitler launched a surprise attack on French territory with the goal of recapturing the vital harbor of Antwerp from Allied forces.

The resulting battle, dubbed "Battle of the Bulge", resulted in the largest and bloodiest battle of the war for the Americans. Over 70,000 U.S. troops were wounded, and 19,000 more were killed.

Melba listened to the reports about these new war situations as they poured in from radio station KPAB in Laredo. With Clarence away so much of the time and her concern for Toby's health, Melba had to force herself to stay focused and not panic. Just a few weeks ago, she thought, it looked like the war would soon be over. She realized the hopes of thousands of families had been destroyed with the latest news from the European War Theatre; the loss of American lives was simply unbelievable. When the war first started, any thought of so much bloodshed would have subjected the chump who dared to voice such a thing to ridicule from his friends and family. Back then it seemed the United States was not just invincible, but far above any potential for mass casualties, yet recent news reports made clear the erroneous nature of such assumptions. Melba felt heartsick.

The December days were not filled with holiday cheer. Storefront displays of glittering trees, gaily wrapped packages and Santa's elves were lacking their usual luster. Buying restrictions tightened, and more foods, clothing and dry goods were rationed. Consumers' thoughts were with the soldiers. It seemed this Christmas would come and go unnoticed.

There were lots of radio and newspaper ads for "audiograms" and "v-cards", and it seemed everyone was sending these to family and friends who were in the battle zones or stationed in conquered territories. It was not a time to think of anything except all those in the middle of the conflict.

On Christmas Eve, however, Clarence came into the house grinning from ear-to-ear. "Come see what's on the front porch!" he called.

Melba and Toby hurried to the doorway. Toby shrieked, "Kissmas tree!" as she ran, hands clapping, and reaching out to touch the branches.

"Oh, honey!" Melba exclaimed. "I didn't expect to have a tree this year; it's beautiful!"

"Those smiles are MY Christmas gift!" Clarence said, laughing. "Just seeing you and Toby so happy is enough to make me flip my wig!" Clarence used his "silly voice" and ruffled his hair when he said this, making Melba and Toby giggle with glee. The rest of the evening was spent decorating the tree and writing a letter to Santa.

Before Toby was down for the night, they told her stories about the Christmases they remembered from their childhoods. Melba recited "The Night Before Christmas" at least four times, much to Toby's delight, and the little family managed to stay happy for this tiny snippet of time they were able to spend without thoughts of the war.

Christmas Day of 1944, Toby's second, passed quickly. The only gifts were a Kewpie doll and a little sack of balls for Toby; Melba and Clarence did not exchange gifts.

On the radio, Melba and Clarence listened to President Roosevelt's greeting to all the soldiers fighting overseas:

"On behalf of a grateful nation, I send to the men and women of our armed forces everywhere warm and confident wishes this fourth Christmas of war. On Christmas Day more than any other day we remember you with pride and humility, with anguish and with joy. We shall keep on remembering you all the days of our lives. It is, therefore, with solemn pride that I salute those who stand in the forefront on the struggle to bring back to a suffering world the way of life symbolized by the spirit of Christmas."

Although the fighting was scaled back at Christmas, it was not halted, reports confirmed. The fact that many of our troops fought on Christmas Day, 1944, made all those listening to the news broadcast realize one thing: peace on earth was only a distant dream. War reporters like Robert Vermillion, Charles Arnot and Norman Corwin told a captive American audience that troops not actively engaged in battle were treated to a special Christmas dinner and some type of "contrived" entertainment and merriment, but that many soldiers retired to a solitary place to spend their Christmas night rereading letters from home, looking at well worn photographs, remembering a Christmas past or dreaming of a future one. The war zones were not happy places.

In the same broadcast, these invincible reporters painted vivid, shocking, pictures of battles to the death throughout Belgium, Luxembourg and France. The cold was not limited to a siege of severe wintry weather.

With the radio's continual broadcast of war news throughout the day and evening on Christmas Day, the normal celebratory feeling of the holiday was missing for Melba and Clarence. It was missing for people throughout the world, Melba thought.

Melba and Clarence liked Roosevelt's Christmas message, and they spent Christmas afternoon talking about what it would mean if the war actually came to an end in the next few months. It was hard to imagine the job of getting all the armed forces back home!

"No telling how long it's likely to take to return our troops", Clarence said, "but I do know it will happen just as fast as possible. The entire country will be on edge…"

"Oh… My Heavens!" Melba exclaimed. "Waiting for our boys to get back will be excruciating! I can think of at least 15 guys that were in school with G.W. and Lindell who'll be coming home, and I just pray they all make it back…And Lindell will get some time off, too. I just hope it's sooner than later. I know Mama's floor-pacing will get worse before it gets better! Just seeing our hometown troops will be…simply beyond great!!

It was truly hard to imagine having all the armed forces back home! The next few days saw everyone in town watching the news and discussing radio broadcasts. Everyone hoped the war was almost over, but there was certainly much fear regarding the battles going on "over there". The *Laredo Daily Times* featured headlines about the battles in France. It was reported that a major German offensive campaign had been launched in the densely forested Ardennes region that included land masses in Belgium, France and Luxembourg. The news media said the assault on Allied forces in the Ardennes was an attempt by Hitler to recapture an important harbor in Antwerp, Belgium in order to get vital supplies to the German troops.

It was reported that Allied forces were completely surprised by this attack and that United States forces incurred their highest casualties of any operation of the war to date. The news reports had a solemn effect on citizens of Laredo, the majority of whom had relatives fighting in Europe.

Thankfully, within a few days, reports came back about the heavy losses sustained by the Germans. The news stated that the battle severely depleted Germany's armored forces on the western front, crippling them. German personnel and their Luftwaffe aircraft also sustained heavy losses. Reports came back from the war zone that Allied ground counter attacks began on December 28th and were expected to increase into January. Although the news was reassuring concerning the debilitating effect of the battles in the Ardennes on the German military, knowledge that so many American lives had been destroyed left those waiting at home in a solemn frame of mind. Depression hung in the air like a heavy fog.

CHAPTER 53

On January 4, 1945, Toby woke her parents in the middle of the night. Her cries sounded wrong, and both Melba and Clarence instantly feared the worst. Sure enough, Toby was sick again. She had a high fever and a bumpy, irregular rash that was mostly on her back and chest. It was 2:30 a.m. and they decided to wait until morning to contact the doctor.

At 8:00, Melba called Dr. Garcia, frantic because Toby was crying and obviously miserable. She refused to eat or drink and her eyes were glassy and dull. The doctor wanted to see Toby immediately, so Melba and Clarence bundled her up in a blanket and drove to Mercy Hospital's clinic.

Dr. Garcia's nurse greeted them as soon as they entered the clinic and took them back to an examining room. Melba held Toby whose head rested listlessly on her shoulder. She was ominously quiet, not crying or even whimpering. Dr. Garcia came in and took Toby from Melba, laying her on the exam table. There was no protest from Toby. The exam was relatively brief: a look at the rash, a look at Toby's throat and ears, and a temperature check (it registered 103.2 degrees), a check of her reflexes, and palpation of her lymph nodes for signs of swelling, tenderness and pain, and a few questions for Melba and Clarence regarding Toby's behavior, her usual sleep patterns and her willingness to eat and drink.

Melba was thinking, none-too-kindly, that it didn't take a medical degree to see that Toby was a very sick child.

Finally, Dr. Garcia said, "She is having a relapse of the throat infection, and we'll start her back on Prontosil and Disprin; I'll need to see her everyday for the next week. If her fever spikes any higher, I'll need to hospitalize her. Use cool baths when the fever is 101 or higher, and call the office if it reaches 104 degrees. If that should happen over the weekend, take her to Mercy's Emergency Room and have the doctor on duty call me.

At that point, Clarence spoke up, saying, "Look, Doctor, I'm not feeling good about this illness being 'a relapse' of the strep throat she had last month. She seems much sicker now than before!"

Dr. Garcia looked at Clarence, shaking his head to indicate his disagreement. "Her throat is red and swollen, she has white spots in her throat and on her tonsils, and she has swollen lymph glands in her neck. It's classic Strep Throat! The drug I've prescribed will clear it up within a week."

Clarence nodded, but he was determined to get a second opinion if Toby didn't start feeling much better by Monday, January 8th. He would be contacting the doctors his friend at work told him about. Of course, getting Toby to Scott and White Hospital in Temple would be difficult, but he would find a way! Feeling heartsick with worry, he helped Melba get Toby back to the car for the trip home.

The next three days were nightmarish; Toby cried and fussed almost constantly, and her fever hovered between 102 and 103 degrees most of the time.

On Monday, Clarence made an appointment with Colonel Kelley. The first thing he said to his boss was, "My baby is very sick, so sick that she may die if I don't get better medical treatment. I'm asking for leave time so I can take her to Scott and White in Temple."

"What's happened here to make you so sure her care is lacking?" Col Kelley asked. His tone of voice relayed the concern of a father; Kelley had three of his own children.

"Dr. Garcia is Toby's pediatrician, and he has been quite good up until now. It's just that he still wants to treat Toby's sickness like a simple sore throat. This is the second time she's had similar symptoms, but the medicine isn't helping. She's miserable and so very sick..." Clarence's eyes betrayed his intense concern.

"Do you know something about Scott and White that makes you want Toby treated there?" Kelley questioned Clarence.

"As a matter of fact, I do have good reason for taking Toby to Temple", Clarence stated without hesitation. "My brother-in-law was treated there last year for cancer, and Harvey is now in remission from Hodgkin's Disease thanks to his team of doctors. Scott and White was the first hospital to be named a cancer and diagnostic treatment center in Texas, and the hospital is living up to its fine reputation. Surely, my baby's malady can be identified and treated there! I'm convinced she has something other than just a simple childhood illness!"

With that declaration, Clarence had to clear his throat and work hard to keep tears from trickling down his cheeks. "She HAS to get well!"

Colonel Kelley nodded at Clarence, stood up and extended his hand. "You are cleared to go to   Temple.

Godspeed!" The two men shook hands and Clarence almost ran out of the building. It was time for action!

Simultaneously, in Europe, soldiers were entrenched in battles that raged continuously, even in the midst of bitterly cold, wet and icy weather. Conditions were so severe that many wounded men froze to death before medical teams could get to them. More than 76,000 Americans were killed or maimed as an avalanche of German fighters surged into Belgium and Luxembourg to attack the Allies. Reports of defeat poured into radio stations from the Mutual Broadcasting System, causing outcries of panic and horror in towns and cities across the states.

Remarkably, late in the day, a retraction of the word "defeat" was made and reports began to surface that German forces were retreating.

Clarence and Melba heard the news over the car radio as they traveled up highway 35 in route to Temple. Melba held Toby, hoping to comfort her as they drove, knowing the long trip would be torturous. Passing through the towns of Dilley, Pearsall, Divine and finally San Antonio, they noticed lots of smiles and groups of clearly excited people in each place. They were shouting, hugging and waving to passersby. It seemed the war news equaled and exceeded birthday, Christmas and wedding celebrations, combined!

"It would be nice to feel the excitement this war news is generating," Melba stated with just a hint of bitterness in her voice. "If Toby's health was back to normal, I'd be shouting with joy from the rooftops!" As she said this, guilt about her neutral feelings concerning the war made her feel even more miserable. Tears slid down her cheeks, but she tried to hide them from Toby.

"It's okay, baby", Clarence soothed. "We have every right to be focused on our child! Hang the war!!"

"But I DO care about our men in uniform…it's just that right now I feel so beaten down, like a field of grain after a violent storm. I need to see some sunshine in our lives!" Melba's words were hard to hear; she spoke softly, almost whispered, yet her pain was unmistakable.

The couple listened silently to the non-stop radio broadcasts they were now able to pick up from San Antonio's more powerful stations. The news was truly answering millions of prayers, worldwide, and it did insert a bit of relief in the souls of the frazzled pair. Toby finally fell into a deep sleep, and her little mouth relaxed, making her appear like any other normal child instead of a child fighting a battle against an unseen enemy, disease.

"She looks so peaceful", Melba said, speaking softly. "I would give anything to help her get over this vicious sickness!"

"Me, too", Clarence agreed, "Me, too!"

Late that afternoon, Clarence pulled into the emergency room parking at Scott and White Hospital. Toby was awake, but listless, and she felt hot. Melba said, "It's time for more Dispirin, but let's wait and see what the doctors here recommend."

Entering the emergency room's reception area, the couple walked quickly to the desk. "We have a very sick daughter!" Melba exclaimed. "We're from Laredo, and have driven all day to find someone who can help her. Our doctor in

Laredo insists she has strep throat, but this is the second time she's had it in the past six weeks and she keeps getting worse! She won't eat and we can barely get her to take any fluids. And she's covered with a terrible rash!"

Clarence was registering Toby as a patient, and he finished the paperwork just as a young doctor came up from a back room. "I've heard what's going on. Bring the child to the second examining room", he said, pointing toward the room.

Dr. Johnson motioned for Clarence and Melba to follow him, as he carried Toby into a small, brightly lit room where he laid her on a child-sized exam table. He spoke softly, telling Toby who he was and smiling at her reassuringly. While telling her he needed to see her rash and look at her throat, Dr. Johnson's hands were feeling her lymph nodes and forehead, running them over the rash, all with the agile movements of a very practiced physician. He asked Toby to open her mouth and say "Ahhh", and, to Melba's surprise she complied without a whimper! A quick swab was taken from the back of Toby's throat. The nurse checked her temperature, saying "It's definitely elevated…almost 104 degrees!"

Dr. Johnson nodded as he rubbed Toby's wrists and ankles, noting they were swollen and tinged a deep shade of pink. Then he listened to her heart, continuing to move the stethoscope around and checking both her chest and her back. Although he smiled at Toby and teased her into a wan grin, both Melba and Clarence could see his concern.

"I've requested a STAT report on the throat swab and blood test. I'd like the three of you to rest right here until I hear from the lab. Nurse, please administer 165 MG of

Dispirin right now, and we'll start an antibiotic intravenously as soon as I'm sure of the diagnosis." Dr. Johnson stated all this very matter-of-factly, seeming to know Toby's parents were prepared to do anything necessary. Then he left, saying, "I'll be back soon."

In less than an hour, the lab results were back and so was Dr. Johnson. "I have both good and bad news", he said. "The bad news is your child has Acute Rheumatic Fever. The good news is we can treat it and she will get well!"

"Oh, my God!" Melba exclaimed. "I knew something bad was wrong! Tell us everything! How did she get this? Why didn't Dr. Garcia diagnose it correctly?"

"I'm confident our treatment will work wonders, but she has a long way to go…Rheumatic Fever can damage the heart and heart valves. I'm hearing a murmur when I listen to her heart, and it is beating faster than normal. There's some fluid around her heart that has to be reduced and eliminated. I'm starting some potent medications right now. I'm including a mild sedative to help her stay relaxed; we want her to sleep as much as possible." Dr. Johnson's voice was calm, but he conveyed the seriousness of Toby's condition. Melba and Clarence were terrified.

"What can WE do, doctor?" Melba asked this, but she intuitively knew what the doctor would say. Melba had picked Toby up and was cradling her in her arms, swaying back and forth and crooning, "Shhh…It's alright, baby girl!"

Dr. Johnson held up a finger to indicate "wait just a minute". He gave directions to the two nurses in attendance before turning back to Melba and Clarence. "You are doing everything Toby needs! Just be here for her, love her and soothe her. We need to let the medications start working. I'll be in the hospital tonight, and I'll be checking in frequently. Please give one another breaks, and please take advantage of the hospital cafeteria on the third floor. I'll see you soon."

With that, Dr. Johnson left the room. Clarence said, "Thank God we came here! I do believe Dr. Johnson's diagnosis, and I know our baby is going to beat this!" His eyes shimmered with unshed tears, but his voice was strong.

Melba gingerly sat in the rocking chair with Toby, being careful not to dislodge either of her IV tubes. Toby was about to close her eyes in sleep, but Melba could not bear to lay her on the bed; she wanted to keep her close to her heart for a little longer. She finally said, "Thank you, Lord! We are blessed to be here, and we just pray for Dr. Johnson as he administers to our little girl. And thank you, Clarence, for bringing us to Scott and White!"

CHAPTER 54

For the next week, Toby's hospital room and a cot in the waiting room were "home" for Melba and Clarence. For awhile, Toby remained listless and unresponsive. Finally, five days after being hospitalized, Toby woke up without fever! Eyes sparkling, she said, "Mama! Wake up! Let's play!"

Melba was sitting in the chair beside Toby's bed and had drifted into a deep sleep; she was exhausted! Toby's voice, an angel bringing good news, woke Melba. Listening without opening her eyes, she worked to place the "noise" and understand what it meant.

Almost instantaneously, Melba blinked and sat up. "Oh, Baby! You're feeling better! Holy mackerel! Is it true? Come see Mama!" Saying these words, Melba stood up and held out her arms to Toby, swooping her up and enfolding her in a long and tender embrace.

"You feel COOL, Baby! Your fever is down! Daddy and Dr. Johnson will be so happy!" Melba swirled in a circle, holding Toby and laughing. "It's a miracle!" Toby giggled at her Mother's antics; she clearly felt much better.

Over the next few days, the fever never spiked above 101 degrees, and it remained normal most of the time. Toby began to eat and drink without any issues. She began to play, talk, sing and want out of bed; her parents were ecstatic!

Two weeks after entering the hospital in critical condition, Toby was released to her parents and was discharged to go home. Dr. Johnson, having conferred with a cardiologist as well as with a rheumatologist, told Melba and Clarence that Toby needed time to completely recuperate from the Rheumatic Fever. He explained that Toby's heart was "enlarged" from the infection, but seemed hopeful that her future health would be "reasonably good".

"Toby has mitral valve prolapse, which means the heart valve doesn't close tightly and allows blood to seep through between heart beats. She may never have significant issues, but should be seen by a cardiologist periodically." Dr. Johnson delivered this information calmly, but it was still as unsettling as a punch in the gut to Melba and Clarence. They said nothing, simply clasping hands and nodding as the doctor spoke.

"I'm confident your little girl will continue to improve. She's pretty headstrong! I consider that quality to be a positive characteristic. Toby has a lot of living to do; I predict she will excel at life." Dr. Johnson then assured Clarence and Melba that he and his team of doctors would be available for follow-up visits and questions. He gave them some literature to read, then shook their hands and bid them a safe trip home.

It was January 16, 1945. Toby's parents knew they had to make some important decisions about Laredo and their future. The long drive home became a life-altering "conference call" for the couple.

As soon as they tuned into the local radio station, news of the war dominated the broadcast. While ensconced at Scott and White, neither Melba nor Clarence had really paid close attention to war news. Now, however, both of them were intent on hearing about the latest action. Both wanted to see an end to the war! They listened quietly for a long time and learned that Japanese Kamikaze attacks had increased against U.S. Naval forces, causing untold deaths to both Allied and Axis forces. They also learned that an amazingly large contingent of German troops were storming Alsace, France in what was thought to be the first plan in an offensive strike against Strasbourg, France. Strasbourg was currently under Allied control; this German offense had the potential to upset the Allies' position in the region.

"These new attacks sound like desperate efforts to make a come-back", Clarence stated. "Hitler and Hirohito are feeling the Allie's heat and ordering their troops to make 'ultimate' sacrifices. That's just crazy!"

At the same time, reports were pouring onto the airways that Hitler was "in hiding" in Berlin. News of his "secret bunker" dominated the airways, and was charged with rumors about the Fuhrer and his mistress, Eva Braun.

"Can you believe all this is happening?" Melba asked. "It seems simply ludicrous that Hitler would be hiding out. I thought he was so brave and powerful…"

"I know", Clarence agreed. "It sounds like he realizes it's over! The Allies have successfully carried out their job; he's DONE!"

The next news feed proclaimed the official end to the Battle of the Bulge! This was amazing news and Clarence pulled off the road to hug his wife, saying "Maybe the end is truly in sight! Do you believe it, Melby?"

"Oh, honey!" Melba exclaimed. "If only you are right! It would mean a REAL new start for all of us…!"

They sat on the roadside for a few more minutes until Toby said, "Daddy, what's wrong?"

Clarence looked at his daughter, smiled and stated, "Nothing, sweetie, nothing at all. Mother and Daddy just heard something that makes us almost as happy as getting to take you home. We're just happy because Uncle Lindell, Uncle G.W., cousins Wayne and Guy Leo and a lot of other soldiers may be coming back to us soon. It's hard to believe! Your mother and I are just...happy!"

Clarence's expression was a mixture of delight coupled with a little bit of apprehension. After all, the war was not officially over, but the end of the nightmarish Battle of the Bulge was a big victory for the Allied Forces. Yes, he and Melba were happy about the news from Europe, but both of them knew, in hearts that had born so much pain, that this war would claim many more lives before it was truly over.

As though reading his mind, Melba touched his hand and said, "We'll take every battle ending in victory as one more step to the final triumph of 'good over evil'; we know the Axis Forces will eventually be defeated. We just have to keep believing! And I know the world will be a better place for our Toby and all the other children living during this harrowing time...It simply must be better!" They nodded solemnly, and Clarence put the car into gear, quickly re-entering the traffic on highway 35 and continuing the drive home to Laredo.

Although Toby was far from out of danger from the disease that had plagued them for months, her prognosis was better than either parent had dared expect. And now the war was being won by the Allies!

After a time of listening to the radio and hearing even more about the War in Europe, conversation turned to decisions they had to make. Their voices were animated and sometimes emotionally-charged as Melba and Clarence discussed what lay ahead. Clarence was fiercely determined to take care of Toby, no matter what else happened.

"I will simply resign my Border Patrol position! After all, I'm a civilian. You know I joined the Patrol to help protect our state as well as the others bordering Mexico from illegals, and I'm proud of my service. But Toby is my first priority! After she's really "out of the woods", then I can get back into BP if we're still at war, but not before! Clarence asserted this firmly, like it was a definite decision, but Melba interrupted him.

"You just can't leave your team like that, Clarence! They depend on you for so many things, and the gunnery trainees need your experience when they are in the field. You know as much about the way the machine guns are mounted than the guys who designed the B-17 planes, and you FOR SURE know everything about how to use all the weapons designed for those bombers! I've seen you assemble and disassemble .30 and .50 caliber machine guns, and you're faster than the instructors! If Chief Kelly has his say, you won't be leaving anytime soon! Besides, Toby is doing okay. We'll be HOME, so I know she'll sleep and eat better. The war may really be over soon, and then your resignation won't be such a problem for the patrols stationed in Laredo. And when the Allies WIN, we'll be able to move back to Kilgore or Oklahoma City." Melba spoke with conviction, and her words made sense to Clarence. There was still much to consider, he knew, but what she said was right.

"Okay. I'll wait awhile, see how Toby does and keep our options open. But it doesn't mean I'm not ready to leave Laredo! If Toby has any signs of a relapse, we'll be out of here!" Clarence gave Melba a quick look that let her know he was compromising, not simply agreeing.

That was okay, Melba secretly mused. Options were good, and they should never close the door on them. Melba knew the importance of focusing on "the big picture", and could still hear Papa's voice telling Mama to "hitch your wagon to a star"… Melba refused to focus on the sun when all the other stars and galaxies were demanding her attention. And the possibilities of future options intrigued her.

CHAPTER 55

Being home DID make a big difference in Toby's recovery. Her appetite improved as did everything else; she was back to "normal", even though it was true that Rheumatic Fever's effects would forever cast a shadow. Toby WAS resilient, and her journey back to good health was certainly worth celebrating. And celebrate, they did! Both Melba and Clarence knew how lucky they were; Toby was their little miracle.

Then, just ten days after returning to Laredo, another, much larger, miracle occurred in Europe: the Soviet Army marched into German-held Poland. Without much resistance, radio broadcasts proclaimed, the Red forces defeated German opposition, liberating Lithuania from their control.

Melba met Clarence at the door that afternoon. "Did you hear the news? Lithuania's been liberated! The Soviets are in control, and it sounds like our troops are joining them. Germany is about to go down; Hitler's regime is bushwa!" Melba proclaimed with unfiltered glee. Clarence laughed when he heard Melba's excitement…and her use of 'bushwa' to describe Germany's coming downfall.

"Yes, I heard the news! Germany IS 'booshwa', and how!" Clarence said as he picked Toby up, grabbed Melba's hand and gave both of them hugs and kisses. "It's the best war news yet, and I'm sure the next news flash will bring an even better report. Germany is going down!"

The next three months were bittersweet, however, as news from Europe and the Pacific Theater filtered into

American papers and airways. Instead of the ferocious wave of victory Melba and Clarence had anticipated, widespread and devastating battles raged on, some of them in unexpected places.

Unbelievable reports came back from Poland. To the horror of people throughout the world, news of what invading Soviet Troops discovered in Poland was unfathomable. Hellish death camps at Auschwitz, including more than forty-five "satellite" camps, held grisly proof of nightmarish events within the confines of their barbed wire fences.

The Red Army uncovered other atrocities that included "death marches" carried out by Nazi captors in attempts to hide the genocide within the camps. More than 150,000 weak, emaciated prisoners were forced to walk hundreds of miles from Auschwitz in icy winter weather. Most died of exhaustion and starvation; those who fell or stopped because they could not keep walking were shot by Nazi guards.

Soviet troops, sadly, uncovered even more verification of inhumane atrocities in "Labor Camps" such as those outside of Poland, Ravensbruck (which held only women) and Theresienstadt. The realities of mercilessly brutal human "medical" experimentation performed on young children as well as women and men sickened the soldiers. Reports found their way to newspapers and radio stations and reactions exploded around the world. Even more countries declared war on Germany and Japan.

South American "newbies" included Ecuador, Paraguay, Peru and Venezuela during early February. These formerly neutral holdouts were followed by month's end by

Egypt, Turkey and Syria. The Axis Powers, thank God, had no new support; both Germany and Japan staged unprecedentedly massive and brutal (often suicidal!) attacks on the Allies. By March, Finland declared war on Germany and Japan. The last "neutral" South American country to declare war on the Axis forces was Argentina.

Another unanticipated "hot spot" was the Philippines, and in February U.S. and Filipino Armies advanced into Manila to drive out approximately 15,000 Japanese soldiers who remained on the island without authorization. This contingent was a largely rogue force, and the atrocities committed by those men were abominable. While the battle raged for weeks without Axis surrender, some renegade Japanese troops committed violent mutilations, rapes and massacres in schools, hospitals and convents throughout the city loosely based on the following unverifiable orders:

> *"The Americans who have penetrated into Manila have about 1000 troops, and there are several thousand Filipino soldiers under the Commonwealth Army and the organized guerrillas. Even women and children have become guerrillas. All people on the battlefield with the exception of Japanese military personnel, Japanese civilians, and Special Construction Units, will be put to death."*

Another Japanese order dated February13, 1945, read:

> *"When Filipinos are to be killed, they must be gathered into one place and disposed of with the consideration that ammunition and manpower must not be used to excess. Because the disposal of dead bodies is a troublesome task, they should be gathered into houses which are scheduled to be burned or demolished. They should also be thrown into the river.*

Reports of the horrors in Manila made headlines in cities everywhere and fueled disgust for the Axis nations. Blatant disregard for rules of military engagement made censorship of Japanese and German acts of inhumanity a reasonable outcome. Worldwide, people with any remnants of morality were enraged. Further escalation of combat in the Pacific Theater followed with he Battle of Manila.

Corregidor Island in Manila Bay was the scene of a major offensive move by the Allies. Corregidor was occupied by Japanese troops after U.S. Army forces were defeated by them in 1942. The attack by Allies in 1945 ensured repossession of the strategically important land for American and Filipino troops; Japanese forces were ousted after their decisive victory.

Additionally, the Allied conquest of Budapest, Hungary was hard-won, following a bloody, months-long defense of the city. Budapest had been under German occupation for more than a year since Hungary attempted to withdraw from its alliance with Germany. The Battle of Budapest was one of the most debilitating fights of the War, with more than 150,000 Soviet casualties and as many German/Hungarian deaths and injuries. Civilian casualties in and around Budapest were severe with more than 38,000 deaths either from starvation or military action. It was another nightmarish event.

As the months preceding the end to the worst war in history came and went, the death toll increased exponentially.

Civilian casualties skyrocketed... Dante's description of hell was given a real-life rival.

CHAPTER 56

By the second week in March, Melba and Clarence had lost the optimism they'd enjoyed in January. "Do you remember when we laughed about Germany going down and Hitler's regime being 'booshwa'?" Melba reflected as the little family enjoyed a warm Sunday afternoon on their front porch.

"How could I forget that, Melby? Until that day, I'd never heard you say anything like 'booshwa'; I was almost shocked!" Clarence's laugh was contagious, and they both chuckled. It was nice to have something funny to remember. News stories were not bringing smiles to anyone these days.

Melba continued her thoughts with her next question. "Do you see any signs of an end to this crazy way of life, of accepting WAR as 'normal', of listening to radio broadcasts that calmly talk about THOUSANDS of deaths as though it's okay? I'm frazzled just having to hear the news reports and cannot even imagine what the folks who live in places like London and Manila are experiencing! It's worse than distressing, and I'm sure my frustrations are beginning to affect Toby." She waited for Clarence to think about her question, meanwhile entertaining Toby with silly faces as she played with her dolls.

"Wish I knew what to tell you, Honey", Clarence answered, considering his response thoughtfully. "I know the Allied leaders keep meeting and it seems like they're trying to force Germany and Japan to surrender. I'm surprised they haven't already given up, but each and every country in this conflict has already suffered unspeakable damage and loss of life. We just have to keep on praying for an end that leaves the world still intact. No matter what, the road to recovery for all of us is gonna be another nightmare!"

Those prayers weren't answered during the remainder of March as German soldiers "dug in" to protect Berlin and the Fuhrer. Reports from the front implied that Allied forces were closing in on Germany and that their defensive tactics were seen as less and less effective, but the death toll continued to rise.

After hearing about the attacks along the Rhine and the weakened German forces, Clarence told Melba, "Victory in Europe is inevitable now! The German bastards are going down, no doubt about it. Sounds like Eisenhower, Bradley, Patton and Montgomery are earning their 'keep' as our leading generals. I'd wager some tactical maneuvers are going on that will outfox Hitler's men and get the job DONE, once and for all!"

"I'm sure you're right." Melba responded, "What I've read about those generals is impressive. They've had to learn from mistakes, but they have utilized their knowledge. I agree, things sound a bit hopeful!"

"Yeh, and news about the Red Army sounds good, too. They're supposedly advancing on Berlin, but the reports don't give details." Clarence affirmed his confidence in the way things appeared. "It seems obvious that Hitler has no real strength left to stop our Allies, but I'm sure the fights will be brutal; he won't admit defeat. When our troops storm Berlin and find his hiding place, it will be VERY interesting to witness his reaction! No matter what, I believe Hitler will refuse to raise a white flag…"

On March 31, newspaper headlines printed a letter from General Eisenhower to President Roosevelt. Eisenhower's words to the President mirrored what Clarence thought.

DEAR MR. PRESIDENT:
The further this campaign progresses, the more probable it appears that there will never be a clean-cut military surrender of the forces on the Western Front. Our experience to date is that even when formations as small as a division are disrupted their fragments continue to fight until surrounded. This attitude, if continued, will likely mean that a V-E Day will come about only by proclamation on our part rather than by any definite and decisive collapse or surrender of German resistance.

Projecting this idea further, it would mean that eventually all the areas in which fragments of the German Army, particularly the paratrooper, Panzer and SS elements may be located, will have to be taken by the application of or the threat of force. This would lead into a form of guerrilla warfare which would require for its suppression a very large number of troops.

Of course, if the Government of Germany or any group that could take over a political control would make a national surrender, then all armed bodies remaining in the field would, in my opinion, no longer be classed as soldiers of a recognized government, but would occupy the status of brigands or pirates. Since, if captured under these conditions, they would not be entitled to protection afforded by the laws of war, it is my conviction that, except for extreme fanatics, they would largely surrender. But so long as any of the Hitler gang retains a semblance of political power I believe the effort will be to continue resistance not only throughout Germany, but in all of the outlying areas, including the western port areas of France and Denmark and Norway.

To counteract this eventuality our local propaganda stations are constantly pointing out to the Germans that they should now be planting crops for next winter's food instead of fighting. In addition, I am hopeful of launching operations at the proper time that should partially prevent a guerrilla control of any large area, such as the southern mountain bastion.

It is, of course, always possible that there might be in Germany a sudden upsurge of popular resentment against the war, which would lead to a much easier pacification than that described above. My opinion is based upon the supposition that our experience to date provides our best basis of future prediction. At best we should be prepared for the eventuality described.

DWIGHT D. EISENHOWER

CHAPTER 57

General Eisenhower's predictions about Germany's refusal to surrender would prove accurate over the next weeks. German forces continued to fight with undaunted intensity, even as Allied forces tightened their positions surrounding Berlin...

Then, on April 12, 1945, the unthinkable happened. Clarence and Melba had just finished supper and were enjoying a post-meal cup of coffee on the porch. Toby was playing in the yard, and the radio was on as they listened to music broadcast prior to the 6:00 news. Suddenly, the music stopped and a solemn-voiced announcer said, "America, we have tragic news. FDR is dead! Our Commander-in-Chief, our beloved President, died today of a massive cerebral hemorrhage. He was in Warm Springs, Georgia at 'the little white house' when he collapsed. All efforts to revive him failed, and he was pronounced dead at 4:28 p.m. A time of silent reflection and prayer will be follow. Please join together as a nation to pay respects to our great leader." The next minutes were filled with music as all commentary ended for the next four minutes.

Melba and Clarence heard the horrifying announcement in silence, other than the background sounds of Toby who continued to play in oblivion. The looks on their faces were a reflection of the tremendous loss they, along with people throughout the world who prized freedom, were attempting to process.

Finally, Melba said, "Oh, my! We have lost too much! The President was a gift to all of us! What will happen to the War effort? FDR was the rock of democracy during all these years of war; no man can fill his shoes!" Her voice was shaking, and tears streamed down her face.

Clarence embraced Melba, nodding in agreement. When he spoke, his words were a whisper. "This damned War! It was the crushing weight of it that wore him down..." Melba looked into Clarence's face and saw a mixture of pain and anger, and she understood what she saw. She felt it, too. They stood on the porch, trying to internalize the reality of such loss.

Suddenly, Toby seemed to notice something was wrong. She ran over to the porch, climbed the steps and wrapped her little arms around both parent's legs. "Mama, Dadda...! It's okay! Don't be sad!"

Clarence lifted her into his arms. "Yes, sweetie, yes. It will be okay, but right now being sad is right and good. We have to say goodbye to a very special man. President Roosevelt was called to Heaven today. He's with the Lord, and we will miss him."

The radio announcer resumed what would be a days-long broadcast about everything related to FDR's death, the funeral processions and tributes, world-wide responses, and the quietly carried out inauguration of the new President, Harry S. Truman.

Melba and Clarence listened intently to the reports of Truman's Oath of Office. The new President of the United States was sworn in to serve as America's 33rd Commander-in-Chief in the Cabinet Room at the White House.   The radio broadcast shared that witnesses of the ceremony included Truman's wife, Bess, his daughter, Margaret, Mrs. Roosevelt, members of the Cabinet, and Speaker of the House, Sam Rayburn. It was, reportedly, an immensely solemn service, one that was required by Federal Law and the Constitution to ensure the uninterrupted continuation of supreme leadership in the United States. The ceremony lasted only minutes, and President Truman did not speak to reporters. An almost immediate Cabinet Meeting was called by him, to convene after a 45 minutes break.

Clarence's first comment was, "The weight of the world is on that poor man's shoulders. What a terrible way to start his Presidency!"

Melba nodded, saying, "The War is what killed FDR, and poor Truman is the one who has to 'step up'. I feel so bad for him! Can you imagine what his wife and daughter are thinking? It must be especially difficult for them! And what is going to happen with the War effort now? Do you think our military leaders will be able to keep the pressure up and defeat Germany? What about Japan? I'm really worried!" Melba's expression as she looked at her husband said everything. It was, indeed, a time of terrible upheaval, change and uncertainty.

CHAPTER 58

Time did not stand still, and the ensuing weeks were a period of suffering while the forward momentum aimed at ending the War continued. No soldier was "at ease"; all were aware of the necessity to keep on fighting without let up. It was a bloody but determined time for both Allied and Axis troops. No one wanted to cease and desist, no one wanted to admit defeat, and Hitler demanded his forces fight to the death. Those "at home" felt every bullet, understood what each advance of troops could mean. It was as if the world was holding its breath in anticipation of the next "event", and the tension was felt both by the soldiers in the field and by their loved ones at home. The riveting question: "When will it end?" echoed from town to town, from city to city, as all waited for some kind of resolution to the hellish years of war.

April did not herald spring in the usual way in 1945. It was not a "new beginning", but a continuation of fighting, mutilation and death. Melba and Clarence tried to remain upbeat for the sake of Toby, but daily conversation always included reviewing war news and waiting for the next troubling announcement from "over there".

Unspeakably horrible reports came over the airways about the liberation of prisoners from "death camps" like the one in Ohrdruf, Germany, the first such camp to be found and dismantled by U.S. troops. News of the grisley discovery went to Generals Eisenhower, Bradley and Patton; the three men traveled to Ohrdruf in central Germany (about 330 kilometers southwest of Berlin), to see for themselves. Eisenhower's cabled report of the distressing scene reached General George C. Marshall in Washington, and it wasn't long before what he described found its way to the media.

In Eisenhower's words, "The most interesting— although horrible—sight that I encountered during the trip was a visit to a German internment camp near Gotha. The things I saw beggar description. While I was touring the camp I encountered three men who had been inmates and by one ruse or another had made their escape. I interviewed them through an interpreter. The visual evidence and the verbal testimony of starvation, cruelty and bestiality were so overpowering as to leave me a bit sick. In one room, where they were piled up twenty or thirty naked men, killed by starvation, George Patton would not even enter. He said that he would get sick if he did so. I made the visit deliberately, in order to be in a position to give first-hand evidence of these things if ever, in the future, there develops a tendency to charge these allegations merely to 'propaganda'. I have never felt able to describe my emotional reactions when I first came face to face with indisputable evidence of Nazi brutality and ruthless disregard of every shred of decency.... I have never at any other time experienced an equal sense of shock."

In short order, the Bergen-Belsen and Dachau camps were found. None of the discoveries were anything except painfully grim. The few remaining prisoners were in distressing condition.

Melba was reading aloud to Clarence; they had the latest edition of *The Laredo Daily Times*. On the front page, the headlines read "General Eisenhower Exposes Nazi Atrocities". As Melba read the words Eisenhower purportedly cabled to General Marshall detailing the grievous evidence of Nazi inhumanity at the Ohrdruf Death Camp, the anger in her voice spoke volumes.

"How could these things happen? Where were the 'good people'? How could they hide the smell from the fires? Can fear be so extreme that evil just takes over? I'm beyond horrified! I hope the American government joins with all the Allies to make sure all the Nazis are punished! They deserve NO grace!!"

"Agreed!" Clarence asserted with venom. "They deserve nothing but HELL for eternity, but first they should die a slow and painful death!"

"The thing that scares me is the idea that some of the worst perpetrators will undoubtedly escape. I wouldn't be surprised if the ones with enough money are already living somewhere else far away from Europe with fake names and fake identities. It makes me sick…!" The veins in Melba's neck and forehead were bulging with the internal pressure of her fury. Her fists were clenched, and her eyes were narrowed. Clarence had never seen her so flipped out, but he DID understand; he felt the same way.

CHAPTER 59

Just when it seemed good news was a pipe dream, on the last day of April, 1945, the Fuhrer, Adolf Hitler, committed suicide in his hidden bunker in Berlin. It seemed surreal after all the histrionics about the heinously powerful man who began the worst war the world has ever known to hear the words, "Hitler's dead!" But the whole world heard them...

It was a Monday and Melba was home with Toby when the announcement came over the radio: "America, news from Germany just hit our airways. Adolf Hitler is DEAD! He was found in his bunker along with his mistress, Eva Braun. Hitler and Miss Braun both swallowed cyanide capsules, then Hitler turned his gun on himself. More news will be forthcoming."

"Oh, my God!" slipped out of Melba's mouth as Toby looked on. "Oh, Lord! Thank you, thank you, thank you!" Then she ran to Toby, picked her up and raced out the front door. Other neighbors were in the street, waving, laughing and yelling things like, "Hot damn!" and "I knew Hitler couldn't last forever, not with our boys hot on his trail!", and "Holy mackerel! Those Germans best give up NOW!" Melba found herself laughing and crying at the same time; it was a really good feeling, and she could hardly wait until Clarence got home...

It seemed the entire population of Laredo celebrated into the night with dancing, drinking, laughing, crying and sharing stories (whether truth, fiction or fantasy) about der Fuhrer. Clarence and Melba enjoyed the festivities until Toby was asleep in their arms, then returned to the house. They were almost giddy with excitement; the death of Hitler would surely mean an end to the War! With Toby asleep and in her bed, the couple spent the next hour listening to the steady flow of news about the end of Hitler's reign. Unexpectedly, the world became privy to a bevy of intimate details about the man so many reviled.

"It's hard to understand why Eva Braun loved such an evil man, and it sickens me that she actually married him just days ago so she could be his wife when they committed suicide! How disgusting!" Melba spat. "If what we're hearing is true, she had to be delusional if not downright crazy. Her father was a school teacher, for Heaven's sake! She came from a good family, had two sisters, and she even attended a Catholic school. Her 12 years in the background, being HIS mistress, must have been worse than strange", Melba mused.

"Yeh, I don't get it, either!" Clarence agreed. "You have to wonder what her family thought about it! I doubt she ever saw her parents or sisters after she took up with the monster."

"Well, I can't say I feel sorry for the woman!" Melba asserted. "She HAD to know SOMETHING about the heinous things her lover cultivated and carried out over the past five years. How could she simply look the other way? The War, itself, was fueled by his lust for power and domination…"

"Yes it was", Clarence acknowledged. "His 'legacy', I'm sure, made the Devil proud!"

CHAPTER 60

While America mourned the loss of FDR, the country rallied behind its new leader. Harry Truman did not flinch from the monumental and sometimes downright monstrous decisions he had to make. After learning about the top secret "Manhattan Project", he gave the directive that scientists were to continue their work. Three months later, this decision would bring an end to the war with Japan.

With Hitler dead, the Nazi Regime quickly collapsed, and the first week in May brought an end to gunfire, bombings and mayhem throughout Europe. On May 7th, Germany surrendered to the Allies in Rheims, France. On the 8th of May, a ceasefire was declared in effect at one minute past midnight.

That Tuesday, May 8th, began like most other days in Laredo. Melba and Clarence were up early and having breakfast with Toby when they heard a now-familiar announcement over the radio: "BREAKING NEWS!" They immediately turned up the volume, moving closer to the speakers. Because so many newscasts beginning this way brought bad news, their tension was palpable. The announcer continued: "Germany has surrendered to the Allies! Great Britain has declared VICTORY IN EUROPE!"

In unison, the couple screamed, "THANK GOD!! HALLELULIAH!!!" as they embraced, spinning in circles around the room. Toby reacted by screaming, too, "Yaaaaaaaaaay!!" Then they all dissolved in laughter.

At the same time, roars of cheer and exultation were heard through the open windows as Laredo broke into almost crazed merriment. Clarence threw open the front door and they ran into the yard, waving and screaming and laughing and weeping; it was OVER!! After the recent partying over Hitler's death, this news was almost anticlimactic, but it was still SIMPLY FANTASTIC! This day, everyone knew, would forever be celebrated in history books.

For a few days, euphoria mesmerized people around the world, and, even if it was secretively, many of those living in Axis-controlled countries felt jubilation. The ceasefire agreement brought the first semblance of peace to the war-ravaged European countries. It also gave Americans hope that victory over Japan would soon follow.

Euphoria was nonexistent for the thousands of U.S. Marine, Navy, Air Force and Army troops who, at the same time, were engaged in some of the most intense and deadly combat of the entire war. Japan was the target; the death and destruction they began with the attack of Pearl Harbor would finally come home…

CHAPTER 61

Melba and Clarence, their lives still in limbo, had to continue daily routines like every other American civilian. But routine did not keep them from wondering what would happen in the "Pacific War Theatre". News of massive battles in places like Okinawa, the Solomon Islands, Kure, Yokosuka, Kyushu, Swatow, and even Hong Kong and Shanghai poured into the Office of War Information in Washington, D.C. and was quickly spread to media centers around the world. The news on July 19, 1945 about Allied attacks on Japanese military installations in Nojima Saki, Honshu and Hamamatsu were both chilling and encouraging.

However, it was the continuous loss of lives that kept Melba awake at night. She could only imagine the effect the aggression against Japan was having on families across the entire world; it was worse than sad. As Melba thought about these tragedies, she realized her opinions were not shared by most Americans. She understood that the overwhelming sentiment about what was happening to the Japanese was, "They're getting what they deserve, the bastards!" Her thoughts would have to remain one of those secrets stored deep within…She had no one, not even Clarence, who would understand her mixture of hatred for the Japanese leaders and sympathy for the people who, having no choice in the matter, were born and raised in the island nation that had savagely caused so much widespread death and destruction over the last four years. The nightmarish news that the battle for control of

Okinawa was estimated to have cost the deaths or injuries of over 50,000 American troops and the deaths of over 150,000 Japanese soldiers and civilians made Melba feel physically ill. Reports of the massacre of American prisoners of war by the Japanese enraged the world. The devastation to so many families in the States was appalling. Would this war NEVER end?

The news release out of Washington on July 26, 1945 was astonishing; hope surged in the hearts of Americans. The reports stated that President Truman and England's Minister of Defense, Clement Attlee, and the Premier of the Soviet Union, Joseph Stalin, with concurrence from China, had written an ultimatum for Japan. It was clear that there would be no negotiation; the Potsdam Declaration was a "take it or leave it" demand. It clearly told Japan to surrender or face total destruction. When Melba and Clarence heard the broadcast, they were stunned by its demands, but they were also relieved. The determination of President Truman was unmistakable:

"The prodigious land, sea and air forces of the United States, the British Empire and of China, many times reinforced by their armies and air fleets from the west, are poised to strike the final blows upon Japan. This military power is sustained and inspired by the determination of all the Allied Nations to prosecute the war against Japan until she ceases to resist.

The result of the futile and senseless German resistance to the might of the aroused free peoples of the world stands forth in awful clarity as an example to the

people of Japan. The might that now converges on Japan is immeasurably greater than that which, when applied to the resisting Nazis, necessarily laid waste the lands, the industry and the method of life of the whole German people. The full application of our military powers, backed by our resolve, will mean the inevitable and complete destruction of the Japanese armed forces and just as inevitably the utter destruction of the Japanese homeland.

The time has come for Japan to decide whether she will continue to be controlled by those self-willed militaristic advisers whose unintelligent calculations have brought the Empire of Japan to the threshold of annihilation, or whether she will follow the path of reason.

We call upon the Government of Japan to proclaim now the unconditional surrender of all Japanese armed forces, and to provide proper and adequate assurances of their good faith in such action. The alternative for Japan is prompt and utter destruction."

"The Japs really don't have a choice!" Clarence declared with certainty.

"I disagree," Melba uttered quietly. "Emperor Hirohito has shown no concern for his people! Just think about all the Kamikaze pilots he's sent to their deaths. And he must not care about the civilian population; look at the thousands who were killed during the bombings of Okinawa last month! No matter what the Allies have done, Japan just seems to 'dig in' even more. It's like they WANT to see their country destroyed...!"

"True, but I believe THIS statement from Truman and the Allied leaders will scare them into surrendering. I know Hirohito keeps his Prime Ministers from making the decisions. It's gonna happen this time!" Clarence asserted confidently.

Melba just shook her head. The reality of what might be happening so far away made her head spin and her heart pound. That the War's complete and final end seemed near was an overwhelming thought. She sat silently, staring at nothing, immersed in her own musings.

CHAPTER 62

The days following news of the Potsdam Declaration seemed to happen in slow motion. Continual postings in the Laredo newspaper about the greatly increased Allied offensive in the Pacific were disconcerting. Islands in the Marianas that had been under Allied control for months, reports stated, were faced with frequent attacks by Japanese forces. The Japanese attacks focused on stopping (or at least crippling) raids on their mainland which were fueled by a large fleet of Allied B-29 bombers based in the Marianas. War Department information assured U.S. citizens that the air and naval offensive was destroying Japan's ability to receive supplies. News reports focused on assurances that American and British troops had the "upper hand" and that nothing could stop the Allies from victory. Finally, news leaked back home about warning leaflets that would be dropped by Allied planes on heavily populated areas of Japan. These were purportedly intended to give civilians in the cities marked for destruction 72 hours to flee to safety.

When Melba heard this, she blurted, "That's outrageous! Those people...old men and women, babies, little children...can't escape. Why are we playing games with them? Whose brain-child came up with this idea?" She was clearly distraught by what she viewed as a ludicrous plan.

By the first days of August, 1945, it became evident that untold numbers of Japanese people would die simply because their government refused to surrender. The leadership was comprised of Prime Minister Suzuki Kantaro and his cabinet ministers. The ministries these men headed were filled with antagonistic factions; no agreements could be met. The "ruling elites" included Emperor Hirohito and his Court, as well as those in the Supreme War Leadership Council. Although the emperor held conferences during which the majority of his advisors expressed strong and urgent reasons for bringing the war to an end, Hirohito was the only one with "sovereign power" to decide the issue and make the final decision. He did nothing. It was as if he was in a catatonic state; he seemed like a statue instead of a living man.

Of course, the American public only got "tid-bits" of real information. Those in charge were careful to protect any salient truths about plans. People understood the need to protect "state secrets", but the waiting to see how things played out was torturous.

What happened next was, for the most part, totally unexpected. Although the Potsdam Declaration stated, "The alternative for Japan is prompt and utter destruction", not even the most annihilation-prone Americans really understood the meaning conveyed in Truman's message to the Japanese.

On August 6, 1945, the city of Hiroshima, Japan was literally leveled when a B-29 bomber, "Enola Gay" dropped a 9,000 pound uranium-235 bomb on the center of the city whose population was around 90,000 people. The explosion immediately wiped out around 90% of the city and killed at least 80,000 citizens. The aircraft, flown by Colonel Paul Tibbets and 11 other men of the United States military forces, had just dropped the first atomic bomb ever used in combat.

As soon as President Truman issued the following statement, heard all over the world, the reactions literally flew from person to person, from state to state, and from country to country:

"Sixteen hours ago an American airplane dropped one bomb on Hiroshima and destroyed its usefulness to the enemy. That bomb had more power than 20,000 tons of TNT. It had more than two thousand times the blast power of the British "Grand Slam" which is the largest bomb ever yet used in the history of warfare.

The Japanese began the war from the air at Pearl Harbor. They have been repaid many fold, and the end is not yet. With this bomb we have now added a new and revolutionary incease in destruction to supplement the growing power of our armed forces. In their present form these bombs are now in production and even more powerful forms are in development.

It is an atomic bomb. It is a harnessing of the basic power of the universe. The force from which the sun draws its power has been loosed against those who brought war to the Far East.

Before 1939, it was the accepted belief of scientists that it was theoretically possible to release atomic energy. But no one knew any practical method of doing it. By 1942, however, we knew that the Germans were working feverishly to find a way to add atomic energy to the other engines of war with which they hoped to enslave the world. But they failed. We may be grateful to Providence that the Germans got the V-1's and V-2's late and in limited quantities and even more grateful that they did not get the atomic bomb at all.

The battle of the laboratories held fateful risks for us as well as the battles of the air, land and sea, and we have now won the battle of the laboratories as we have won the other battles.

247

Beginning in 1940, before Pearl Harbor, scientific knowledge useful to us was pooled between the United States and Great Britain, and many priceless helps to our victories have come from that arrangement. Under that general policy the research on the atomic bomb was begun. With American and British scientists working together we entered the race of discovery against the Germans.

The United States had available the large number of scientists of distinction in the many needed areas of knowledge. It had the tremendous industrial and financial resources necessary for the project and they could be devoted to it without undue impairment of other vital war work. In the United States the laboratory work and the production plants, on which a substantial start had already been made, would be out of reach of enemy bombing, while at the time Britain was exposed to constant air attack and was still threatened with the possibility of invasion. For these reasons, Prime Minister Churchill and President Roosevelt agreed that it was wise to carry on the project here. We now have two great plants and many lesser works devoted to the production of atomic power. Employment during peak construction numbered 125,000 and over 65,000 individuals are even now engaged in operating the plants. Many have worked there two and a half years. Few know what they have been producing. They see great quantities of material going in and they see nothing coming out of these plants, for the physical size of the explosive charge is exceedingly small. We have spent two billion dollars on the greatest scientific gamble in history...and won.

But the greatest marvel is not the size of the enterprise, its secrecy, nor its cost, but the achievement of scientific brains in putting together infinitely complex pieces of knowledge held by many men in different fields of science into a workable plan. And hardly less marvelous has been the capacity of industry to design and of labor to operate, the machines and methods to do things never done before so that the brainchild of many minds came forth in physical shape and performed as it was supposed to do. Both science and industry worked under the direction of the United States Army, which achieved a unique success in managing so diverse a problem in the advancement of knowledge in an amazingly short time. It is doubtful such another combination could be got together in the world. What has been done is the greatest achievement of organized science in history. It was done under pressure and without failure.

We are now prepared to obliterate more rapidly and completely every productive enterprise the Japanese have above ground in any city. We shall destroy their docks, their factories, and their communications. Let there be no mistake; we shall completely destroy Japan's power to make war."

It was to spare the Japanese people from utter destruction that the ultimatum of July 26 was issued at Potsdam. Their leaders promptly rejected that ultimatum.

The Secretary of War, who has kept in personal touch with all phases of the project, will immediately make public a statement giving out further details.

His statement will give facts concerning the sites at Oak Ridge near Knoxville, Tennessee, and at Richland, near Pasco, Washington, and an installment near Santa Fe, New Mexico. Although the workers at the sites have been making materials to be used producing the greatest destructive force in history they have not themselves been in danger beyond that of many other occupations, for the utmost care has been taken for their safety.

The fact that we can release atomic energy ushers in a new era in man's understanding of nature's forces. Atomic energy may in the future supplement the power that now comes from coal, oil, and falling water, but at present it cannot be produced on a basis to compete with them commercially. Before that comes there must be a long period of intensive research. It has never been the habit of the scientists of this country or the policy of this government to withhold from the world scientific knowledge.

Normally, therefore, everything about the work with atomic energy would be made public. But under the present circumstances it is not intended to divulge the technical processes of production or all the military applications.

Pending further examination of possible methods of protecting us and the rest of the world from the danger of sudden destruction, I shall recommend that the Congress of the United States consider promptly the establishment of an appropriate commission to control the production and use of atomic power within the United States. I shall give further consideration and make further recommendations to the Congress as to how atomic power can become a powerful and forceful influence towards the maintenance of world peace."

Three days later, a second B-29 dropped another A-bomb on Nagasaki, killing an estimated 40,000 people.

Six days later, on August 15, 1945, Emperor Hirohito conceded defeat and Victory Over Japan Day (V-J Day) was proclaimed by the Allies.

CHAPTER 63

By October 1945, Melba and Clarence were making plans to return to Kilgore; it was finally time to go home! After the War ended and the massive movement of troops back to the States started in earnest, Clarence was reassigned to Border Patrol duties. Now, seven weeks after the war ended, his resignation was accepted and it was time to return to civilian life.

"I'm just glad my service to the Country could be done here rather than overseas", Clarence affirmed more than once. "What Lindell and Buron, Uncle George and Cousin Kelly endured makes me grateful the Patrols wanted me and we ended up here! But I think it's safe to say we are ALL ready to get away from Laredo and start a new life back home!"

Laughing, Melba said, "Oh, honey! I'm gonna be so sad to leave this beautiful town and our fabulous house!" Even Toby knew her Mama was being silly. She clapped her hands and giggled. They were all feeling especially chipper about their soon-to-happen move, and Toby's gleefulness was incentive enough to get ready without delay.

"It's lucky for us that Papa's able to drive down here to help us move! I can't believe Bobby's already 14 years old! It will be SO amazing to see him; I'm happy he's coming with Papa to help!" Melba exclaimed. "Today's the 18th, and Papa says he'll be here this Saturday. That's just TWO DAYS from now!! We have a lot to do, Mister Winters!"

Clarence said with mock seriousness, "No, honey. YOU have a lot to do!" Then he reached out for a quick hug, and their smiles lit up the room.

In truth, the few belongings they had would easily fit into theirs and Papa's pickups. Melba, always organized (SHE would never be like Mama!), had many "nonessentials" boxed and ready to go. She was pleased that Clarence would be working for a man in Kilgore named "Doc" Shoemaker who owned a small trucking business; he wanted Clarence to make hauls between Kilgore and New Orleans on a regular basis starting the week of November 5th. Shoemaker had a loosely-defined partnership (he had 5% interest) with a man named Everett Lowrance who owned a produce business called the Oklahoma Banana Distributing Company, Inc. Lowrance was an Oklahoman, but he currently lived in New Orleans and needed Shoemaker to truck loads of bananas to markets in the East Texas area. The job seemed too good to be true, but Clarence, ever the optimist, insisted it would be "fine".

The other good news, thankfully, was the way the couple found a place to live. One of Papa and Mama's friends at the First Baptist Church had a vacant rental house ready for occupation. They would move into the house owned by Cecil Moyers. Mr. Moyers told Papa the house was "nothing special", but clean and ready for renters. Melba and Clarence were more than happy to be "the renters"!

Arriving in Kilgore with two weeks to spare before Clarence's job began was sweet, Melba thought. Having him home to help with setting up the house would be a blessing, and, Melba also mused, he'd experience all the family and friend "reunions" that were sure to happen. She was getting revved about finally being HOME; the fresh, clean smell of the pines, the rolling hills, the beauty and shade from all the oak, elm and sweet gum trees, the heady scent of the brilliant white blossoms on the magnolias all seemed to beckon her to "hurry".

Moving in the fall when the deciduous trees flaunted rich colors of red, orange, purple and every shade of yellow caused Melba to smile as a panorama of her memories about the year-round beauty of nature in East Texas flowed through her brain. She loved each season, and welcomed being back to the part of Texas that actually had FOUR distinct times of year. Hopefully, Toby would see her first snowfall in December or January. It would be so special to see her reaction to the cold, crisp and breathtaking splendor of a snow-covered landscape. Just thinking about how Toby would squeal with glee made Melba happy. Good times were coming; she just felt it "in her bones".

Bobby and Toby immediately bonded. Bobby bounced into the house while Papa spent a few minutes situating the pickup for easier loading. After giving a cursory "knock", he pushed the door open while hollering, "We're here!"

Melba was in Toby's room, packing the last few items. Toby ran out to see her "Uncle Bobby", and he took one long, surprised look at her before grabbing her for a big hug.

"Oh, my gosh! You've grown up since I saw you two years ago", Bobby declared with real astonishment in his voice. "I know you don't really remember me, but I'm Bobby", he said with a big grin on his face. "Where's your Mama?"

"Bobby!!" Melba exclaimed when she ran into the living room. "Oh, Bobby!" With arms outstretched, she reached for her "little brother" who was no longer LITTLE. Their hug was what Melba always called a "bear hug"; it was SO good to see Bobby, and neither sibling had dry eyes. For the next few minutes, they just exchanged comments and banter about all that had changed, about the War's end, about Bobby's first year in high school and about the rest of the family. Clarence, who had been outside talking to Papa, finally came in, greeting Bobby with a hug.

Papa, not even stopping to hug Sister, walked over to Toby, picked her up and kissed her cheek. "My, my, my!" he exclaimed. "Aren't you just the cutest little thing? Your Granddaddy has missed you SO much!"

Toby really won his heart when she said, "Toby missed you so much, too, Gran-Da!"

Her smile is simply adorable, thought Melba while watching the exchange between her baby girl and Papa. Homecoming was off to a great start!

That night, the little group enjoyed a home-cooked meal together. Melba was feeling festive despite the boxes of packed belongings, and she made fried chicken that was always a favorite with all the men in the family. She'd made rice pudding on Friday, another of Papa's favorite dishes. They sat around the table and shared stories about everything. They talked about the way they heard the news about V-E and V-J Days, news about friends and neighbors who lost loved ones "over there", news about soldiers who were coming back into town, stories about new babies born while Melba and Clarence were in Catoola and Laredo, details about friends who were sick or who had died, and so much more! Melba realized they could talk all night and still not even begin to discuss everything, but finally she murmured, "Hey, guys. I think we'd better call it a day and hit the hay; tomorrow's gonna be busy! Papa, I have a cot for you in the living room. Bobby, I've made a bed on the couch for you. Toby wakes early, so we won't need an alarm clock!"

They said goodnight. Clarence was snoring before Melba even lay down, but she had trouble sleeping. Thoughts about their days in Laredo and in Catoola kept her mind spinning; they were leaving friends who had shared the war years with them, friends who had been there for support when Toby was sick, had watched Toby grow from an infant to a sturdy toddler, friends she would miss. It was bittersweet. Finally, Melba drifted off to sleep with the shocking realization that this was their last night in Laredo, Texas.

CHAPTER 64

By 9:00 Sunday morning, the trucks were packed. Furniture was carefully stacked and covered with blankets and quilts, boxes were wedged into every crevice in between, and stacked tightly. Amazingly, everything fit! At 9:20, the two pickups rolled out of Laredo on highway 35 N, heading toward Austin. It would be a very long day; they planned to drive the almost-500 miles with minimal stops. Thankfully, Toby was an incredibly good traveler. Melba prayed she would sleep at least a few of the hours to help ease the tedium. As it turned out, Toby was a "dream child"; she slept from noon until almost 4:00. When she woke from her nap, they were just a few hours from Kilgore.

It was just a little past 8:00 when the tired little group pulled into Papa and Mama's circular gravel driveway. Although it was already dark, there was a full moon, and the stars twinkled brightly in the clear sky. Melba exhaled a long, weary breath as she climbed out of the pickup. Toby held out her arms and said, "Mama, are we HERE?"

Melba couldn't help but laugh as she answered in the affirmative, "We sure are! Come on, let's go see your Mummy!" (Melba liked the name G.W.'s kids had bestowed on Mama; it was different than "Grandma or "Me-Maw". In fact, Melba knew no other grandmothers who went by "Mummy".)

Mama had cooked a big meal for the travelers, in keeping with her belief that food was the best way to show your love for others. Her cooking was first rate, and Melba could hardly wait to have a home-cooked meal made by Mama! The smells as they entered the kitchen were mouth-watering, and ALL of the travelers "oohed and aahed" over her chicken fried steaks, macaroni and cheese and fresh-from-the-garden green beans! Mama also had a BEAUTIFUL apple pie sitting on the cabinet. The greetings were over in short order since everyone was famished!

After dinner, they talked about so much for such a long time that it was difficult to stop and bring in the items everyone needed for the night. Toby, though, was dozing off in her chair. It was time to get her in bed.

Monday dawned with a beautiful azure blue sky dotted with a few fluffy white clouds. By early afternoon, with lots of help from family and friends who could take time from work, the Winters family had all its belongings in the newly-acquired house owned by Mr. Moyers. Toby was entertaining herself by exploring all the "nooks and crannies" in the house, opening all the closet doors, peeking into cabinets, and going out front to swing on the porch swing. She loved the new place, and her giggles and silliness made Melba and Clarence happy, too.

Within the next few days, Clarence had moved furniture into places that suited Melba, organized the one-car garage, built some new shelves for storage in the kitchen, and met with Doc Shoemaker about his new job. He was feeling swell about being in Kilgore; he knew this was what Melba wanted, and he agreed. Kilgore was turning into a really nice place since the early days of the boom. City planners had made sure nicely paved streets were constructed with curbs and sidewalks. The recently completed Kilgore Heights Elementary

School was located on Broadway. It had a beautiful brick exterior, and large classrooms with polished wooden floors. The playground was huge, and the grounds around the building were manicured and lushly landscaped with greenery and decorative shrubs. Kilgore High School was also open and a showplace. Oilmen, like well-producer Shack Laird, helped fund the construction of the public schools. They wanted only the best for their offspring, and "the best" started with quality construction of the buildings and esthetically pleasing designs. The schools were both beautiful and functional; they were also filled with highly qualified teachers.

Clarence and Melba knew the reputation of Kilgore's schools, and they were confident that Toby would be both happy and well-educated when she attended them. Their knowledge that Kilgore schools had a reputation for academic rigor and a no-nonsense curriculum was certainly comforting. They had no doubts about Toby's educational future in Kilgore!

Clarence started his job at Shoemaker's on November 5, 1945 as planned. Doc told him a little about Everett Lowrance, calling him an entrepreneur. He explained that Lowrance lived in New Orleans and ran a banana importation business. Wanting an East Texas venue for sales of his produce, Lowrance had met up with Doc and worked a deal. Doc now had two truck and trailer rigs and needed a second driver. It was a piece of sweet luck for Clarence, and he was feeling really good about snagging the New Orleans "gig".

Melba was feeling just fine about being left alone during the week; she had family all over Kilgore! After Laredo with no family nearby, her life in Kilgore was simply easy. And by the end of November, Clarence's work routine became fairly consistent.

His schedule involved a weekly six hour run to the Crescent City, going to the dock to meet with the dock foreman and, not infrequently, also meeting with Lowrance to determine the size and price of the load. (This varied weekly, depending on weather conditions in places like Honduras, Costa Rica, Guatemala and Panama.) Occasionally, Clarence got to spend the late afternoon and evening exploring places like the French Quarter, eating some Cajun catfish and doing a little gambling over games of Black Jack, Craps or Horseshoes.

Typically, however, the ships were ready to unload their cargo, and the grueling task of transferring the heavy banana stalks (bunches) from the boats to the trucks began immediately. The bananas were hauled on the stalk, hanging from hooks attached to the inside roof of the refrigerated trailer, and the usual load would be at least 2.5 tons. Loading could take several hours, even with the help of a lot of dock "bums" who worked for pennies. Then the long drive back to Kilgore would begin. Melba learned to expect Clarence to arrive at home sometime in the "wee" hours of the morning, and she knew he would be exhausted.

Shoemaker's routine was to meet the trucks (usually both of his haulers traveled in tandem on the New Orleans runs) when they arrived. It might be midnight or later, but the bananas had to be unloaded into a big freezer vault so they could be stabilized at around 60 degrees Fahrenheit to keep them green. The ripening process would begin only when the fruit was ready for delivery to markets all around Kilgore.

Generally, Clarence started the ripening process within a day or two of getting the fruit to Kilgore. Although tricky, Clarence became adept at the procedure, and Shoemaker soon expected Clarence to handle the process on his own. The first step involved lowering the internal temperature of each banana (the pulp had to test at 15 degrees Celsius, 59 degrees Fahrenheit), and to accomplish that, the vault's temperature had to be lowered to between 48 and 50 degrees Fahrenheit for 12 to 16 hours. Humidity had to be at or above 90%, so Clarence used commercial humidifiers in the vaults. He also sprayed water on the concrete floors, keeping them moist, to assist in infusing extra moisture into the vaults' air. He measured the temperature and humidity hourly during the entire ripening process. When all conditions were "right", Clarence discharged ethylene gas into the vault at a concentration of .02%. (The gas was a catalyist for initiating the hormonal process that started the ripening.) He kept the room closed off for 24 hours, then opened the doors and ventilated the bananas thoroughly. After the ethylene gas was removed, Clarence closed the vaults and controlled the temperature inside at 15 degrees Celsius for three to four days. The humidity was kept at about 75% during this part of the process. At the end, the vaults would be opened and thoroughly vented and the ripe fruit would be removed and packed for delivery to stores.

CHAPTER 65

During those first months in Kilgore, Melba had time to enjoy Toby and make sure she was well-acquainted with her cousins. G.W.'s four kids, Larry, Jean Ann, Gary, and Carole Lou spent a lot of days with Toby. Larry, being the "oldest" at 7 years of age, was definitely a favorite of Papa and Mama, and the family often gathered at their house where the grandchildren were, officially, spoiled by "Mummy". She made them all sorts of yummy treats, like fresh-baked donuts and fried pies, and she liked to take them outside to feed the chickens, tend the flower garden and chase the squirrels. Jean Ann was just a year younger than Larry, so, at 6 she acted like the "mama" to her younger cousin and siblings. Gary was just old enough, at 2 years, to get into mischief constantly, and Carole Lou was the baby. Toby fit right in. She was a bouncy 3 year old, and adored her "best friends".

G.W. had just returned from California in September following a last-minute call to serve his country. With four children to feed, he had been exempted from active duty during the first four years of the War, but ALL able-bodied men were called to active duty throughout the early months of 1945 and into the summer when fighting escalated. Intense and deadly conflicts, like The Battle of the Bulge, the fierce fighting by American troops in taking control of Manila, Philippines, the weeks-long bombing of Dresden, Germany, the Battle of Iwo Jima, Japan, and the virtual destruction and capture of Okinawa had caused so many casualties on all sides that new troops were desperately needed. G.W.'s draft notice came from the Navy in June, and he was sent to San Diego, California for boot camp.

Ozelle and the children stayed in Kilgore while G.W. was away, Ozelle taking on the role of "head of the house". She earned the respect of everyone in the family by handling her heavy responsibilities with surprising serenity and amazing astuteness considering she'd never had to take care of all the finances, shopping, and child care independently. Ozelle and G.W. did a lot of celebrating that August when Japan finally surrendered and World War II was finally REALLY over!

With G.W.'s return to Kilgore, Ozelle could reclaim her role as wife and mother, leaving a lot of the other home- related jobs to her husband. Ozelle was heard to say, "Thank the Lord!" more than once!

G.W.'s oilfield days had ended with the onset of war, and he was actively looking for continued work in Civil Engineering. The end of fighting opened a whole new job market for civilians, and G.W. intended to ride the wave of opportunity that followed the War. Cleanup and preservation of the "spoils" of war were high on the list of massive jobs to be done, and it seemed likely that he and his young family would be moving away from Kilgore in the near future.

Melba and Ozelle became close friends almost immediately after she and Clarence moved back to Kilgore. G.W. was busy job-hunting and Clarence was away several days and nights each week, so the two women just naturally gravitated toward each other. The fact that being together was never an option in the early years of their marriages made them appreciate the "sister" thing. The women realized they had a lot in common. Both had endured the Depression as young girls, and they also understood all the sacrifices and sadness of war. Each woman took motherhood seriously, and both loved their offspring. Melba was a bit jealous of how easily Ozelle seemed to get pregnant and how simple giving birth appeared to be for her, but she tried to ignore the envy she felt. Ozelle was four years older than Melba, but the age difference presented no problems. Melba was "old" for her years; she had seen a lot...

On a day in mid-December, Melba decided to confide in Ozelle that she and Clarence were "trying" to have another baby. "I just don't understand why I have so much trouble!" Melba said almost tearfully. "Mama never seemed to have any issues; it's just not fair!"

Ozelle, ever the pragmatist, told Melba, "Listen, silly! Just stop worrying about getting pregnant and it'll happen. Trust me, it's always better to stay upbeat about that kind of stuff. If I had to guess, Clarence isn't worried about it!" With that, Ozelle and Melba both giggled; men were always the same...MEN!

The two spent the next hour watching the kids and speculating whether Melba's next child would be a boy or a girl. Melba insisted it didn't matter to her, but Ozelle thought that wasn't exactly "honest"; Melba liked dressing Toby in cute clothes, styling her hair in Shirley Temple curls, having "tea parties" and make-believe "debutante balls". More than the immediate "girly" things she enjoyed with Toby, Melba liked to talk about her hopes for females in the future. Ozelle, secretly, believed Melba would be happier if she had another girl. As for herself, Ozelle admitted to being a little partial to her boys.

The holidays that first year without war were truly special. Being back in Kilgore meant having family together for the first time in five years, and everyone enjoyed the special get-togethers they shared. Bobby, a typical teenager, was always surrounded by a bevy of friends. Anna Jean and Buron were on vacation and had taken the train in from New York City. Lindell and Nedra had married two years earlier while he was participating in his 12 week Army Navigation School training in Hondo, Texas. He and Nedra were living in San Angelo while awaiting his next assignment, and Lindell continued to make strong progress with his recovery from war injuries. They were home, too!

The derricks in downtown Kilgore were transformed into a "city of lights" after they were draped with thousands of Christmas lights. It was an amazing sight that would become a much-loved Kilgore tradition.

Meanwhile, the entire nation embraced the Christmas Season as millions of veterans finally stepped back on American soil, and the National Christmas Tree lighting in Washington D.C. was resumed after five years of war. President Truman lit the tree, and his message was broadcast throughout the world. His words were heard by millions of physically and emotionally exhausted, bereaved citizens, who listened intently as he said, "This is the Christmas that a war-weary world has prayed for through long and awful years. With peace comes joy and gladness. The gloom of the war years fades as once more we light the National Community Christmas Tree."

Truman was correct about the relief and hope bubbling up in the hearts and minds of survivors; it was an almost-surreal time for more than a few.

CHAPTER 66

Christmas could only do so much to give renewed hope to hundreds of millions of people throughout much of the world. The truth, even when softened with rhetoric about humane acts of compassion and helpfulness, was terribly hard to accept when considering the aftermath of World War II. Much of Europe and Asia had been destroyed, food supplies were virtually nonexistent, sanitary drinking water was scarce, and there was virtually no industry to help rebuild the ruined towns, cities, factories, hospitals, churches, schools, and housing. The roads, the transportation systems…EVERYTHING was in wreckage from country to country and from city to city. It was a ghastly time in the world's history.

But Americans had the ability to block out the horrors of what they left behind all over Europe and Asia because they did not come home to devastation. In fact, the surviving Americans found burgeoning post-war growth and a much-improved economy when they returned to their former cities and towns. The United States quickly entered what is now called the "Golden Age of Capitalism".

Almost immediately after the war, U.S. companies expanded to include overseas markets in places where rebuilding was urgently needed. Most of the rebuilding would be funded by the "Marshall Plan" which, by 1947, would pump over 17 billion dollars into assistance for the Allied countries as well as for the Axis foes. Not everyone was pleased that aid was going to Axis countries, but most reluctantly agreed it was one of America's "hallmarks" to assist the downtrodden, even when the aid was needed by former enemies.

Secretary of State George Marshall proposed his plan during a speech he gave at Harvard University. His idea was to provide a post-war European aid program that would send humanitarian aid in the form of money to Great Britain, France, West Germany, Italy, the Netherlands and Belgium to help those countries rebuild. Within a year, Marshall's plan was approved by congress and put into place.

As Marshall, himself, stressed, "Our plan is directed not against any country or doctrine, but against hunger, poverty, desperation and chaos."

Fortunately for the millions of people who benefitted, the plan worked! The Marshall Plan created an economic miracle in Western Europe. By the end date of funding, four years later, Western European industries were producing twice as much as they had been the year before war broke out. A perk for America came in the form of record levels of trade with our firms, fueling a postwar economic boom in the United States.

In truth, the Marshall Plan was much more than a humanitarian effort. It was meant to help contain the spread of communism, and it succeeded. The Cold War worked itself into place, and communism was held at bay.

History would give the first ten years following the War an interesting title, one that failed to surprise the millions of happy couples who found themselves blessed with a child, or with SEVERAL children. This era was called the "Baby Boom", and it aptly described a phenomenon of World War II:

new life! Perhaps a result of the years of suffering and the misery of all that had happened in the world, millions of soldiers reunited with loved ones and families quickly expanded. With the passing of the GI Bill of Rights in 1944, veterans could obtain low-interest loans to purchase homes and farms AND benefit from either a very low down payment, or none. The American Dream became reality!

In keeping with America's success story, Clarence, still with Shoemaker and working long hours in his trucking business, had adjusted to life in Kilgore. He loved it! Toby was growing into an expressive, witty, and, quite simply, adorable child. Her presence, her health and her exuberance about everything made both Clarence and Melba happy. Life was good.

Clarence worked for Shoemaker for almost two years, and during that time he learned a lot about bananas! He was Shoemaker's "man" for ripening all the fruit brought in from New Orleans, and that skill, alone, made him invaluable. At the same time, he became acquainted with the grocers all around East Texas in little towns like Gladewater, Henderson, Palestine, New London, Tatum, Carthage, Hallsville and Rusk making sure they knew him and, most importantly, liked him. Clarence had a plan, so when "old man" Shoemaker told him about his desire to retire, Clarence was ready!

By early January, 1946, G.W. and Ozelle were in Ohio. The job at Wright-Patterson AFB in Dayton was just what G.W. wanted. Of course, Melba hated losing her first, "oldest", sis-in-law and her adored brother. But she was busy with life in Kilgore…

The unexpected news that Jeannie and Buron were moving to New Jersey after their "temporary hotel homes" in Chicago, Washington D.C. and New York left Melba feeling truly dejected; she had hoped Jeannie would be back in TEXAS, at least, but that was not to happen. Buron wanted a home outside the big city, but close enough for a daily commute into Manhattan, and he and Jeannie liked the town of Madison.

Clarence and Melba were making repairs and upgrades to the little house next to Mama and Papa's out on Danville Road. They planned to move there in order to save money so they could eventually purchase a house. Papa and a few friends had constructed the house when his mother and father needed a place to live after Papa Aycock got sick. The house had stood empty for several years; Grandmother Aycock was living in the extra bedroom inside Papa's house now.

At the same time, Clarence's new venture was in the works; he was working on a deal that would enable him to open his own business within the next three months. He would be the owner/operator of the Kilgore Banana House! Shoemaker was ready to retire, and he encouraged Clarence to utilize his contacts to help give the newly-formed banana-import business a head start.

During the last weekend in January, the pieces all seemed to glide into place.

"Honey!" Clarence called out. "Come in here! I just hung up the phone after talking to Sterling down at the bank. They're gonna give me the business loan!" Clarence's tone was beyond excited, and he grinned that lopsided grin Melba loved. "We're in business, Mrs. Winters!" Clarence wrapped his arms around Melba, kissed her long and hard, and whispered, "It's really happening, baby. We're finally going to make it!"

Melba could barely breathe. She was elated, but at the same time secretly afraid. The "what ifs" were pushing their nasty little thoughts into her brain, but she determined to fight them away and be positive. After all, this WAS a dream she and Clarence had nurtured over the past year. "Oh, honey! I'm SO happy for us!" Melba exclaimed. "You will be the best businessman in Kilgore!"

CHAPTER 67

The new adventure began with a bang! All sorts of things had to happen before Clarence could "close" on the loan. Of primary importance, the "market" for his product had to be ready. Fortunately, working for Shoemaker had given him a solid business base. Shoemaker was perfectly happy to see someone else come in and continue to provide the East Texas area a consistent supply of fresh bananas.

Clarence had already located a double refrigerated warehouse on Broadway Street, near Kilgore College. It had been used by the recently closed Kidd Dairy business and would accommodate storage and preparation of the huge shipments of banana bunches, some with as many as 200 individual banana "fingers", he'd be transporting from New Orleans and occasionally from Galveston, to Kilgore. The owner of the warehouse had accepted an earnest money payment to hold it for a month, and the banker was a long-time acquaintance. Clarence had actually had an account at Kilgore National Bank when working in the oil business back in the '30s. He had been a "kid" at the time, but he wanted to establish an account; it just seemed "right". He realized now the "smarts" of working with the bank when he first moved to Kilgore. It was paying off!

Clarence obviously needed at least one refrigerated trailer and truck, and it had to be in good condition. For the refrigerated banana storage areas, industrial-grade humidifiers were required, along with upgraded cooling units and temperature gauges. He knew he'd have to purchase tanks of ethylene gas and generators for disbursal of the gas to facilitate the ripening process. The warehouses had an attached "office" area out front, so he would have a place to handle transactions, set up a filing system, install a telephone and do all his paperwork.

It took the rest of the spring to get ready for the business to open, but finally all the planning was complete and all the equipment had been ordered. The terms of the loan were finalized, and the last few meetings in New Orleans with Everett Lowrance and the shipping company managers were held. Everett was instrumental in getting Clarence set up with the importers and introducing him to all the key players necessary to actually RUN the business. It felt amazing to see the plans materialize! As for Toby, she just liked running around in the vaults and listening to her voice echo off the bare walls. She had a new playground: "Daddy's work"!

Clarence hired Jimmy Watters, his nephew, to help with the business; it would take both of them working long hours to get the business up and running. Fortunately, Jimmy and his wife, Jackie, were already in Kilgore since Jimmy had been working as a roughneck for several of the oil companies. ("Thank the Lord for small favors!" Clarence thought more than once!) It was definitely a "shoestring" operation. Several "handymen" who hung around the oil fields looking for jobs were happy to have part-time work unloading the truck and assisting with the detailed care of delicate and newly delivered bananas. The first full load of bananas arrived the last week in May, 1946.

Initially, contracts had been worked out with 20 grocery stores, all within a 50 mile range from Kilgore. Getting the newly-ripened (but still partially green) banana stalks to the stores was another aspect of the business that required drivers and pickup trucks. Since Jimmy was usually on another "run" to New Orleans, Clarence made most of the deliveries. Sometimes he needed to hire other drivers to assist, but the bulk of the work fell on him. The summer of 1946 was a whirlwind of activity for the new business, and it seemed the entire family got involved. Estel helped out anytime he could, even doing some of the maintenance on the trucks and learning about the proper care of all the bananas. Melba's dad helped out by making deliveries to some of the smaller grocery stores that were scattered across communities in close proximity to Kilgore.

Clarence's mother, Ina Belle, offered to stay in the little house that came with the purchase of the two warehouse vaults and the office space. She would handle the walk-in customers, selling sacks of single bananas for 30 cents a dozen. (Clarence's sister, Nellie, was living with Ina in the Tulsa house, so this arrangement worked well for her immediate family; they would have the house to themselves while Ina was in Kilgore.) The little house beside the warehouses had been the residence of Herman Kidd, the manager of Kidd Dairy, the previous business, and was in fair condition. All Clarence and Estel needed to do was purchase a new stove and install new linoleum in what would be called "Grandma's Cottage". Clarence and Melba were pleased that Toby's other grandmother would be living in Kilgore; they wanted her to enjoy some special times with her granddaughter!

CHAPTER 68

About the time the cottage was ready for Ina Belle to move in, Melba and Clarence learned they were finally expecting their second child! It was late September, and it seemed time had simply evaporated since the business opened. Even though Melba had vowed NOT to use Dr. Allums for another "birthing" experience, she ended up going to see him to confirm her pregnancy.

"Yes, ma'am, Melba", he said with a twinkle in his eyes, "you are definitely pregnant. I estimate you will be giving birth sometime in April of next year." As he spoke these words, his always-kind and caring face spoke volumes; he had not forgotten TOBY'S birth and the fact that Melba had asked for "natural" childbirth. It was clear he expected to be told HE would not deliver THIS baby. In fact, the next thing he said was, "Would you like a recommendation for an obstetrical specialist?"

Melba was a bit surprised that he even offered to recommend another doc, but she said, "I guess that would be a good idea, Dr. Allums. I'm not sure what I'll decide, but I do appreciate that you remember my issues with Toby's birth."

"Currently, Kilgore Hospital does not have an obstetrician on staff, but I know of two fine doctors who practice in Longview," Dr. Allums continued. "I'll get their contact information for you. Of course, should you decide you want to continue your prenatal treatment here, I'll be available to help."

With that, Dr. Allums left the room. Melba stared at the door after it closed for what seemed a long time, finally getting herself dressed and ready to leave the clinic. She was really torn about who to select for this baby's delivery; it seemed ridiculous that she had to make such a decision when she trusted Dr. Allums for everything else. It was just the birth of Toby that made her wonder...

That night, she brought up her mixed feelings to Clarence, saying, "I feel really upset about not asking Dr. Allums to handle this pregnancy."

"Oh, honey, I can understand why you're still angry with the doc!" Clarence stated. "It was wrong, especially since you ASKED him to let you try to have Toby without medications! You read all about natural childbirth and that's what you wanted. If Dr. Allums had really tried to work with you and there was some big complication, I would have understood his use of morphine and forceps. Problem is, he just wanted to do his 'normal' stuff. Of course you still resent the fact that he gave you sedation and delivered Toby from your unconscious body with forceps!"

"So now I have to decide what to do about THIS pregnancy, Clarence, and I just don't know the best answer", Melba groaned. "I mean, Toby was born healthy and I had no real problems after she arrived. Maybe I'm just being ridiculous about this and should just tell the doctor I want him to take care of me but that I insist on natural childbirth this time. Surely he will agree to let me give it a try...!" Melba's eyes told Clarence how much she wanted to have the decision made. It was clear that the indecision was causing her a lot of distress.

"Let's talk to Dr. Allums together as soon as we can get an appointment. If he seems okay with what we want, we'll use him this time, too. But he has to let US decide about any drugs or the use of forceps." Clarence's voice as well as his words soothed Melba, and she finally relaxed. She laid her head on his shoulder and he pulled her close.

Both of them were relieved because they'd made the first decision; if the doctor wasn't receptive, they'd find someone else.

Five days later, Melba and Clarence had their meeting with Dr. Allums. After hearing both of them talk about why they believed a "natural" delivery was best for the baby and for Melba, he agreed to do everything possible to fulfill their wishes. He told them the hospital staff would need training since the expected protocol at Kilgore Hospital did not include following the advice of Dr. Grantly Dick-Read!

With a twinkle in his eyes, Doc Allums said, "You know MY philosophy is to keep laboring women from undue suffering. My use of medication is intended to make birthing less traumatic… but, I do understand the good that can come of more natural birthing, and I aim to help you experience it even if it means I have to walk away and leave you with a midwife for awhile."

"That's fine with me", Melba insisted. "Thank you for giving me the opportunity to attempt it, and, most of all, for listening to my concerns about being heavily medicated and the use of forceps. I trust you to talk to me about any problems during labor and let Clarence and me have choices."

After the meeting, Melba felt like a huge weight had been lifted off her chest; she honestly found breathing easier! The stress of deciding whether or not to keep Dr. Allums as her doctor for both prenatal care, the birth and postnatal care had been harder on her than she'd realized. As Melba and Clarence left the clinic hand-in-hand, both were smiling. Life was, once again, good!

The very next week, Estel drove to Tulsa to get his mother and bring her back to Kilgore. She was only bringing her bed and a 2-door chifforobe, clothes and personal items, so while Estel was gone, Clarence and Melba shopped for the rest of the things she would need to "set up house".

They found a used kitchen table and four ladder back chairs with woven cane seats for $25, a floral print, overstuffed platform rocking chair for $40 at Sears Roebuck, and a small davenport covered in navy blue corduroy that cost them $35, also at Sears. Mama had a few extra pots and pans she "donated" for Ina. At the Five and Dime store, Melba got a set of utensils and a few other kitchen and bathroom necessities. After all the preparation, she was ready to welcome her mother-in-law.

"Holy Mackerel! If I'd realized how much time and effort it would take to get things ready for Mom's arrival, I might have changed my mind about having her come to Kilgore!" Melba groaned this admission to Jackie. "I really wasn't thinking about all the things she'd need. I must have been out of my mind when I told Clarence having her here would be swell!"

"You know it'll be good after the baby gets here, Melba", Jackie declared. "I still think all this is gonna work out, so please stop stressing! After she gets here this afternoon, you'll feel better. When Ina walks into the cottage and sees the way you've got it fixed up, she'll be happy. I can't wait to see her face! You know Jimmy and I haven't seen her since we left Tulsa last year."

"Hope you're right, my dear", Melba told Clarence's niece. "I think I'm just tired; maybe I should try to remember that I AM pregnant!"

Two hours later, Estel pulled up at the Banana House. Clarence was actually present and accounted for, and Jimmy, Jackie, Melba and Toby were all standing outside the cottage. Mom opened the door of the pickup and stepped out, her face the image of happy anticipation. She stretched out her arms to Toby and Toby allowed her "new" grandmother to pick her up and give her a big hug; this was the first time they'd met! The hugs, smiles and absolute delight they all shared was definitely a good sign, Melba mused.

Besides, Mom DID love her "digs", and that made Melba feel really happy! When they walked into the tiny kitchen, Mom's reaction was, "Perfect! I can cook a meal for the family on Sundays, but the size is just right for me on a daily basis. And, by the way, I love the stove!"

After they toured the cottage, Mom's comment was, "I could stay here forever! The size is just right for me, and I even have a screened-in porch so we can bring my birds down here! You know the only reason I hesitated about this move was leaving Polly and Molly behind. I suppose you've figured out by now that SOMEONE will have to make another trip to Tulsa to get my parrots!"

The looks exchanged by Clarence and Estel were, well, a little strained. Still, it appeared that the brothers were pretty pleased with their mama's comments.

Ina settled into her new house and job without any difficulties. She loved being able to see Toby almost daily, and she was amazed with the way the business was running. The first time she witnessed a haul of bananas coming in, her reaction was, "My gosh, Clarence! I've never seen so many bananas in my life! I had no idea you were bringing such a huge truckload to Kilgore at one time! Can you really sell all these bananas?"

Clarence assured her he not only could sell the truckload of bananas, but that Jimmy was on the way back from New Orleans with another three tons of the fruit.

The way things would work for the next decade was quite an eye-opener for the little lady who had been a sharecropper's wife on a small, struggling farm in Kentucky. Seeing the size of Clarence's cargo was mind-boggling for a farmer's wife who grew a few bushels of vegetables in one season and managed to recoup, at best, two or three dozen eggs per day. She had no way to mentally compare her "boy's" business with others that were similar.

And Clarence was right with his predictions, selling his bananas was, almost, a breeze! Most people in East Texas had rarely even seen a banana, and to be able to buy them every week was considered quite "the thing"! The appearance of bananas in groceries all over East Texas was simply amazing, and people soon began to think buying tropical fruit was something worthy of bragging about or even grandstanding to friends and neighbors! Piney Woods residents began to take desserts like banana pudding and banana pies to social gatherings, making the popularity of the fruit even more contagious. It was as if bananas advertised themselves!

By the time Christmas rolled around, Molly and Polly were comfortably settled into their new digs on the porch, and Clarence had covered the screens with plastic tarps so the little area could be heated during the winter months. He added a small space heater and discovered it worked just fine for keeping the birds in a tropical-feeling habitat.

The holidays were good that last month of 1946; life was getting back to "normal". Melba was five months pregnant, and Dr. Allums assured her the baby was progressing just as expected. Actually, Melba felt good, and she and was especially delighted because Anna Jean was expecting, too! It was Jeannie's first baby, so she was always pestering Melba for details about the birthing process. The phone bills for both families were higher than they'd ever been; calls were made almost daily!

For the first time in many years, the sisters were able to really be best friends and share all the amazing changes women experience during pregnancy. They reveled in talking about EVERYTHING, and the laughter they shared made both of them happier than either had been during the war years. The most wonderful thing for both sisters was the fact that their babies were due at around the same time in April! To top it all off, news from Ohio was that Ozelle was expecting another child, her FOURTH! It was almost too much good news at once; two more cousins for Toby! The fact that such long distances separated the "girls" was a constant source of discussion and the only disappointment they shared.

"Jeannie", Melba said during a conversation one afternoon, "you know I'd like to have a boy this time, but I'll still be thrilled with another girl. Do you have a big preference?"

"Naw, not really. I mean, I'll be happy as long as our baby is healthy. It would be nice to have a boy, but if we BOTH have girls, they can be best friends just like us!" Jeannie's voice transmitted her smile. Then both women giggled as they shared this moment. Things were good, even "long distance"!

CHAPTER 69

Over the next few months, Melba enjoyed spending time with all the family, and she tried to appreciate the last weeks she would have to enjoy Toby as an "only child". Toby, always quite the precocious one, claimed she knew all about the baby that would soon be joining them. She prattled on and on about what would happen when Melba went to the hospital, saying things like, "Daddy's gonna take Mommy to the hospital and then she'll get a new little baby and she'll bring her home." Toby was determined "the new baby" would be a girl, and she proclaimed to anyone who asked, "Our baby is a GIRL!" Her belief regarding the gender of the baby may have had more to do with the fact that Melba did have a lot more girl "stuff", clothes and blankets and toys she'd saved that were Toby's when she was little, than anything else. Even when Melba and Clarence tried to explain that the baby MIGHT be a boy, Toby just shook her head back and forth, pursing her lips in defiance of any other possibility. It was funny and cute, but they just hoped Toby would be okay if the life within Melba's womb turned out to be of the "male persuasion"!

April that year was extra-nice, weather-wise. There were plenty of showers, but those were followed by warm sunshine and cool breezes. Melba was grateful for the beautiful days and pleasant nights. To say she was "ready" for the big day to hurry up and arrive was a definite understatement!

As it turned out, Anna Jean went into labor first. It was early in the morning (3:30!) on April 10th, 1947. Buron called Clarence. Clarence called Mama, Papa, and Lindell. Then the waiting began for the Kilgore family; not being at the Morristown, New Jersey hospital with Jeannie was like some form of inhumane torture! Buron called again around 9:00 a.m. to tell the waiting family that Jeannie's doctor had just come out to inform him it would be "awhile".

Jeannie was already 5 centimeters dilated, though, and that made everyone happy. No one wanted this first baby to give their "little sis" a hard time.

Ronald Steven Thomas was born at 11:30 a.m. He weighed 7 pounds, 3 ounces and, according to Buron's telephone message, was a strong and healthy boy. Buron seemed beside himself with pride, and his excited voice described little Ronnie from the top of his head to the bottom of his tiny feet. Buron, with obvious relief, told everyone in Kilgore that Anna Jean was doing well, too, and he promised to have a picture of Ronnie to send really soon.

Buron told Melba to call Jeannie later that afternoon, and that's exactly what she did:

"Hello, Mommy", Melba teased. "I know you look beautiful, little sissy! It's the natural beauty that only comes with motherhood; I'm so excited for you! I know Ronnie is adorable! Buron said he has a lot of dark hair just like you did when you were a baby, except yours was curly and his is totally straight. And we're told his eyes are dark brown, like Mama's hot cocoa. Buron thinks Ronnie looks a lot like you, but says his face is angular and long like his. He's a 'sweet patootie', for sure! And I'm totally jealous…! You beat me!!"

A week later, Melba went into labor.

Terri Lee Winters was born at 5:20 a.m. on April 17, 1947.

In spite of all the natural childbirth issues and the fact that Melba and Dr. Allums failed to see eye to eye about the best way to deliver a baby, Melba actually accomplished a non-medicated, no forceps delivery. The price she paid was an extremely long labor; it was 25 hours from the time contractions began until Terri's birth. Added to the prolonged labor, Terri was a tiny baby, weighing barely 5 pounds. But Melba felt vindicated because, had medication like morphine been used, Terri might have died.

Melba learned things were not much different this time than five years ago when Toby was born. The nurses were still domineering, and tried to stress the "need" for both Melba and Terri to be isolated from contact in between feedings. The current "trend" still had mothers rejecting breastfeeding as something practiced by the uneducated and those of "lower classes", so Melba was encouraged to allow the nurses to bottle-feed Terri. After all, she had opted to have a HOSPITAL delivery!

Melba was exhausted after her long hours of laboring, so she offered little resistance to anything for the first two days. Besides, she was fearful for her baby when the dangers of the low birth weight were explained. Dr. Allums believed the best course of action involved bottle-feeding the tiny infant, using a new formula made of evaporated milk with added nutrients to expedite rapid weight gain and growth.

The nurses were definitely "pro-bottle", and they succeeded in convincing Melba to abandon any attempts at breastfeeding. By the third day post-partum, Terri was fed formula only. Despite the richness of formula, she lost 8 ounces those first few days. By the time Melba was ready to go home, Terri weighed in at 4 pounds, 8 ounces and admonishments from the nursing staff caused a lot of unnecessary worry.

Melba left the hospital on April 21st, her newborn daughter in her arms. Of course, she had to fight the hospital's "requirements" in order to go home in the family car, but Dr. Allums knew to respect her decision.

"I'm so relieved to be out of there!" Melba stated emphatically when Clarence pulled away from the hospital. "It makes me crazy to be surrounded by all those matronly nurses who think they have the right to tell me what to do! This is the first time I've really been able to relax with my baby in my arms; in the hospital the nurses stood around like guards and I never had any private time. Thank God, we're going home!"

Clarence nodded his understanding, reached out and touched his baby girl's head that was covered in soft, almost transparent, pale tufts of hair. His smile conveyed his contentment, and he said, "It will be so much fun to watch Toby's reaction when she sees her new sister! I know Mom has read her Golden Book story, *The New Baby*, a bunch of times! Of course, Toby has the book memorized. I think it's for the best that we had another girl; Toby might have given us fits if our 'Terri' had been 'Terry'!" Clarence chuckled as he said this, and his glance Melba's way made both of them laugh. It was SO nice to share these private moments on the drive home.

CHAPTER 70

The months simply flew by. Terri grew way too fast, and Toby became the official "little helper". The Banana House also grew; soon, Clarence was hauling two loads TWICE a week, selling the stalks of fruit almost before he could get them ripened. He added more full-size grocery stores (Piggley Wiggley, Brookshire Brothers, Lucky Seven, and Winn-Dixie) in both Longview and Tyler to his list of contracts, and was soon having difficulty keeping them supplied with the amounts of bananas they could sell.

By the end of the year, Clarence had added two new drivers to assist Jimmy and himself, and he'd also hired delivery men to distribute bananas to all the stores. In fact, before the first of 1948, The Banana House had eight fulltime employees, not including Mom Winters and Estel, who helped out quite often. Even Papa and Mama Black made deliveries when things got extra-busy. Clarence was making more money than he'd ever thought possible; business was swell!

By the time Terri was 18 months old and Toby was in first grade at Kilgore Heights Elementary, many of the dreams Melba had secretly harbored for so many years were coming true. She and Clarence had joined the First Baptist Church and were making lots of friends in that fellowship. Melba was volunteering both at Toby's school and at the church, and she even joined the prestigious Kilgore Garden Club where so many of the "rich" ladies spent time.

Melba, always determined to "fit in", sometimes worried too much about being accepted by the women she admired in Kilgore. Those early years in Damon and at Kilgore High had traumatized her, and injured self-esteem is hard to overcome. Nevertheless, Melba knew she was attractive. She was smart, too, using her intellect to study the social trends as well as the politics in Kilgore. Melba scrutinized and researched everything, reading books that taught her about debutante and socialite norms. In truth, it was all easy for her; she simply absorbed social rules and understood them as clearly as if she'd been born and raised by a wealthy elitist family such as the Crims or the Lairds.

Melba still used her innate abilities as a seamstress to create stylish clothes that were one-of-a-kind. Clarence also encouraged her to shop at the two ritzy dress shops in Kilgore, Jordan's and The Toggery, and he even took her to Dallas where she found the most beautiful clothing she'd ever seen at two big department stores, Neiman Marcus and Sanger-Harris. Following that excursion, Melba never loved shopping ANYWHERE except in Dallas!

In letters to Nedra and Jeannie, Melba tried to realistically explain the wonders of shopping in the Dallas stores. She wrote, "You can't imagine anything like Neiman's! It takes up a whole city block and the displays are snazzy; there are even LIVE models walking around in the most gorgeous outfits. I feel like I'm in Heaven when I walk through the doors! It even SMELLS ritzy!"

Nedra wrote back, "Of COURSE the store smells ritzy! I'm sure they spray Chanel No. 5 all around the displays to

288

entice women AND men!" When Melba received her letter, she laughed out loud. It was such fun to have Nedra to gossip with about Neiman Marcus and write "catty" comments about the mega-rich dames who visited the tea room during their shopping sprees!

Melba just wanted to enjoy an occasional trip to Dallas to spend the day in the luxury of such fabulous stores! After all, she mused, the women in the "elitist circles" in Kilgore would never know she really wasn't in their league as long as she kept her secrets to herself! Of course, she did get those occasional trips to Big D, and she even enjoyed plenty of lunches in the "Tea Room"!

It wasn't long before Melba gained recognition as a master flower arrangement designer. The Kilgore Garden Club met at the Community Center twice monthly, and their mission was simple: "set high standards of artistic excellence, increase knowledge of horticulture and share the beauty of gardening with fellow members and the public".

Most of the members were from families that struck it rich during the oil boom years, and Melba never talked about her background. She really didn't want the others to know her dad started out as a roughneck and was still working as a pumper, so she always talked about Clarence's IMPORT business and his "connections" to plantation owners in Panama, Honduras and Guatemala. She knew it sounded good, and that was what she intended. And because she was savvy and self-taught, the other women relied on her knowledge about flowers and plants; they liked to copy her arrangements and they envied her creativity. It wasn't exactly what Melba wanted, but some acceptance was better than none…

Having earned a place in social circles meant Melba had little time to worry about her secret dreams. As had always been the case, plans beyond her current circumstances were on hold. Thankfully, Clarence's business continued to prosper. In fact, Clarence and Estel were working out a deal to open a second Banana House in Hot Springs, Arkansas! Estel would be the manager; he and Ruby would be moving there with their girls, little Dorothy and Paulette.

With the addition of another business operation, Clarence was rarely at home. Even so, Melba's own activities kept her too busy to complain. Their membership at Kilgore's First Baptist Church advanced Melba's involvement in all sorts of church activities. By the time Toby was in kindergarten, Melba was holding down the position of Sunday School Director for the entire church! Fortunately, whenever Clarence was at home on Sunday, the family attended services together. In fact, the fifth row back from the front, center aisle, first quarter of the pew, was their self-designated spot. And the close friendships they developed with six special couples would last the rest of their lives. That fact was the one thing that always made Melba smile. She loved their friends, and the love and laughter they all shared had no price tag.

CHAPTER 71

After living next door to Mama and Papa for two years, Melba and Clarence at last had enough money to buy a house. Toby was seven years old and in second grade; Terri was an active two year old. The family needed more space, so in 1949 they were actively looking for their "dream home". The first time they walked into the two-story house just down the street from Kilgore College, and two blocks from the Banana House, they knew it was the one!

The house was a beautiful two-story frame structure with pine green shutters, a huge screened-in back porch that ran the length of the house, three bedrooms and two bathrooms. It was located on Simmons Street and shaded by tall pines and oaks. There was even a creek out back named "Turkey Creek". They both thought it was simply perfect. Within a few weeks, the house was theirs!

With Clarence totally involved in the banana business, getting the house set up fell to Melba, and she was delighted! Finally, she reflected, FINALLY her dreams of "nice things" were becoming a reality. Melba spent a lot of time just thinking about the house and how she wanted it to look. She even made sketches of furniture layouts and lists of exactly what she wanted to purchase. Of course, the decorating was something she was really keen to do. Colors danced through her head like sweet treats danced through the heads of the children in the "Sugar Plum Fairy" scene from *The Nutcracker*! Melba believed all properly decorated houses MUST have a splash of some shade of red, and she was very partial to a rich shade of burgundy. She was "chomping at the bit" to go to the biggest fabric shop in Dallas and find just the right cloth for her drapes and furniture upholstery; there would be no "as is" sofas or chairs in HER living room!

After what seemed an endless amount of time, a day came when Clarence could go with her to shop for furniture! (It was about time, Melba fumed.) They were moving into the house on Simmons Street in 3 weeks! The day they were to close on the house was August 4th. They decided to drive to Dallas where they visited the eighth floor of the huge Sanger-Harris Department Store.

Melba had heard Sanger-Harris carried some of the best furniture in the nation. When they walked into the showroom, they were immediately treated like a king and queen! Fortunately, Clarence thought, Melba had a plan! She told the salesman exactly what she expected to find, and let him know that if THIS store couldn't satisfy her expectations, she would look elsewhere.

For the next several hours, Clarence and Melba were shown around the massive store. They looked at an amazing number of living room "ensembles", but Melba wanted to be creative and make the furniture HERS, so she finally asked to be shown only pieces that could be upholstered in specialty fabric. She was adamant about looking at heavy pieces made of either mahogany or oak, and she wanted her choices to be both beautiful and functional (but mostly beautiful!).

They spent several hours talking with an interior decorator at Sanger-Harris and Melba looked through books of fabric samples. With her usual ability to visualize things, it wasn't long before every room in their new house was mentally decorated. Selecting drapery and upholstery fabrics, coordinating materials for accent cushions and cornice boards seemed to energize Melba. She was so motivated, Clarence wondered if he'd ever get her out of the store! At the end of the day, the excitement in her voice assured Clarence that Melba loved their selections, and since the choices were HER brain child he simply said, "Good job, honey!"

"I'm sure our house will look fabulous! I just can't wait to see the sofa and chairs covered in our fabrics! And the children's furniture is beautiful! I simply fell in love with the French Provincial bedroom set. Toby will grow into it... I'm so glad you plan to make a built-in desk for her room; it will complete the "look" and she'll have a place to do her homework", Melba gushed.

Clarence had never seen her so keyed up about stuff. He felt, momentarily, like the husband of the year and it made him smile. It was the first time he'd ever experienced the addictive power of having money to spend on his wife...

Like clockwork, the countdown to possession of the house was steady and relentless; it seemed there was too much to do and nowhere near enough time. A week before moving day, the draperies, blinds and cornice boards arrived from Sanger-Harris. With the help of Estel and Buron, Clarence installed the blinds and shades. Melba showed the men how the cornice boards had to be installed, after which they were able to hang the draperies in the living room. Melba planned to sew curtains for the kitchen and bedroom windows. She was still worried that the new furniture would be delayed. Amazingly, though, moving day arrived and only a day later so did the new furniture.

The house was just the way Melba had imagined it; she was delighted that her decisions created this special "look". Maybe her self-esteem notched up just a bit with all the kudos from family and friends, and for Melba ANY improvement in self-confidence was a good thing. Of course, she would never let others know she ever doubted herself. Why let that dark secret rear its ugly head? It was something even Clarence did not know about his wife.

The move to Simmons Street changed so many things. There were new neighbors, new opportunities to host events (something from Melba's dreams!), and new playmates for the girls. The business kept Clarence away too much, but it was agreed that such was the price of enterprise. It was all good.

CHAPTER 72

The remainder of 1949 simply flew by, and Christmas in the new house was delightful! The entire family was home for the holidays, even Nedra and Lindell to the great joy of everyone! The family finally got to meet little Richard, their son, who was born all the way around the world in Fukuoka, Japan where Lindell had been deployed after Japan's surrender. Nedra, bless her soul, had traveled ALONE (well, almost alone with a 3-month old baby!) from Fukuoka to San Francisco on a ship. Lindell had been forced to travel separately using military transport and they had been reunited in San Francisco. For the past year, California had been their home, but after Christmas they would be moving to Shreveport, Louisiana! Lindell's assignment to Barksdale Air Force Base made the Texas family happy; they would be just a little over an hour away from Kilgore!

The reunion in Kilgore was simply amazing! Finally getting to meet each other's little ones was the highlight for everyone! Ronnie and Terri were two and a half years old, Ozelle and G.W.'s youngest, Donnie, six months younger, had just turned two and Nedra and Lindell's Richard was a busy 18 month old. With Ozelle and G.W.'s four other children and Toby, the kids played nonstop. It was as though they'd been together from birth, and laughter, excited shrieks and noisy play filled the house.

Melba hosted Christmas Eve dinner, baking a 25 pound turkey and mounds of cornbread dressing with gravy. She made "coke salad", a gelatin favorite with walnuts, white and red cherries, and, of course, Coca-Cola. Additionally, decadent mounds of candied yams vied for attention on already-full plates.

As if ENOUGH food wasn't consumed that night, everyone went over to Mama and Papa's house on Christmas day. Mama still loved to cook for her "brood", and she made tons of the goodies they all adored: her famous sugar cookies, all the favorite pies, including pecan, pumpkin, cherry and even rutabaga and mincemeat, and a huge ham served with sides of sweet potatoes, fresh green beans, cornbread and fruit salad. The entire rest of the holiday week, there were so many leftovers no one had to cook!

It was SO fine to spend the end of 1949 with family. The War was ancient history, or so it seemed. No one wanted to tell war stories; instead, all talk was about new babies, new jobs and the good things happening in America. Truman had been re-elected, and both Melba and Clarence believed he would keep the country out of harm's way. His campaign against Republican Thomas Dewey would become legendary; Dewey was considered a "shoo-in". When he was defeated by Truman, it was a surprise to all except Harry Truman! The only political talk involved jokes about the Chicago Tribune's huge faux-pas in printing the headline "Dewey Defeats Truman" the morning after the election. Papa LOVED telling and retelling that story!

After a week with everyone in Kilgore, it was painful to have to say goodbye. G.W., Ozelle, and their children and Anna Jean, Buron and Ronnie had long trips back to their homes in Ohio and New Jersey. Lindell, Nedra and Richard would retrace their path to California, then get packed up for their move to Shreveport. Still, all agreed the time together had been truly special. The early morning of December 29th came too soon...

Fortunately, preparations for New Year's Eve kept Melba busy for the next two days, and then they enjoyed the BIG celebration: welcoming in the new decade of the "fifties". Everyone in America, it seemed, was eager to usher in a new and, hopefully, war-free half-century! Melba and Clarence were among the merry-makers in Kilgore that night, going to the recently-built Kilgore Community Center for a huge party hosted by the growing and prospering city. They were joined by both family and friends and Melba looked gorgeous in her new (self-created and self-made!) evening gown fashioned of burgundy taffeta.

The decorations adorning the ballroom consisted of colored clusters of cellophane straws hung from the ceiling and covered with evergreen boughs. Romanesque columns intertwined with lighted greens and glittery silver bells lined the entrance and made a pathway down the center of the room. The celebrants gave 1950 a rousing welcome as revelers bade a noisy farewell to the decade of war that was now behind them. "Infant 1950" brought with him a new half century that stretched before the merrymakers like a heavenly nectar that no one could wait to experience. Showers of balloons and confetti fell on everyone as chimes rang and 1949 was officially bidden farewell with the song, "Auld Lang Syne"

Clarence and Melba's kiss at midnight was heartfelt and sweet. Both of them believed the future "nectar" that lay ahead would be far beyond their dreams. The girls brought unimagined happiness and fulfillment, but Melba, secretly, wanted more. She still did not know exactly what "more" was, but something continued to infiltrate her dreams with ideas that were, perhaps, irrational. Melba knew the things she wanted were dependent on more education, but how could that ever happen?

Following the New Year's Party and the end of holiday events, things settled back down to normal. Toby loved school at Kilgore Heights, and Melba enjoyed having the school hours during which she devoted her energies to Terri. They had "play dates" with the children of friends from Kilgore Baptist. Terri played with Russ Morgan, Jimmy Mayfield, and Lindley Vann who were close in age. Melba and their mothers planned picnics and outings for the children interspersed with play time at their respective houses. It was always fun to watch the little kids interact, and it was clear the kids had fun, too. Melba sometimes worried about Terri being the only girl, but it didn't seem to matter; they all played well together!

Although Melba enjoyed her friendship with the women in this group and the garden club ladies, she knew her current life would never be enough. Little did she know that the "women should embrace staying at home and being wives and mothers" theme of the '5o's would spawn changes that had never been imagined. Melba, in truth, did not agree with the current role assigned to females, staying home and being a "good wife". She knew there was much more she needed to accomplish to find fulfillment.

Because Melba was an avid reader, the works of a controversial British female author, Virginia Woolf, caught her attention around this time. She was mesmerized by Woolf's intelligence and her high expectations for herself as a woman.

Life in Kilgore certainly flirted with "high society". Clubs existed that appeared glamorous and upscale, such as the Junior League, the Kilgore Garden Club, the Meadowbrook Country Club Women's Group, and the Kilgore Women's Club. Melba continued to work hard to gain acceptance and the privilege of membership in all of the clubs (no more "Melba-Smellba" nonsense!), and she persisted in leadership roles at Kilgore Baptist, too.

Her service as Sunday School Director enabled face-to-face interaction with the pastor, Howard Bennett, as well as with other male church leaders. Always ready for questions and some degree of disrespect from the predominately male church leadership, Melba prepared for every possibility. She knew her materials, was a learned Bible scholar, and analyzed every possible "issue" the men might bring forward. Because she knew her "stuff", Melba rarely faced defeat; her suggestions gained approval more and more often, and her ideas about programs for all departments of Sunday School began to receive accolades and acclaim from the entire congregation. The acceptance of Melba as a leader by MEN in the church seemed meaningful, and Melba allowed herself a bit of self-pride based on her church-related experiences... Further, she firmly believed women could do ANYTHING. Throughout history,

MEN held them back. She really did not fault the men; it was simply the accepted culture. Regardless, Melba had other plans both for her own future and the future of her girls!

Her leadership experiences earned in the garden club and at church, eventually paved the way for reasonably easy admittance into the Junior League and the tight-knit Kilgore Women's Club. Clarence's money opened the door to membership in the Women's Group at Meadowbrook! ("Whatever!" was the only comment she allowed herself to make about the "in" crowd to which she now belonged, at least for the time being. Melba had no illusions about how she'd be treated if the money "disappeared". THAT was a "no brainer"!)

And admission to the many women's organizations meant one thing: time. Melba's days became even more cluttered with all sorts of commitments. She enjoyed most of the "stuff", but she sometimes longed for peace and quiet! Fortunately, most of the members also had young children. Babysitting was usually available, or Melba left Terri with Ina Belle in order to honor her agreements. Thankfully, Toby was in school a good part of each weekday, and that certainly helped!

With no sympathy for the rapid-fire passage of time, 1950 came to an end almost before the bustling town of Kilgore could assimilate all the changes, both city-wide and in the country. "Cold War", a new term that defined the tension between the United States and the Soviet Union, explained much of the thinking during the '50's; Western leaders passed their worries down to the populace regarding the so-called expansive tendencies of the Soviets.

The growing paranoia caused by fears that communism was spreading into America and elsewhere created the belief that democracy and capitalism were at great risk and that the only way to protect these values was with diplomacy that was backed by threats and force.

Melba DID worry about communism. After all, the horrible events of World War II were a constant and recent reminder of how governments can become the perpetrators of inhumane and evil behavior. The last thing she wanted was a communist takeover. She and Clarence talked about some of the frightening things that were being done in Washington, such as the investigations of American citizens, including many high-ranking government officials, by Senator Joseph McCarthy.

"You know, Clarence, all this talk about the communists taking over is frightening." Melba said this during dinner one night. "Do you think that Senator…McCarthy…is right to say he has proof that some of our leaders like General Marshall actually SUPPORT communism? I just have trouble believing such a thing is possible!" Melba declared her incredulity with vehemence.

"Well", Clarence asserted, "I tend to agree. The only thing I really know about General Marshall is his dedication to the Truman Document. I do believe McCarthy is trying to protect us from communist subversion, but it seems like he's on a witch hunt."

"What's a witch hunt, Daddy?" Toby asked.

"It's when somebody treats others unfairly by punishing them because they THINK they have opinions believed to be dangerous or evil. You'd be on a 'witch hunt' if you said the lady next door wanted to hurt us." Clarence stated.

"The sad thing", Melba asserted, "is good   people who've done NOTHING wrong are being vilified.   I understand this "Red Scare" is causing loss of jobs and even the destruction of families for some who are being targeted!   It's just not right!"

Clarence nodded his agreement, but they stopped the discussion because it seemed to be bothering Toby. He knew Terri was oblivious since she was only four years old. She was listening, though, and it seemed best to change the subject...

CHAPTER 73

The girls' birthdays provided a time of celebration! It was April, 1951, and Toby had her first real party not just with family planned for her 9th birthday. The party was held at home, and all the girls were invited to dress as "hobos". Melba planned lots of games and Toby got to invite 10 friends.

They played "Decorate the Box" (The girls were divided into pairs and given large cardboard boxes to make into a "house"; prizes were awarded.); "Name that Hobo" (Each girl came up with a "hobo" name while sitting in a circle. After revealing the names, each girl took turns naming ONE hobo name, continuing until all names were recalled.); "Hobo Scavenger Hunt" (the girls paired up and went house-to-house trying to get the most items on a list…tin cans, empty or full, an old pair of shoes, a comb, an old cup, etc.) Toby loved the party! All but one of the invited girls attended, and all attendees stayed overnight for the "camp out". Melba and Clarence thought it was simply grand!

Then, for Terri's fourth birthday, they invited her church friends and their parents to the house to celebrate. Clarence made ice cream in the hand-cranked ice cream freezer; that was a favorite activity! The party was a great hit! The future would complicate life with "comparisons" between the two girls, but their age difference, Melba thought with relief, made pleasing each of them easy. Life was good…

Later in the month of April, 1951, Melba began to recognize the unmistakable signs that another little one was on the way! A visit to Dr. Allums confirmed what she already knew: baby number three was, indeed, "in the oven". Clarence was delighted, but Melba was feeling overwhelmed. Another child would mean more waiting, and the waiting had nothing to do with the pregnancy. She realized, with a sinking heart, the secret ideas swirling in her head could not come to fruition anytime soon.

"I feel", thought Melba "like writer and feminist Charlotte Gilman must have felt when she became pregnant and realized her condition did not make her happy!" (Melba had recently read *The Yellow Wallpaper*, a semi-autobiographical short story written by Gilman after the birth of her only child. The story was painful to read because of the way Gilman's severe post-partum depression was handled by her husband and doctor.)

Melba drifted further into her dreamlike state of abstract thought, wondering, "Is motherhood to be the sole accomplishment of my almost 32 years on this earth? It seems so unfair when I think of all the other things I might have done with my life!"

Melba could think of dozens of stories about women and their struggles to be heard in the world of MEN. After all, women did not have the right to VOTE until 1920!

Another of her recently read books penned by Virginia Woolf was an essay-novel, *Three Guineas*. Melba vehemently agreed with Woolf's pacifist philosophy espoused in this book when she compared fascism and dictatorship to "a worm that poisons both sexes equally …we have in embryo the creature, Dictator as we call him when he is Italian or German, who believes that he has the right, whether given by God, Nature, sex or race is immaterial, to dictate to other human beings how they shall live; what they shall do."

In mulling over what her current condition would mean in terms of longed-for endeavors, Melba quietly and surreptitiously grieved about the forces that ruled women's lives. It just wasn't fair…

"Why was I born a WOMAN?" Melba moaned. At the same time, oddly enough, she knew her life as a mother was quite precious. The juxtaposition was perplexing, to say the least.

Fortunately, there was way too much going on in her life to allow the distress caused by being "with child" to interfere with continuing to focus, as always, on the here and now! Summer even included a vacation to Galveston, Texas. Although Melba and Clarence had visited the island with Ozelle and G.W. years ago, Toby and Terri saw an ocean for the first time. The experience was simply delightful for all of them. Just seeing the girls' awe when they first stood barefoot on the beach, giggling as the waves splashed over their toes, created never-to-be-forgotten happy memories for both Melba and Clarence.

"Just look at them, honey!" Clarence exclaimed. "Those smiles tell me this trip was one of our best ideas ever!"

"It IS grand to see their delight...makes me appreciate our ability to bring them here."

Melba's voice was wistful when she added, "When WE were children, doing something like this was as impossible and foreign as living in a palace and wearing golden crowns!" She laughed at this thought, and Clarence nodded his agreement with a chuckle.

"Yep, that's a fact", he agreed. "I never thought I'd SEE an island, much less take a vacation on one! I guess we're pretty snazzy, Mrs. Winters!"

Five days flew by with sandcastles, wave-jumping, shell collecting, bird watching, picnics on a big quilt in the sand, and flying kites on the long stretches of beach in front of their motel, The Jack Tar. Returning to Kilgore in mid-July, the girls were a little melancholy for a few days, but their usual love-of-life made a roaring comeback as they played in backyard shade provided by towering pine and sweet gum trees. Life was good; Melba felt a gratifying and soothing acceptance of her current circumstances.

School started the day after Labor Day in September, and Toby entered fourth grade at Kilgore Heights Elementary. Terri started Kindergarten at the First Presbyterian Church. It was a half-day program; Melba insisted she needed the interaction with other children her age. Clarence had no reason to disagree with Melba's logic; he trusted her opinions about the girls and about education.

The remaining weeks of "waiting" seemed to fly! With school events, fall celebrations, Clarence's non-stop work at the

Banana House and preparations for the new baby, Melba's due date became imminent almost before they were ready.

On December 9th, Melba felt some contractions. Thinking they were just Braxton Hicks and not "real", she tried to ignore them. However, later in the day she realized the contractions were becoming more regular. Melba called Dr. Allums and he told her to meet him at the hospital...

Lucinda Ann Winters came into the world at 4:25 a.m. the next morning, December 10, 1951. She was simply beautiful, another perfect baby! The entire family welcomed her with open arms; she would be the impish "little sister" that Toby and Terri adored. Happily, Melba's labor was much shorter than with Terri and no drugs or forceps were used.

As Melba and Clarence held their newborn and looked at every finger and toe, they were, once again, enchanted by the miracle of life. Cindy's arrival added another layer to their existence, and the new layer started with her birth had unexpected meaning for the entire family. Cindy was the last, and she would greatly enrich their lives.

CHAPTER 74

The New Year began without much in the way of "different". The celebrations were fitting for the times: local parties, fireworks, family gatherings, special church services. Because Melba and Clarence had a newborn baby to care for, Mama, Papa and Ina Belle joined them for a quiet New Year's Dinner. The older girls played happily in their rooms after getting some special attention from their grandparents, and the adults enjoyed "oohing and aahing" over little Cindy. It was nice to welcome in the new year at home; everyone felt relaxed and at peace.

Eventually, talk focused on the latest events in the news, and Papa said, "I know you've listened to the radio and heard the reports about Korea. Bobby's been paying a lot of attention to talk about communism and what's going on over there. He told me he's heard we're about to be in another WORLD war because the Soviets won't back off."

"I'll talk to Bobby, Papa", Melba declared. "He's too much of a hot-head; he needs to calm down!"

"Do what you want, Sister", Papa stated, "but you won't change his opinion. He's already making plans to enlist in the Marines!"

Clarence jumped into the conversation, saying, "Bobby's right to be worried, and I know he's itching to get in the military. After all, he grew up during the war and he hates communism! If he DOES decide to enlist, we need to support him."

"You're right, honey", Melba agreed unenthusiastically, "but it will be hard. The last thing this family needs is another wounded soldier!"

In reality, peace was, at best, nebulous; the "Cold War" situation between the Soviet Union and the United States held actual combat in check, but the entire world quivered on the "sidelines" with terror that the odd truce might come to an end at any time. The fact that North Korea had invaded South Korea after a series of skirmishes at the "border" fueled concern that Soviet and American troops might be deployed to help. North Korea, ruled by Dictator Kim II Sung, had communist support from the Soviet Union and the South, ruled by anti-communist Dictator Syngman Rhee, had the reluctant support of the United States.

President Truman was not ready to engage in another war, but there was great pressure from many top officials to get involved. In fact, a National Security Council report months before recommended "the United States use military force to 'contain' communist expansionism anywhere it seemed to be occurring, regardless of the intrinsic strategic or economic value of the lands in question."

When Truman spoke to the nation saying, "If we let Korea down, the Soviets will keep right on going and swallow up one place after another", he committed American troops. At almost the same time, the North Korean army pushed into Seoul, the capital of South Korea. Seoul, and the small contingent of American forces present at that time, met defeat. Almost immediately, the Korean Conflict became a war against communism, itself!

Bobby enlisted in the Marines. Having spent his teenage years living with the specter of a communist takeover, his decision to become a Marine was quite natural. Bobby's "rough and tumble" nature also gave impetus to his decision to join the military branch known as the "toughest". His training in San Diego, California, scheduled to begin on January 29th, was fast-approaching. News about fighting in Korea came with renewed angst that the "Cold War" with its scarcity of physical conflict could escalate into another world war. Melba recognized that Mama was particularly distressed that her youngest son was following the path already followed by Lindell.

As January marched forward, Bobby's imminent departure for California was like a dark cloud hovering overhead. Melba's concern for him continued to deepen the closer his date with the Marines came.

Additionally, her continuing recovery from Cindy's birth hit some snags that had Dr. Allums limiting her activities. Most difficult for Melba, she was advised to stay downstairs because going up and down the steps was dangerous; she was still experiencing post-partum bleeding.

During the early morning hours on January 18th, Melba woke to the cries of a hungry baby. She got out of bed and went across the room toward Cindy's cradle. Sudden lightheadedness hit her before she reached the cradle, the room whirled, and Melba fell unconscious to the floor.

Cindy continued to cry, and the pathetic newborn wails soon awakened Clarence. The rest of the events that followed were a blur of frenetic activity: Clarence saw Melba and rushed to her side. Thankfully, she moaned and responded to him. He picked up the distraught baby, trying to calm her; he ran to the telephone and called for an ambulance; he called Dr. Allums…Cindy continued to cry and Clarence knew nothing would calm her except a bottle of formula.

When the paramedics arrived, they examined Melba and determined she was suffering a hemorrhage. The bleeding had to be stopped. As they moved her to the ambulance, the driver spoke to Clarence in a firm tone of voice, saying, "Mr. Winters, your wife needs to be at the hospital. You must tend to your baby. Who can we call to help you?"

"Call my wife's dad at 931. He's not too far away…" Clarence looked frantically at Melba's still form on the gurney. "Is she going to be okay?"

Reassurances were hurriedly given by the medics as they loaded Melba into the ambulance.

"Come to the hospital as soon as you can, Mr. Winters. Dr. Allums will meet us there, and we'll do everything possible to help Mrs. Winters." With that, the ambulance roared away, lights flashing and sirens blaring.

Clarence felt as if he'd been punched in the gut; his first reaction was anger that this was happening. Almost simultaneously, though, he recognized the necessity of feeding Cindy and calling Ina Belle. Holding the phone in one hand while cradling and feeding his baby daughter with the other, he contacted his mother, telling her Kenneth would pick her up in just a few minutes. Then he called his nephew who, thankfully, lived just a few houses down the street from Ina Belle's cottage at the Banana House.

"I need you NOW, Kenny!" Clarence demanded. "Melba's in trouble! The ambulance drivers took her just minutes ago and she's at the hospital. She was bleeding something awful…! Please go get Mama and bring her here. She has to watch the girls so I can be with Melba."

"I'm on my way, C.E.!" Kenny told his uncle. "Just get yourself ready; you can leave as soon as I drive up. We'll take care of the girls."

Clarence finished feeding the baby. Thankfully, she settled down and even accepted her pacifier as he laid her back in the cradle. As quickly as possible, Clarence dressed and was standing at the door when he saw Kenneth's lights coming down the street. "Thank God!" he thought with more than a little sincerity. "Come, on, Kenneth! I need to GO!"

Within minutes, Ina and Kenneth were inside. Clarence updated them on the girls, quickly explaining that Cindy had been fed and should be okay for at least the next three hours as far as feeding was concerned. Toby and Terri would likely wake up around 6:00; the current time was 3:30.

Without another word, Clarence raced to his truck, tires squealing as he jettisoned down the street toward the hospital. His heart thumping in his chest, Clarence arrived at the hospital, clambered out, and bolted down the hallway toward the emergency ward.

The receptionist looked up in alarm as Clarence raced into the room and demanded, "Where's Melba Winters? She's my wife! They brought her here about 45 minutes ago!"

"Mr. Winters, she's being attended by Dr. Allums and Dr. Murphy, the on-call emergency doctor. I'll take you back as long as you let the doctors do their jobs without interfering." As the receptionist eyed Clarence to see whether he seemed ready to follow instructions without creating a scene, she walked around the desk and stood beside him.

"Okay! Please take me to my wife! I'll stay out of the way, but I HAVE to know what's going on." Clarence's voice quivered with emotion, but his eyes never waivered from the woman's face. "Please!" he intoned.

The next hour passed quickly. Clarence was able to stand beside Melba's bed and hold her hand. She seemed to know he was there even though her eyes remained closed. He could feel a tiny bit of pressure from her hand.

Dr. Allums asked Clarence to follow him into the hall so they could talk privately.

"Clarence, she has lost a lot of blood. I'm of the opinion that an emergency hysterectomy is needed to stop the bleeding and prevent continued problems." Dr. Allums said these words quietly, but the seriousness of Melba's situation was written all over his face. "I'm afraid we could lose her if I don't operate."

"Lose her?" Clarence almost yelled. "How could this happen? She was feeling good and thought everything was okay; she even mentioned during dinner last night that following your instructions about not going up and down the stairs was paying off. She believed the worst of the bleeding was over!"

"Sometimes hemorrhaging can happen weeks after a woman gives birth. In Melba's case, some placental tissue remained in her womb and ruptured. Everything we've tried to stop the bleeding has failed; it's time to operate. I can't wait any longer. She has lost too much blood already!" As Doctor Allums said this, nurses were already moving her gurney toward the surgical suite.

Doctor Allums continued with, "I need your permission to operate…" Clarence interrupted him, "Of course you can operate! Melba wants to raise our daughters! Do whatever's necessary!"

Two hours later, Melba was in recovery. Clarence, in a state of shock, stood by her side and held her limp hand; she was not fully conscious and he was grateful for her passage of time in blissful ignorance of what she'd been through. Clarence felt like he'd been in a car wreck. What would he say to Melba when she woke up?

CHAPTER 75

As it turned out, what to say wasn't a problem. During the next hour, Melba opened her eyes and looking right at Clarence said, "I know." A tear trickled down her cheek and Clarence bent down to kiss it away. He hugged her gently and whispered, "It will be okay, Melby. The important thing is that you're okay. I love you!"

After sucking on ice chips and drifting in and out of a morphine-induced sleep, Melba started asking questions. Her first was a startled and panicky, "Who has the girls?"

Learning that Ina Belle was at the house with them, she asked, "Is the baby okay? Did Toby and Terri wake up when the ambulance came?"

Clarence reassured Melba that everything was FINE at home. No, the girls did not wake up when the ambulance arrived. Yes, baby Cindy was doing just great; she was content to let her Grandma hold and spoil her. The routines of Toby and Terri were in place thanks to Kenneth. Both were in school at the moment. Both told him they wanted to visit their mother at the hospital.

"I'll ask Dr. Allums when you can see the girls. Meantime, I want you to rest and let the nurses do their jobs. You've been through a lot. Everyone just wants you to recover, and the only way that's gonna happen is for you to focus on YOU. Please, Melba, just this once, think about yourself", Clarence implored.

Melba gave him a weak smile as she drifted back to sleep. Clarence felt a sense of relief that the medication was forcing her to stay put; without it, he was sure she'd be trying to get out of bed and go home!

The next three days were much the same for Melba. She was asleep more than awake, and the pain in her abdomen began to ease. It was a comfort not to have blood pooling between her legs, and as she drifted in and out of sleep she subconsciously allowed relief to filter in that the nightmare of so much blood loss was over. There was also a very slight lingering sadness that she would never have another child. When lucid, Melba knew she had never wanted to be like Ozelle; three children were more than enough! As that realization wafted through her groggy mind, she began to feel empowered. There would be no more worries about any unwanted pregnancies. She had a perfect-sized family, and now the "female factor" did not concern her!

By day four, Melba was up and walking, at least short distances. Clarence received approval from Dr. Allums for the two oldest girls to visit, and that evening he wheeled Melba to the waiting room where Kenneth waited with Toby and Terri.

"Mama!" both girls screamed when they saw Melba.

"Come here! I need lots of hugs and kisses!" Melba cried when she saw her girls. "Tell me what you've been up to!"

The next 30 minutes were filled with stories about school and tales of all the things Grandma let happen at home that Mama did not allow! There was more than a little laughter, and Melba conspiratorially told the girls, "Well, we won't tell

316

Grandma she's made a few mistakes. We want to keep her happy!"

"Grandma lets me stay up 'til 8:30", Toby confessed. "That's kinda cool!"

Melba nodded in agreement, then said, "But when I'm back home, we'll have to 'adjust' that bedtime back to 8:00, right?"

Toby grinned, saying, "I suppose so, Mama."

Terri, who was dancing around the waiting area, giggled and said, "Yeh, Toby! You have to MIND Mother!"

Finally, goodbyes were said and last hugs and kisses exchanged.

When Kenneth left with the girls, Melba declared, "Honey, I hope we can get them back on track without too much effort…if I ever get out of here!"

"It's gonna be fine, Melba. Mother's doing a good job with all the girls, even the baby. I know Cindy's sleeping six hours without a bottle during the night. And the girls are behaving. All's well!" Clarence asserted all this calmly as he pushed the wheelchair back down the hallway to Melba's room.

Ten days after the catastrophic hemorrhage and emergency hysterectomy, Melba's progress was so good that Dr. Allums agreed to release her from the hospital. Not mincing words, the man Melba had entrusted to oversee the births of her three girls stood by her bedside and declared, "Melba, you are one lucky woman! I honestly feel blessed that you survived your complication; it could have ended differently. I'll let you go home today, but you MUST follow my instructions, allow others to do all the lifting and carrying for awhile, and stay off your feet at least most of the day."

Melba was so relieved to be going home that she was ready to agree to ANYTHING, but the seriousness of Doc Allums made her pay attention. "Of course, Doctor", was all she said.

Clarence interjected, "I am finalizing taking possession of a new house. It's a one-story that has all the amenities we've enjoyed on Simmons with the exception of a second story. Bull Barber, assistant manager at the John Young Ford Dealership, wants my house and I want his. It's pretty much an "even exchange"; we're both satisfied. Melba won't be going up and down stairs when we get to Myrtle Street, and our move will happen real soon. Melba will just have to "direct" the move; she won't be packing or moving ANYTHING!"

"Yes, and I'm feeling really good about the move, Doctor. The girls will be closer to Kilgore Heights Elementary, and the house on Myrtle is still close to the Banana House. It's all positive. I promise to take care of myself; I have too much to lose if I don't!" Melba declared all of this with fervor, and the calm expression on her face assured Dr. Allums that letting her go home was the right decision.

Within two hours, Clarence had Melba sitting in the kitchen at their Simmons house, catching up on everything that had happened during her hospitalization as she shared coffee with Ina Belle and held little Cindy. Life would have been beyond good, but Bobby's departure for basic training was the very next day...

That afternoon, Bobby came to say goodbye. Seeing moisture in Melba's eyes, he teasingly said, "Come on, Sister! No tears! You know I'll be back with a whole montage of stories about the Corps that'll have my nieces shouting 'OORAH'! and singing 'From the Halls of Montezuma'!" As always, the visit with her "baby" brother left Melba smiling. Their playful bantering assuaged the dread she'd been feeling about his enlistment. After all, this was Bobby's decision no matter the outcome. Melba knew she would always want to protect him, but he was telling her it was HIS turn to do the protecting. Bobby promised to stay in touch, and he promised to be safe... But his assurances did not prevent the lump in her throat and ache in her heart as he left.

CHAPTER 76

By the time six weeks had passed since her surgery, Melba was in the middle of preparing for the move. Clarence had been honest with Dr. Allums when he said he would do all the packing, lifting and moving of their things, but Melba was definitely involved in the organization and planning. As always, the extended family helped out. Estel, Kenny, Jimmy and Ina Belle all got involved; no one wanted Melba to overexert! Melba kept saying things like, "Please quit 'babying' me! I'm not FRAGILE!" Her complaints were ignored.

On Saturday, April 26, 1952, the big day finally arrived. Without a single hitch, everything was moved from Simmons Street to Myrtle Street, and lots of hands worked to get the essentials unpacked and set up. Toby and Terri, their excitement evident, "helped" with the unpacking of everything that went into their rooms. Toby got the middle bedroom all to herself, and she couldn't hide her pride in having her own stuff in her own place!

Terri and Cindy would share the third bedroom, and it was special because it opened onto a side porch. Terri thought it was "the best". She said, "Cindy will like our room, too, but she's too little to care right now." Since Cindy had just turned four months old on April 10th, Terri's comment about Cindy was accurate. There were no arguments about where toys would be arranged or which bed would belong to which child. Melba and Clarence exchanged secret looks, smiling at the simplicity of childhood.

The remainder of the spring and summer, filled with decorating the new house, getting acquainted with the neighbors, and hosting social events with friends and family, became a blur. Melba's health returned, although she most assuredly pushed the limits on following Dr. Allums' advice. As her strength improved, so did her commitment to make life the best it could be. After all, she reasoned, at 32 years of age she still had time to make a difference beyond the confines of her tidy "domestic paradise"! Perhaps in the doing she could forge a path for HER girls.

Reminders of societal expectations for women were everywhere! Melba simply fumed at many of the advertisements in magazines and on billboards. In fact, she cancelled her subscriptions to both *Good Housekeeping* and *Home Journal* after viewing the ads and some of the articles in each. How could she support things like, "The Chef does everything but cook—that's what wives are for!", as stated in an advertisement for a Kenwood Chef Mixer? Even worse, another ad showed a handsome man in a business suit standing with one foot on top of a woman's head. The woman was pictured as the 'head' of a big tiger rug, adorning the floor of a living room. The ad's printed words, spoken by the man, were "It's nice to have a girl around the house." Then there was the advertisement for a man's sweater, the advertiser's words strewn across the top of the picture of a great-looking young man wearing a tight-fitting sweater: "Men are better than women!"

Reading the 'fine print', Melba realized the ad had to do with Drummond Sweaters, and she was seething when she read,

"Inside, women are useful—even pleasant! On a mountain, they are something of a drag."

Oh, my! The MEN who wrote these ads clearly had no sisters! G.W., Lindell and Bobby all knew how tough Melba could be; they would NEVER say something so despicable and so totally WRONG.

Melba could feel her blood pressure going up as she turned the pages of the magazines that used to bring so much enjoyment. How could anyone think the obnoxious attitudes displayed on almost every page were acceptable??? For women to be treated so disrespectfully made Melba feel sick. Something deep inside was screaming, "Get to work! Do something to make a difference for women! You are raising THREE girls who will grow up facing this kind of horrid discrimination just because of their gender! And it won't matter one whit how smart, how talented, how motivated, or how creative they are!!!

It was at that very moment that Melba knew she would stop waiting for the right time to do that secret something she was meant to do. The idea of waiting was suddenly preposterous and unthinkable. Even if Clarence disagreed, even if he acted like the men in those ads, she would never turn back. After all, she mused, Clarence had never been sexist, at least not in the way all the ads had men acting. Melba knew he loved her, loved the girls, and wanted life to be great for all of them. Regardless of Clarence and his reaction to her decision, she would not change what she envisioned for her future; it beckoned her with a power that took her breath away and made her feel giddy with pure excitement.

Suddenly, the frenetic decorating and shopping for things to upgrade the Myrtle Street house seemed lame. It was July, 1952. Cindy was seven months old and starting to crawl. Her need for constant attention had become much less demanding; she wanted Melba when hungry, tired or sick. Other times, she was content to entertain herself or have Toby or Terri occupy her with toys and music and walks in the stroller.

Soon, school would start again, and both Toby and Terri would be busy with daily classes, friends, school events and all the rest of those things that made childhood special. Toby was moving into fifth grade and Terri into first. Melba wondered how so much time had slipped away; the girls were growing up! With that growth was change. Melba knew her decision to let her dreams become reality was exactly right; it was her time to listen to her heart. It was time for MELBA!

Acknowledging her need for information, Melba determined to visit the Kilgore College campus the very next day. She needed to know the requirements for admission. Although she had graduated from high school, Melba still felt nervous about trying to gain college admission. It had been a long time since she'd attended classes at Kilgore High School! What if she really did not have the ability to handle college course work? What if the high school classes she'd done so well in were really not good enough? Worries and bad dreams kept Melba tossing and turning throughout the night.

Arriving at the admissions office the next morning, Melba asked to talk with someone who could guide her. She explained she had graduated from high school in 1935. Her goal was enrollment in KJC for the fall semester, 1952. She really wanted to take just two or three courses. She needed to see if she had what it would take to continue with a bigger course load, and Cindy was still so young…

Almost instantaneously, the admissions clerk reviewed Melba's high school diploma, noted her high grade point average, and gave her an application. She explained the cost for courses and asked Melba how she wanted to pay. Melba took out her wallet and unfolded the cash. Clarence had given her the money with one comment, "Melba, this is for you to use. I want you to go to school. I want you to make up for all the years you spent doing for everyone else. I want you to be happy. I love you!"

Melba studied the application and looked carefully at the course book. She wanted to take classes that would apply to a degree in teaching, so she honed in on basics that were required for all students.

"Thank you, Mrs. Winters", the admissions lady said with a smile. "I see you've chosen to take both English 1302 and 2326; that combination will certainly keep you busy! And you also want Math 1324, correct?"

"That's right. Thank you for helping me navigate the course lists and determine what I'm qualified to take!" Melba stated. "I guess I'm all set for the first day?"

"Yes, ma'am. Good luck!" the clerk smiled cheerfully.

When Melba went by the Banana House to "collect" Cindy, Ina Belle asked her about registration.

"I'm going to RACE through college, Mom! I have so many goals; this time I won't be held back…! And, somewhat surprisingly, registration was a piece of cake!" Melba proclaimed with a lilt in her voice. "I'm really feeling intoxicated about the future!"

Ina looked at Melba with an expression that registered wariness. Her life had revolved around being the central, but passive, keeper of the household. As a farmer's wife during the early years of her marriage to Clarence's father, her work hours were unending, and her most important roles were wife and mother. It had always been her job to shelter her family from the harsh realities of life outside the home she guarded twenty four hours a day. No matter how bleak the circumstances, Ina's task was to sooth, comfort and provide. To hear Melba talk about "her future" was disconcerting; Ina had ceased thinking about herself MANY years ago.

"I suppose it will be alright, this college thing", Ina said in a quiet voice, "but I can't help worrying that it may be too much on the girls. It may be too much for all of you, Melba."

"No! It's the right thing for me and it's the right thing for the girls. And Clarence is encouraging me to go ahead. I know I can handle my responsibilities AND earn my college degree. It's important to me." Melba's tone of voice left no room for further discussion, and Ina said nothing more. But all this change went against everything Ina believed about being a mother and a wife.

"Besides", Melba continued, "Clarence convinced a very young and impressionable girl to marry him before she turned 17 and move away from her family. He failed to ask me if marriage was 'right' for me at the time, and I also failed to ask myself the same question. I'd say he OWES me a chance to do more with my life.

CHAPTER 77

September arrived faster than Melba believed possible. Her classes began and her days soon became filled with things she'd either never known or had long forgotten: taking notes while listening to long-winded professors talk about their favorite subjects, reading incredibly long and (sometimes!) boring articles the professors insisted were necessary for full understanding of their courses, writing laborious analyses of all those articles and typing them on the Royal Portable Typewriter she'd managed to purchase from another student at KJC for only $5.00 . (Melba had never typed ANYTHING, so teaching herself how to work the daunting machine was an amazing feat in and of itself!) Getting to classes early so she could talk to other students and attempt to stay "on top" of assignments all took more time than she had ever believed possible. Of course, Melba was also balancing her "mom duties" and "wife duties" while attending class. It was tougher than she'd imagined.

The days flew, reminding Melba of Cindy's rapid growth. (In truth, she'd almost forgotten the truly miraculous changes Toby and Terri had demonstrated from birth to six months!) She experienced the pain of missing out on quotidian milestones, simple though they might be; it hurt to miss all those little nuances that were shaping Cindy's emerging personality.

By Thanksgiving, so many other issues demanded Melba's attention that she determined to complete these   three courses and then wait until Cindy turned four to continue school. Bobby's short visit home in April had been stressful. Deployment of his unit to Korea, scheduled for mid-May, had happened as expected. Since the six months following his departure, Mama and Papa, stressed and edgy about news coming from Korea, seemed more despondent than during the BIG war! Especially worrisome, the North Koreans remained strong and fearsome combatants even with the newly-formed United Nations demanding a peaceful cessation of battle. Korean forces continued fighting the armistice demanded by the U.N. and agreed to by American leaders.

Mama cried a lot and kept saying things like, "Buster, what will happen to us if Russia and China get even more involved with Korea? What if the mess over there brings on World War III?"

Of course, almost every question Annie posed involved BOBBY and her fears for him.

Almost more distressing to the family than the actual fighting, news from Korea spoke of other horrors most Americans could not even imagine. Soldiers, described as dehydrated and overheated, and unable to get drinking water were drinking contaminated water used to irrigate crops. The contamination was with human feces, used in Korea as fertilizer. Terrible sickness and numerous deaths were blamed for this common practice, but with no other water source the choice was simple. Soldiers suffered with dysentery, shigellosis and typhoid fever all because clean drinking water was not available. Other reports spoke of complicated injuries that necessitated extreme measures in the war zone portable hospitals, the M.A.S.H. units. News was grisly…

Melba tried to keep her focus on the girls and on completing her first semester of college with high marks, but the stresses over Bobby, her parents and Clarence's expanding business territory made her feel she was going crazy! Not soon enough, it was January.

Classes ended and her grades were exceptional, Mama and Papa became a bit less overwrought after hearing from Bobby, Christmas was over, and the two banana houses were making money. With a sigh, Melba realized being home was RIGHT for now; she would see to it that Cindy had just as much attention as Toby and Terri had enjoyed at her age. There was still time for fulfillment of dreams. Besides, the space between now and Cindy's entrance into pre-kindergarten was really very short, Melba ruminated. By focusing on the girls and all her outside leadership roles while mentally preparing for earning a degree in just three years by reading, keeping up on current events and sharpening her study skills, the real deal would be much less harsh. In fact, Melba realized she could say without hesitation, "I understand what she meant!" when thinking about a quote she'd read that had been attributed to the famous female pilot, Amelia Earhart:

"The most difficult thing is the decision to act, the rest is merely tenacity. The fears are paper tigers. You can do anything you decide to do. You can act to change and control your life; and the procedure, the process, is its own reward."

Yes, Melba realized, the decision to postpone more college was hard. Knowing that it would not be a long hiatus comforted her. She knew the rest would be a mixture of pure pleasure and perseverance, the first step in her unspoken, secret plan.

CHAPTER 78

The first few months of 1953 were, Melba realized, quite peaceful! She truly enjoyed play dates with other mothers and their youngsters, especially those with one of her best friends, Ollie Ford. Although Cindy was six months older than Ollie's middle son Jack, the two were "joined at the hip". Both kids were exuberant and outgoing, silly and adventuresome, and as cute as kids can be. It was great fun to watch them play and listen to their banter. Melba and Ollie planned a lot of time together since the Fords had three boys near in age to Cindy and Terri. When their oldest, Hank, and Terri were not in school, play dates were especially delightful.

The relationships with friends were strong during this time. Melba was especially close to June Morgan; the two women had lots in common. But there were others with whom Melba and Clarence formed close relationships, and all these friends really became strong cement as the events of the next years unfolded. (By 1958, four of the families had moved away from Kilgore: the Fords to Shreveport, Louisiana; the Vans to San Angelo, Texas; the Mayfields to Houston, Texas; the Morgans to Meridian, Mississippi.)

In the future, Melba would reflect on those she knew and loved during this time. She would eventually be dishonest with them, spinning stories that were far from true, but lies enabled her to preserve the dignity she'd longed for as a child...and that longing "won out" when her "perfect" life began to unravel with the loss of the banana business. But the

331

important families would continue to get together year after year until almost all their children were grown. They became "The Labor Day Group", meeting at chosen places with all the kids the last long weekend of summer vacation, Labor Day.

And then there was family with all its "drama" added to the mix. During the years from 1946 to 1951, Jeannie and Buron lived in Madison, New Jersey with their growing family. Ron was born in 1947, and John in 1950. Buron worked for Bell Laboratories/AT&T, and although visits were rare, Melba and Jeannie kept up through letters and frequent phone calls.

During 1952 and 1953, Buron made a very prestigious sojourn to White Sands, New Mexico to work on the development of rockets that were predecessors of the Nike Zeus and other huge rocket systems. These early rockets were instrumental in paving the way for space travel. Previous to actually living in White Sands, Buron occasionally visited the missile base as a consultant.

Those temporary assignments during the first post-war years of the late 1940's were noteworthy. They allowed him to engage with a group of German scientists recruited by the United States after the War, men who came to the United States in exchange for their freedom, an event dubbed "Operation Paper Clip". One of the men, Werner Von Braun, was one of the most well-known and sought-after scientific academics of the time. The fact that he was a member of the German Secret Service and Nazi Party doing work for Adolf Hitler notwithstanding, Von Braun pledged allegiance to the United States and would eventually become a U.S. citizen.

It was clear to Melba that her brother-in-law harbored mixed feelings about working with these men. Much later, Buron wrote several memos about his experiences with the German scientists:

"Immediately at the end of WWII in Europe, U.S. engineers were sent to Germany to 'encourage' Werner Von Braun and a group of his rocket engineers to come to the United States. I imagine these 'volunteers' came quite willingly because living conditions in Germany were not so good at that time. They were sent to White Sands, New Mexico where they could continue working and experimenting on their V-2 rockets. Also, a quantity of V-2 rockets, spare parts, testing and support equipment were rounded up and shipped to White Sands so the Germans could continue their work. Of course, the U.S. was very much interested in learning all we could about this rocket development, since the Germans were ahead of us at that time. Von Braun's group assembled and test-launched V-2 rockets from White Sands until they ran out of spare parts. Then they were sent to Redstone Arsenal, Alabama, to continue other rocket development."

Continuing his memoirs, Buron wrote, "In 1948, when I was at White Sands Missile Range, I was invited to a meeting in a Quonset Hut one night where Von Braun would speak about rockets. There were possibly 25 or so people there including Bell Labs and Douglas Aircraft engineers, a few support engineers and some military officers. We met Von Braun and chatted informally while the group was gathering. He literally radiated self-confidence. He spoke good English with a 'British' accent. His presentation was about putting a

333

rocket into space for an earth orbit, rather bold new-frontier stuff at that time! He said the rocket would be a 3-stage missile, launched east from White Sands to take advantage of the earth's rotation. The first stage booster would separate and fall to earth near Big Springs, Texas and the second stage would land around Meridian, Mississippi. Then the third stage would take over and place the missile in earth orbit."

"After he had finished explaining, in rather elaborate details, just how such a mission could be accomplished, someone in the group spoke up: 'But, Dr. Von Braun, don't you think the people in Big Springs and Meridian would object to such a launch trajectory?'"

"Von Braun didn't even hesitate." He said, 'I wouldn't worry about that. There is a very small probability that anyone would be hit.' His answer was interesting, but somehow we were not prepared to accept his philosophy!"

Buron's early interactions with Von Braun and fellow German engineers gave him first-hand insight regarding the intricacies of rocket development. Philosophical differences aside, he could not help admiring Von Braun's brilliance.

At Bell Labs, Buron helped complete some amazing top-secret projects during the Cold War. During the 40's, test firing the long-range ballistic V-2 missiles continued under direction of the Germans. The missiles were brought over to Fort Bliss, Texas from the Peenemuende Launch and Development Center in Germany as well as from seven combined production-launch bunkers in both Germany and France. White Sands provided the site for these rocket launches for the next five years, as the Army fired dozens of V-

2s, establishing high altitude and velocity records that reached to the very edge of space. It was an exciting time!

Buron, a prolific writer and record-keeper, penned more essays about his experiences at White Sands:

"When Werner Von Braun's group would get a V-2 assembled, they would test it by launching it so it would impact on the northern end of the White Sands Missile Range. One day, however, something went wrong. After a normal vertical launch phase, instead of bending over and heading up range, the missile turned its trajectory toward El Paso, Texas, about 50 miles away. So some Germans and our military officers jumped in about a half-dozen jeeps, headed for highway 70, and over the Organ Mountain Pass toward El Paso. When they got about halfway, they stopped at a filling station and asked the attendant, 'Did you see a rocket come by here?'"

"The attendant said, 'Yeah, it looked like it was going toward El Paso.' They asked the same question on the edge of El Paso and got a little different answer: 'It looked like it was going down to the Rio Grande River.'"

"At the international bridge that connects El Paso to Juarez, Mexico, the Mexican police escorted the caravan from White Sands to a cemetery in the outskirts of Juarez where the missile had impacted. There was no warhead in the V-2, but the residual fuel exploded and blew a large hole in the cemetery. The White Sands military was very concerned about a possible international incident, so they hurriedly brought some heavy equipment down, filled the hole and dressed up the area. There were rumors around the base that some local police and politicians were handed some bribe money to minimize the incident. In any case, by the time the news had filtered through the Mexican bureaucracy to Mexico City, the whole affair had been quieted down, and the White Sands military could breathe again."

Buron's memoirs about White Sands would become family treasures. Melba and Jeannie sometimes talked about the oddity of Buron's involvement in rocket science. They both knew him best as a man who loved music and theater. He was always soft-spoken and gentle, exceptionally caring and solicitous, and a fine father. The sisters shared their incredulity over Buron's involvement in ballistic missile development and, thus, his knowledge of military secrets. It seemed unreal! Sometimes, Jeannie admitted, Buron might seem like an odd ball, but she insisted he was just a "good guy"! Melba agreed with her sister; Jeannie was blessed to be married to such an amazing man.

Meanwhile, Nedra and Lindell were living in Shreveport, Louisiana since returning from Japan. They left Sacramento, California in 1951 when he received his assignment to Barksdale Air Force Base. The base was located in Bossier City, Louisiana, just seven miles from Shreveport where they bought a house. Barksdale became a SAC base (Strategic Air Command) after World War II, and Lindell's training made him a viable candidate for this post. Melba was just glad she was close enough to her brother for weekend visits, and there were many! She and Clarence regularly took the girls and made the 72 mile drive to visit Lindell, Nedra and three-year-old Richard. Of course, Lindell also brought his family to Kilgore frequently to visit all their relatives (both sets of parents, Melba and

Clarence, Bobby and Patsy, Nedra's sister Billie Kathryn, lots of aunts, uncles and cousins). It was an especially joyful time for everyone. Lindell's almost-miraculous recovery from his injury in the Philippines still made Melba's heart sing!

Fittingly, those early fifties years found Melba admired by friends and family for her accomplishments in Kilgore. She always dressed beautifully, refusing to leave the house without "doing" her hair and makeup. All her efforts, however, failed to bring the sense of self-pride Melba still both wanted and needed. She kept trying to achieve more, much more…and she never confided her secret plans to anyone, not even Jeannie or Nedra.

CHAPTER 79

Without warning and moving with destructive, unrelenting intent, a great storm approached the richly forested rainforests along the Caribbean Coast of Central America in September of 1955. The banana plantations situated in these paradise-like locations where temperatures remained high year-round, rainfall was predictably moderate to heavy, and the soil was highly fertile, richly volcanic and alluvial, were directly in the path of a massive storm soon to be named "Janet".

The savage storm had already moved through the banana groves, villages and forests of Central America before Clarence even knew about it. At 4:00 in the morning, he got a call from Everett Lowrance, and the tone of his voice told Clarence the news was bad.

"Clarence, it's Everett. Things are bad in Honduras and Guatemala; they've had a violent storm, a category 5 hurricane. There's destructive river flooding and the plantations are in ruins." Everett didn't even sound like himself. Clarence's heart sunk and he felt like he'd been punched in the gut.

"Oh, God! All I'd heard was a hurricane was headed that way, but nothing about it being a category 5! Why didn't we hear more?" Clarence, frustrated, was almost unable to talk. "Thanks for the heads up, my friend. I'll call later." With that, Clarence hung up the phone. He sat there for awhile, not really knowing what to do or how to tell Melba.

Before he could move from the phone, it rang again. This time it was Estel who was in Hot Springs. "What's going on?" Estel roared into Clarence's ear. "The news reports about this damned hurricane sound grim. What have you heard?"

"Look, brother, I just got a call from Lowrance down in New Orleans. He says it's worse than the news is saying. I'm afraid we're doomed; the banana trees were destroyed. It takes at least a year for new plants to produce fruit, and we can't wait that long. Unless there are areas down there that survived the storm, we're out of luck. I'll talk to our men in Guatemala and Honduras this week. It may be awhile before there's any phone service, so just hang tight until you hear from me. We have two truck loads coming in today with bananas off ships that beat the storm and got out before it hit. That's all I know." Clarence said all this without optimism. It was clear to Estel that the future they'd believed in yesterday looked bleak today.

"I'll call Kenny and let him know. He's not gonna believe it!" Estel groaned.

"Thanks" was all Clarence said.

As updates about Janet hit the news, Clarence learned more unsettling reports about the Yucatan. Quintana Roo and British Honduras were literally devastated. Only five buildings in Chetumal, Mexico remained intact, and over 500 deaths were estimated in Quintana Roo. Predictions of double that number of casualties were on the airways; it sounded bleak. Although he kept trying to get a call through to his contacts on the peninsula, all phone lines were down. He would just have to be patient and wait. Meantime, he had to tell Melba what was going on, and this task was the last thing he wanted to face.

Clarence had been awake when Everett called, so he answered the phone in the kitchen. Melba was still asleep when he went into their bedroom. Standing beside the bed, Clarence looked at her peaceful face, knowing that the news he had to share would cause terrible distress. It felt as if his heart would break, but he also knew Melba. She'd be strong; she'd help him make the tough decisions that lay ahead.

For the next hour, they talked. Clarence, voice tight as he grappled for control, said, "Melby, I have some bad news. It's about the business." With that, the horrible news about Hurricane Janet gushed out in a flood of words that expressed his utter dismay and his desire to pretend he'd been visited in his sleep by a hellish nightmare, that none of this was reality. Melba held his hands and locked her eyes on his. "We'll be okay", she stated. "No storm can wash US away. We have each other and the girls. We'll figure out what to do, and it's not over, not by a long shot! I refuse to simply throw in the towel!"

"Now we have to play a frustrating waiting game", Clarence groaned in an ominously quiet voice, almost a whisper. "I just don't know what to do!"

"We will just be strong, honey", Melba stated in a matter-of-fact voice Clarence had rarely heard before. "You know there's nothing we can do until we talk to Mr. Ortega in Guatemala and Mr. Vera in Honduras, and they may not have any way to reach us for weeks. The only thing I can see to do is take care of the shipments coming in this week and let the stores know there will be availability issues because of the hurricane. They'll have to understand, and I'm confident they'll work with you."

"I guess they will, but what if I can't find another distributor? It sounds like all the plantations are devastated; there may not be any fruit for a very long time." Clarence expressed his heartfelt dismay. He looked like the storm had literally battered him, and not just figuratively. It hurt Melba's soul to see him this way.

"Just imagine what it's like for our workers down there", Melba said. "I just pray the storm didn't claim any of their lives...or their families!"

Clarence sighed and pulled Melba close. They sat on the side of their bed for a few minutes without talking. It would be a difficult time, but each of them had endured a long list of difficult times. Intrinsically, both Melba and Clarence knew they would survive. Would that knowledge make survival any easier?

CHAPTER 80

Almost two months later, Clarence was able to lay the facts out on his desk and see the "big picture": it was not what he had hoped, but over the past weeks he'd determined that going to the bank was a possibility. Maybe, just maybe, if he could procure a big enough loan to see him through the months ahead and allow him to pay his employees he could leave the business without devastating regrets about the way he'd handled things. He knew his spirit would take a big hit, but he also realized Melba would stand by him, regardless. Both of them wanted to leave no one unpaid; taking care of all debts related to the Banana House was first and foremost. They discussed the possibility of filing bankruptcy, but neither of them felt it was "right". Because they did not want to leave any of their debtors in a bind, the task became HOW to pay debts in a manner that allowed them to maintain some degree of dignity.

Within a week, a loan had been procured at Kilgore National Bank. Clarence agreed to an amount that enabled him to pay the distributors in New Orleans and the plantation managers in Honduras and Panama, his employees in Kilgore and Hot Springs, the landlords who owned his business property in both towns, and all the others who had any stake in his banana business. It was a stressful, disturbing and downright depressing time for both Melba and Clarence.

The decision to continue to run the business at a loss for the next 36 months was painful, but ethics won out in the end. As a relatively young couple with a lot of "work" years ahead, losing the business they'd worked so hard to start was almost more than either could endure, but doing what was right seemed to clear the air and make the other decisions less difficult.

In the end, Clarence opted to sell everything he'd purchased for the Hot Springs store, including the three tractor-trailer rigs, the building and double cold-storage vaults, the two commercial humidifier units, and a long list of additional materials needed to run the business in Arkansas. He also sold four of his Kilgore-based truck and trailer rigs, his tandem bobtail, his single-axle bobtail, and all but one of his pick-ups. He was forced to lay off all but one driver, Kenny (his nephew), and all his delivery drivers for in and around Kilgore. Clarence took on all the store deliveries and Kenneth made the weekly hauls to New Orleans for the single loads of bananas they managed to purchase from plantations in northern Columbia that had escaped Janet's devastation.

Clarence had to break contracts with all the groceries near Kilgore except those in Laird Hill, New London, Overton, East Mountain and Gladewater. He continued to service the stores in Kilgore that had worked with him from the beginning: Brookshire Brothers, Piggly-Wiggly, Bill Walden's Food Store, Riley's Market, and Blue Top Grocery. Clarence was so grateful to the owners for continuing with him even though the price of bananas sky-rocketed.

Clarence worked hellishly long hours every week just to keep the stores he still serviced supplied with enough bananas to satisfy most of the demand. He never took a day off, and he refused to do less; it was as though the harsh realities of working the business almost single-handedly were providing deserved punishment for failing to consider what could happen if banana crops were destroyed by storms, drought, disease, or any other of the numerous scenarios Clarence now realized had always been possibilities. He believed what happened reflected a weakness in his business acumen, and this belief, right or wrong, was mightily destructive to his self-esteem.

Melba dealt with everything, but not in the same way. She analyzed the failure of their business, but she placed the blame on a lot of factors. After all, she deliberated, Clarence had no real business background. He'd learned much from Mr. Shoemaker, but Shoemaker ran a very small business. His work with Everett Lowrance might have been the lead-in to a better situation, but Everett's "help" was superficial; his real agenda was getting HIS fruit distributed in East Texas, not helping Clarence open a potentially competitive small business venture in the region! The advice and assistance he offered Clarence was minimal and without substance. The bankers in Kilgore were mostly vested in clients who worked the oil industry and shouldered huge amounts of investment collateral; small business loans were relatively unimportant to them. In truth, Clarence's Banana House was insignificant to the higher-ups who handled fortunes being earned with every new oil well.

For weeks, Melba researched the history about the United Fruit Company, owners of virtually all the banana-producing plantations in Central America and the Caribbean. Eventually, she understood the business. Understanding, sadly, did not bring a sense of relief.

What was left of her innocence evaporated with the knowledge that what Clarence had worked to create was controlled by servile dictatorships in third world countries! United Fruit was the "dictator-at-large" and that fact both stunned and enraged Melba! How such goings-on could take place under the direction of one of America's much-admired giants in the food industry seemed all but impossible, but truth is truth.

United Fruit, Melba learned, controlled the country of Guatemala from the earliest years of the twentieth century. That control marked the beginning of its domination of banana plantations throughout Central America. Holdings included hundreds of thousands of acres in Honduras, Nicaragua, Costa Rica, Panama, Columbia and even the island countries of Jamaica and Cuba. As one of United Fruit's first executives once stated, "Guatemala was chosen as the site for the company's earliest development activities because its government was the region's weakest, most corrupt and most pliable."

"Great!" thought Melba. "My husband's involvement in the shipping and distribution of bananas has us intertwined with a corrupt and immoral group of ...men. Are they gangsters?" Heart throbbing, she had to allow these ideas access to her brain and its repetitious deliberations. Her frame of mind left her feeling desperate for more answers. She would talk to Clarence. Surely he'd had suspicions about the business over the past years.

The background facts explaining United's power in Guatemala, Melba discovered, included Guatemala hiring

United Fruit to manage its postal service in 1901. This was followed in 1913 by United's creation of the Tropical Radio and Telegraph Company. By developing the first radio company in the tropics, United could keep in touch with their ships at sea as well as with all their plantations in Central America, an unprecedented feat at that time.

By 1930, United overtook more than 20 rival produce firms including one of the largest, the Cuyamel Fruit Company. Owned by Russian immigrant Sam Zemurray, Cuyamel's success story was legendary. Zemurray's "rags to riches" start detailed his first savy business scheme that involved buying already ripened banana shipments (throw aways) in New Orleans that had to be distributed immediately. Within a few years, Sam bought plantations in Honduras, acquired steamships and became president of the Cuyamel Fruit Company. Eventually, Cuyamel was a thriving business in direct competition with the United Fruit Company. Zemurray, always a bold risk-taker, sold Cuyamel to United Fruit for 31.5 million dollars in stock and retired to New Orleans.

Surprisingly, three years later, Zemurray's concern about poor management at United ended with a hostile takeover of the company that was masterminded and financed by him. As a result, he moved United Fruit's headquarters out of Guatemala, relocating it in New Orleans where the business prospered over the next twenty years. Melba thought everything she learned about the banana business, regardless of which "king pen" was in control at the time, reeked of unscrupulous, even wanton, behavior. Appalled by treatment of the native inhabitants in small Caribbean settlements like

Honduras and Guatemala, Melba's distrust of barbarous American investors grew exponentially and became a constant weight on her heart.

Melba knew Clarence's involvement in the banana business stemmed directly from working for Everett Lowrance years earlier, and now she understood the connections Lowrance had with "the Banana Man", Sam Zemurray. Recalling comments Clarence made, such as "Sam's not someone you mess with" and "Everett knows things about 'the money man', but he keeps it quiet", Melba finally knew enough to realize Clarence's relationship with the real money-makers was rudimentary. The truth about his treatment was unknown to him. And that made Melba even angrier!

When the initial anger and disappointment faded just enough that calm discussion was possible, Clarence and Melba sat down with cups of coffee early one morning after delivering the girls to their respective schools. Melba shared all the things she'd learned in her days at the college library where she'd accessed news articles and read histories about the Central American countries so deeply involved in producing bananas. She shared her conversations with both Everett Lowrance and their banker, Ross Sterling.

The fact that she had made appointments to interview Everett and Ross made Clarence furious at first, but he listened to her explain what she'd asked them and how they responded.

Finally, Melba tired of Clarence's dogged insistence in the honesty of the banker and businessman. With an edge in her voice she stated, "Clarence, you were hoodwinked and manipulated by Everett Lowrance. He thought you'd get into the business, fail almost immediately, and come back to him as one of his dependable middle-men. He wasn't really trying to help you operate a business that could possibly be a competitor."

"How the hell would you know that, Melba?" Clarence demanded with a raised voice that clearly indicated his displeasure. "Everett and I are friends! He's wealthy. The banana importation business he runs is just a tiny part of how he makes his money. I think you're wrong about him!"

"I know what you think, Clarence. But I've talked to Everett. He thought your startup business was unlikely to work out, but he knew you had some background and knew a lot of men at the docks in both New Orleans and Galveston. He told me your ideas were good, but he really didn't believe you'd be able to get the business off the ground. When you DID, he was impressed. But he did not help you when the chips were down after the hurricane. After all, he's obligated to Sam Zemurray, and his import business depends on his connections to United Fruit. Zemurray could care less about fledgling businesses; he's in it for himself and HIS interests, as is Lowrance!"

Melba hated herself for being so blunt with Clarence, but she also knew he needed to know the truth. Clinging to any hope that Everett would come to his rescue was futile, and she could not bear to see the man she loved dragged down any lower.

As they continued to talk about the whole mess, Clarence acknowledged, "I know, Melba. My business knowledge is not based on things I learned at a college, or on learning a family trade. I had no mentors and I never worked as an apprentice. I suppose it's a miracle we did so well for the first few years!" A tear trickled down Clarence's cheek as he said this, but he wiped it away angrily. "I'll make it up to you!" With that, he got up from the table, grabbed his truck keys and left the house, slamming the door behind him with so much force the windows shook. Melba sat still for the next minutes, forcing herself to calm down and realize Clarence needed more time to process their loss.

The remainder of the day passed slowly, and Melba had trouble focusing on anything except the hollow feeling in her chest. Her heart felt like it was breaking, and she fought the desire to climb back into bed, cry for hours and wallow in self-pity. Instead, she forced herself to complete household chores and stay busy.

Clarence did not call, and he did not come home for supper. "Daddy's working", was all she said to the girls. Thankfully, their after-school routines kept Melba occupied. The girls were allowed a bit more play time than usual. "Mama's got a headache", explained Melba when Terri asked, "Mama, what's wrong?" Finally, bedtime came and the house became quiet.

Melba did not hear Clarence come in, but it was after midnight when she found the peace of deep sleep. When the alarm buzzed at 6:00 and she discovered he was in bed, the sense of relief she felt was palpable. She allowed herself a few minutes to think about what would happen next, and her mind raced back to so many other times in the past when life seemed unbearable. Clarence did not wake, and Melba appreciated the momentary peace and quiet of the early morning hour.

Thoughts tumbled about in her brain, and while she dressed she began to sort out her innermost feelings.

Fighting her life-long "it's not fair!" attitude, Melba eventually came to a realistic conclusion. Blaming circumstances, blaming others…those behaviors accomplished nothing. Sure, she realized, everyone can play the "blame game", but in the end it's up to each of us to pull ourselves up by the bootstraps and trudge forward. In fact, the words that came to her that morning were SO familiar and so exactly RIGHT that she nearly laughed aloud. She heard Papa's voice saying, "We must hitch our wagon to a star!"

The usual morning events began with Cindy wandering into the kitchen, her beloved stuffed "kitty" in hand, and with the normal daily activities came a new sense of peace. Gone were the "whys" and "should haves". From that point on, Melba never looked back. The days of moving on became filled with purpose and sometimes lofty goals, but Melba truly would "hitch her wagon to a star". The world was hers for discovery, interaction…and action.

As for Clarence, he entered the kitchen, gave Melba his traditional good-morning kiss, and lifted Cindy into his arms for a "Daddy hug". His eyes found Melba's, and the love they expressed was unmistakable. Both of them nodded, smiling. Life would go on…

CHAPTER 81

Almost serendipitously, the couple agreed to tell "white" lies about the Banana House. With Hurricane Janet as the reason for cutting back by selling trucks and employing fewer workers, the first year was relatively easy. The most difficult part, Melba realized, was keeping the failure from family. Even Ina Belle knew very little about what was happening; Clarence told her the storm made things difficult, but that he would keep the business going. Kenny knew things were bad, but he assumed Clarence would bounce back after the plantations revived. Clarence chose not to tell Kenny that it would be years before production could meet demand, and he chose not to be blunt about what that meant for small outfits like his. As long as he could pay Kenny and keep on functioning, he decided not to be 100 percent honest.

Later, Clarence would pay the price of telling "half truths"; guilt would plague him for years to come. But for the remainder of the '50s and even into the early '60s, truth would remain elusive. Certainly, neither Clarence nor Melba wanted the Kilgore elite to know what was happening. Saving face was paramount; it was critical, especially to Melba, and Clarence both understood and supported her determination to "look good".

When it was time for school to begin for the girls in September of 1956, Melba enrolled in classes at Kilgore Junior College. Taking 18 hours, her time for volunteering all but vanished. Still, she continued with church commitments both because she enjoyed what she did and she knew her leadership roles might be assets when job-searches began.

Toby was in 8th grade at Kilgore Junior High and Terri was in third grade at Kilgore Heights Elementary. Cindy was in pre-kindergarten at the First Presbyterian Church. As always, the age differences in the girls complicated life to some degree, but Melba appreciated the luxury of extra time with each of them afforded by the five years in between. Able to engage with her girls independently was easier since there was little competition between them; all three were at completely different places developmentally.

Life became school, and school became life. Melba found herself intently absorbed in her coursework. Learning was her job; she loved it! Often, she took care of the girls in the early evening, spending time with each of them before tucking them into bed. Then Melba set her alarm clock to wake her at 2:30 in the morning when she could devote undivided time to her studies for the next four hours. It worked for her even though Clarence thought her short sleep time was unhealthy.

Dealing with the secrets she harbored regarding the Banana House consumed more time than Melba cared to admit. She hated the half-truths necessary to cover up the fact that the business was soon to be history, but she still refused to tell family and friends that all they'd worked for was coming to an end. It was better, she reasoned, to keep her head held high while she worked to earn a college degree that might be their salvation. After all, she certainly did not want PITY! So, when talking to family she made comments that indicated all was well.

On a weekend in Shreveport with Lindell and Nedra, the family was enjoying an afternoon outside while the kids played on a new swing set and slide. Lindell was in the kitchen preparing hamburgers for the barbecue pit when Melba came inside.

He said, "Well, Sister, I'm pretty impressed with the way Clarence is handling the business since the hurricane caused such disaster for him! Is he doing okay? He's a hard man to read, but both of you seem okay. Am I correct?" Lindell's gaze was disconcerting, but Melba smiled at him and stated,

"Oh, Lindell! Of course we're alright! In fact, things are looking up and I couldn't be happier since I've started college classes again; Clarence and I know our futures are looking good. But thanks for asking! I'm just glad you and Nedra are finally back close to Texas! I guess we'll have to accept that Louisiana's a pretty cool state since it's next door!"

"Okay, Sis. I'll stop worrying about you two. Just be sure and let me know if ever you need anything." Lindell's sincerity when he said this pulled at Melba's heart, but she gave him a big smile while saying,

"Thanks, big brother! But just remember your sis is a tough cookie and know everything's cool." With that, she refilled her iced tea, taking the diversion to suck in a deep breath and hold back any sign of tears. Then she rejoined everyone else out in the backyard.

Nedra seemed oblivious about Lindell's concerns regarding the Banana House. As usual, she prattled excitedly about Richard and Reagan; Melba heard everything about her nephews, their developmental milestones, funny things they said and did, their favorite toys, games, songs and activities, and, of course, how close to "genius" they were.

The sister-in-laws giggled about the daily routines both women had to embrace as part of raising the next generation, and they compared how school was now to when THEY attended. It was good for Melba to simply relax. Taking a day away from preparing assignments and studying for her college classes was a true delight; she enjoyed every minute. And one thing Melba became adept at doing was being a listener. It kept her from needing to talk about herself or life in Kilgore.

CHAPTER 82

The first full year of college passed so quickly that Melba felt like Dorothy in *The Wizard of Oz*! Had she been transported to Oz like Dorothy, her astonishment about her new circumstances could not have been more transforming.

Suddenly, she was interacting with other students while discussing theories, philosophies and ethics. Just the expectation for exploration was mind-boggling, and Melba felt she'd been given a priceless gift. Not a day passed without experiencing an almost giddy sense of excitement and awe.

Summer school was tempting, but Melba decided spending time with the girls and Clarence was more important. The summer flew by; it was over before she could adjust to a more relaxed schedule. When September of 1956 arrived, it was time for Melba to transfer her credits to a four-year school. Since G.W. and Lindell (as well as Buron!) had attended Stephen F. Austin State College in Nacogdoches, it was a natural choice for Melba. The drive was "doable" at 75 miles; she could leave home and arrive on campus in just over an hour. During the fall semester of 1956, Melba enrolled at SFA and registered for six courses. She was determined!

Clarence proved her mainstay. He managed to get the girls to school everyday, fixed their breakfast, checked their homework, made sure they were happy, all while working long hours at the Banana House. Most days, Melba returned from Nacogdoches late in the afternoon. She managed this by taking classes in the morning and working on assignments in the library afterward. Clarence usually had supper ready when she got home, but Ina Belle filled in whenever necessary. They were a team, and that fact made Melba's days much less stressful. The girls handled their mother's school life without a single sign of anxiety, and their acceptance of the situation soothed her soul. She knew, however, that even if Clarence had objected to her decision to go back to school, it would have happened. She had waited far too long!

During that fall semester, buzz phrases and talk about "equality for women" in the workplace were gaining momentum. Especially on college campuses, whispered messages traveled with lightening speed when news about women's rights surfaced. Melba was attentive to all the talk, including what some considered "gossip". After all, she reasoned, it was impossible to really effect change if you buried your head in the sand! Of course, Melba had read books by Virginia Woolf and Simone de Beauvoir, and she was in total agreement with their viewpoints regarding the treatment of women. Who could throw aside the ideas of these two phenomenal writers and ignore their obvious understanding of the world's despicable history of unethical treatment of women? In truth, Melba had loved what de Beauvoir was advocating even six years earlier when she challenged women to examine their role in culture and question the "comfort" of allowing men to handle their affairs. It just made sense to her; why should men get all the top jobs and have so much unquestioned authority over the opposite sex? Melba knew she was smart, and she knew a lot of other women who were even smarter. It just wasn't fair...

One of the anti-establishment beliefs circulating on the SFA campus was articulated by a female classmate of Melba's during an impromptu after-class meet up. With heat in her voice she said, "I see so many flaws in our so-called decade of peace and plenty! President Eisenhower is the Commander in Chief of the Cold War, and the questionable peace we're enjoying could turn bad without warning. It also infuriates me that so many women are back doing domestic duty after working as engineers, scientists and mechanics during the War.

And we all know what's happening with salaries. Sometimes I question my reasons for being here; a college degree won't mean much for WOMEN grads!"

Another female student agreed, adding, "My mother was employed by a branch of the Kirby Lumber Company in Lufkin; she was a trimmer-saw operator, and she was stronger than a lot of men. But as soon as the war ended and soldiers needed jobs, she was fired. It didn't matter that she was more skilled because, as we all know, MEN should be the bread-winners and WOMEN should be wives and mothers. It's a bunch of hooey!"

"At least President Eisenhower is keeping his promise to include women in high-level government appointments", Melba interjected. "But even with his efforts to honor women, the reality is we are expected to raise the children and make sure our homes are tranquil places for the comfort of our husbands. Why should we continue to give in to this absurd belief? I'm older than all of you, and I've stayed at home with my three girls...but it's time for a change!" The little group of younger women nodded agreement.

One of them, a petite and pretty young lady who was clearly asserting her disagreement with the establishment by dressing in "mannish" clothing consisting of jeans, a sweater and loafers, spoke up. "Just try to keep me at home! I'm not standing for such bunk. Look around at the 'dark' citizens here in Nacogdoches, especially the females. They are living in poverty and if the men can even GET a job, they make a pittance for doing the same kind of manual labor as the whites. It's wrong!"

Another girl said, "Amen!" Then she added in an admonishing tone, "Both blacks and females are treated, at best, as second-class citizens. That's especially true here in the South. Added to all the discrimination we face, there's the constant threat of a communistic takeover by Russia as well as all the fear of atomic warfare. Just look at what the government says about the necessity of building bomb shelters and the stupid bomb drills required in all our public schools! It's a joke! Life has changed, but not entirely for the better!"

After the women exchanged farewells and continued on their separate ways, Melba went to the library. Her economics professor's assignment beckoned. It was to read an article written by Mabel Newcomer, a Vassar professor and nationally acclaimed guru of economics. Interestingly, Dr. Newcomer's work really meshed with the conversation of Melba and her classmates.

In it, she raised questions that underscored the inequalities faced by women, including: Why do we educate only 25 percent of the women capable of college work? Must early marriage deprive women of higher education? Are college

358

educated women contributing their share to American scholarship and art? Is the current shortage of scientists, doctors and educated brains due to a failure to utilize women's potential? The reading assignment underscored Melba's conviction that women both could and SHOULD make a positive difference in the "outside world", not just in their lives at home. She knew there would be some heated debates in Dr. Joseph's Economics class in the coming weeks!

CHAPTER 83

As Melba's academic acumen increased, so did her confidence in the future she envisioned. She had a mission, and her determination was rock-solid. As the days and weeks evolved, so did her career plans. Being a great teacher came first, but she knew there was much more on her professional agenda!

On her daily commutes to and from SFA, her thoughts often turned to family members like Uncle Cecil whose mental retardation had prevented him from living a full life. One of her goals involved finding methods to better educate those with low intellectual ability while also working to bring about legislation that would mandate government aid to families living with handicapped relatives. Cecil, a victim of PKU (a rare inherited disorder that caused the build up of the amino acid called phenylketonuria in his body), was affected by severe and irreversible mental deficits within months of his birth. Melba often imagined ways to make both his life and the lives of his siblings who continued to have to look after him a little easier. It just seemed FAIR.

She'd often wondered why Mama and Papa were Cecil's caretakers. He lived with them and only rarely did any of Mama's brothers or sisters offer to take him even for short visits. As is so often the case, it became Annie's "duty" to take care of her younger brother. The other siblings had their reasons for not wanting Cecil in their homes fulltime, but Annie and Buster just accepted him without any sign of ambivalence. After all, he was Annie's baby brother and that was her attitude.

Cecil thrived in their home because he was treated, as much as possible, like an equal. Annie let him help with chores, and she talked to him about family. Cecil knew every member of his extended family, both brothers and sisters, their wives and husbands, and all the children born to them. It was sometimes mind-boggling to hear him greet family when they visited; he never failed to know who each person was, and he knew a lot about each of them. The fact that Cecil could identify family and make connections was simply amazing to Melba.

Cecil was "labeled" as "feebleminded", an "idiot". The family had long been encouraged to institutionalize him. They were told it was "best" for him, but Papa stepped in after Annie and Cecil's mother, Martha, died in 1964, telling the other siblings he and Annie would take care of Cecil. Melba never forgot her parents' decision; she knew it was the right thing to do, and it made a significant impression that would influence her ideas about mental retardation for the rest of her life. When Melba realized her parents refused to go along with the prevailing societal belief that people born with intellectual disabilities should be segregated and prohibited from living with those of "normal" intelligence, she was proud. But thoughts about Uncle Cecil certainly caused Melba to ponder what becoming a teacher would mean in terms of educating students with mental retardation.

Additionally, she often thought about Dr. Allums and his hydrocephalic daughter, Claudia Kathleen, who was born in 1949. She was a victim of a birth defect that prevented her spinal column from closing and caused fluid build-up in her brain.   Little Claudia was really in a vegetative state. She was

361

both blind and deaf, and unresponsive to stimulation. Dr. Allums and his wife, Geraldine, were caught in a situation no one ever anticipates. They already had two older daughters, Ann and Sherry.

Toby and Terri played at the Allums' house on occasion; the four girls were close in age. Melba couldn't forget the time Terri came home practically in hysterics. Claudia's daybed/cradle had been in the living room by the window, and the girls were playing hide and seek. Terri inadvertently bumped into Claudia's cradle, and, looking down saw her laying there. Although Terri knew her friend, Ann, had a little sister who was "sick", she'd never been close to Claudia. Terri was horrified because Claudia looked so strange; her head was greatly enlarged and her cloudy, colorless eyes were open. Even though Mrs. Allums had tried to help Terri understand that Claudia couldn't hurt her, that she had a "condition", Terri kept crying until Geraldine telephoned Melba and explained what had happened. Of course, Melba felt terrible about Terri's reaction, but it was certainly natural; none of the adults had considered introducing her to Claudia and answering any questions she might have had. Unfortunate as the incident was, Melba never forgot the bigger lesson: handicapped individuals cannot be ignored or overlooked, and ensuring their acceptance is a responsibility of their caregivers. Helping such children and their families was another goal in Melba's growing list of "to dos".

CHAPTER 84

During her years at Stephen F. Austin, Melba's grades were outstanding. In fact, in every course she took except MUSIC, she earned A's or even A+'s. Her only "B" (a B+, actually) was earned in Music for Elementary Majors, a course that was relatively easy. The problem came with Melba's inability to hear pitch and "carry a tune", something that had humiliated her since childhood. Although she had no difficulty with reading music, she simply could not differentiate subtle changes in sound. Talking with the professor about this inability did not help her improve her grade since Dr. Williams required students to sight-read songs and sing them on pitch. He would make no exceptions. In the end, Melba just did the best she could. Music kept her from graduating with all A's. It was one time when Melba's old "it's not fair" mantra was justified!

Melba was proud of making the Dean's List every semester at SFA; it was nice to be recognized for making top grades. This honor did little to inflate her self-esteem, but it at least confirmed Melba's belief in the importance of having a strong work ethic. Completing assignments to the best of her ability was intrinsically rewarding and the very idea of failure made her physically ill; she realized the term "perfectionist" applied to her!

When the final semester arrived, Melba received a letter from Dr. R.W. Steen, President of Stephen F. Austin. In it, he commended her academic success and recognized her status as the student currently holding the highest grade point average in the history of the college. Dr. Steen requested a meeting with Melba to discuss Commencement and her invitation to deliver the Valedictory Address.

Melba was stunned! When she opened the letter at home on the night of April 29th, she gasped in surprise. Clarence looked at her with concern. "What's wrong, honey?" he asked.

"This just can't be right!" Melba exclaimed. "I know there are other students much smarter than me; I'm afraid Dr. Steen has made a mistake!"

"About WHAT?" Clarence demanded.

"This letter from him states that I have the top grades in the entire college, Clarence! That's impossible! Remember the "B" I made in Music? I'm sure there are other students who've earned straight A's!" Melba all but yelled, and there was a tremor in her voice. "It really must be a mistake, Honey. I know I can't have the highest grades; I'm with so many other students who outshine me all the time in class discussions. I'm sure when I meet with Dr. Steen he'll have to apologize for a terrible mistake!"

"Why do you always underestimate yourself, Melby?" Clarence insisted. "I've always known you to be better at everything than anyone else; you're just the cat's meow!" With that, he grabbed Melba in a big bear hug that ended in a sweet kiss. "Now stop the nonsense and realize you ARE the best!"

Clarence's smile was so sincere that Melba smiled back and said, "Well, I'll see if I can set up an appointment with Dr. Steen early next week…"

The appointment proved Clarence was right; Melba learned she truly was the top student in terms of grade point average with a 3.936 average. Dr. Steen told her a poll of her professors confirmed their high esteem for her academia and her personal commitment to excellence; all agreed she should be named the Valedictory Speaker at Commencement.

Melba's response was indicative of the long journey leading to this acclaim. Looking directly into the eyes of Stephen F. Austin's president, she stated, "I'm honored, sir, but I'm also overwhelmed with a sense that I'm just not good enough for this recognition! Earning high grades has never been inordinately difficult for me. I was blessed with a strong visual memory which certainly enabled excellent recall of facts so highly valued by instructors. But I'm a product of the Depression, the Oil Boom and the War, quite a blend of events that shaped my beliefs. One of the reasons I'm here is an effort to rise above the current mindset that women should stay at home, abstain from higher learning, eschew politics, repress personal opinions and elevate masculinity above femininity since men are superior. I simply don't agree with such nonsense, and one of my goals is to use the rest of my life and my career to refute the separation of the sexes based on a list of "cans" and "cannots". If that makes me less of an ideal candidate for the honor of Valedictorian, I understand." Melba even managed to smile as she waited for Steen's response.

Without so much as a moment's hesitation, Dr. Steen leaned back in his chair, rubbed his hands together and smiled right back, declaring firmly "Well, then, it's decided! Please start preparations for your Commencement Address. I, for one, can hardly wait to hear it!"

Melba was taken aback; she assumed her comments would cause reconsideration of which of the top students should be named Valedictorian. Instead, Dr. Steen stood up indicating the meeting was over. "We are proud of your accomplishments, Melba. You have earned our recognition and our esteem. Now go home to your family and let them know you are NUMBER ONE!"

The drive back to Kilgore was over in a flash; Melba drove without one thought about the task of controlling her car. Instead, her mind exploded with memories about all the events that created the woman she'd become. She thought about the secret dreams that began in her earliest years as she competed with G.W. and Lindell. It was clear the competition was for much more than keeping up with her brothers in all their games, races and physical tasks. Melba determined as a child that she would prove "just a girl" capable of anything she could imagine, and her plans for bettering herself started way back in Damon.

Remembered conversations flitted in and out of Melba's mind. All these years, she mused, and I've never stopped trying to prove my worth. She recalled her elementary school days in Damon, hearing once again the hated sing-song chant "Melba-Smellba" and the taunts of girls like Patty about her clothes. Tears trickled down her cheeks as she drove down highway 259. When she thought about Lydia, one of the bullying girls at Kilgore High School, the anger from the day Lydia and her little group "invited" Melba to join them after school for an excursion to the ritzy clothing store, Jordan's, still simmered in her soul! She recalled their syrupy-sweet voices saying, "Maybe you can find something NICE to wear to school since Jordan's is having a big sale!" Their scornful laughter STILL hurt, even after all these years... Never mind the fact that I've worn lots of beautiful dresses from Jordan's as an adult, Melba reflected; the pain inflicted by girls like Patty and Lydia left indelible marks.

Thoughts of her marriage at age 16 surfaced. Yes, she loved Clarence in 1936. Yes, she loved him now. Love did not alter the fact that marrying at such a young age had stood in the way of so much, and she was unable to bury the resentment that boiled up as thoughts of what might have been flickered like embers in a dying fire. "What ifs" streamed through her brain, coming close to ushering in a new stream of tears; thankfully, thoughts of all the good things that DID happen after her marriage won out. How could she fail to remember the wonderful early days with Clarence? They'd had such fun, enjoyed the company of so many friends and relatives, and really embraced life in spite of the hard times and scarcity of money! And even later, after the War started, they'd shared amazing things...Most amazing, she meditated, the births of their three girls! Did it really matter that she was just now completing a college degree? Perhaps the grades she'd earned would have eluded her when she was young; after all, life experiences certainly added a lot of knowledge and expertise no college class or professor could impart!

Melba was almost home when she refocused on the reality of her day and the news she needed to share with

Clarence and the girls. Taking a deep breath, she wiped away the last trace of tears, turned on the radio and revved up the volume…Ricky Nelson was singing "Just a Little Too Much", and Melba began to relax. Everything would be alright, and she WOULD enjoy the good feeling generated by being named valedictorian. Clarence would be proud, and that fact, alone, made Melba happy. She was smiling when she pulled into the driveway. Terri and Cindy, as was often the case, raced down the long front yard toward the car.

Melba could hear them yelling, "Mama!! You won't believe what happened today!!" Even though the girls could make Melba mad with their tendency to "tattle", today's exuberance seemed to be the gleeful sort. Stopping the car, she opened the door and had both children reaching in for hugs. "What DID happen today, girls?" Melba demanded. "It sounds like something special!"

"It was special, Mama!" both girls exclaimed at the same time. "Daddy took us to the Bar-G Stables this afternoon!" Terri said excitedly. "I got to ride my favorite, Star!"

"That's awesome, honey!" Melba affirmed. "Which horse did you ride, Cindy?"

"I rode Miss Nutmeg. She's SO gentle, and I just love her!" Cindy chortled. "Daddy helped me, but I did a lot by myself! Daddy even took the lead rope off when we got out in the pasture."

"Let me guess", Melba stated. "Daddy probably rode Comanche. Am I right?"

"How'd you know, Mama?" Terri demanded.

"Daddy loves Comanche because he never slows down and he's all lathered up before you're 100 yards from the stable! Comanche reminds your dad of a horse he rode in Laredo when he was a Border Patrol Agent. That horse's name was Stormy, and Clarence always insisted he was as tempestuous as his name!" Melba shared this information with a wink and a nod, smiling gleefully as she related this story.

Both girls laughed, and after a few tales about their most recent experiences on the trail, they all decided to go inside and see what Daddy was making for supper.

CHAPTER 85

The next weeks were devoted to completing course assignments, attending classes and, of course, deciding the gist of what she wanted to say at Commencement. Melba spent a considerable amount of time reflecting on the message she hoped would make a positive impact on her audience. After all, her life was almost certainly vastly different from the lives of the majority of others in her graduating class! They were twenty years younger and had grown up in the post-Depression, post-War decades. Melba had to remember that her classmates were closer in age to Toby than to HER. Once again, she wondered what Dr. Steen and the Board of Regents were thinking when they named her the Valedictorian. It still seemed simply crazy!

Melba decided to write down her thoughts. Maybe doing so would give her some valid ideas about the speech she had to make! She mentally reviewed all the things which, in her opinion, had "formed" who she had become. Of course, family was at the top. She'd been raised by Buster Black, a self-made and very independent man with a simple, basic education, and by Annie Black, a woman from a long line of German immigrants who valued women for bearing children and keeping food on the table. Annie, too, had little formal education; she could read and write and do simple math, but other than the basics was uneducated. Melba thought about others in the family. Both Brother and Lindell had gone to college. Lindell had the most formal education as well as all the training he'd received in the military, but G.W. was brilliant and well-educated in his own right. His work experience and training had increased his knowledge base. Melba's early education had been reasonably sound, but her social experiences had scarred her in terrible ways.

Kilgore years had enabled Melba to expand her social expertise; she was a self-taught leader in a wide variety of acceptable ventures at church, the garden club and much more. She had learned to fit in, was better dressed than the vast majority of women, had become "cultured" through her activities and her incessant quest for the knowledge to be gained through books. Hard times and tragedy had peppered her perspectives about almost everything, but her tenacity had kept her from giving up. Melba jotted down ideas and looked back over them frequently as graduation day approached.

On Saturday, May 30, Melba, Clarence and all three girls made the drive to Nacogdoches early in the afternoon. Graduation exercises were scheduled to begin at 6:00, and, because Melba was giving the Valedictory address, she was asked to report to the officials at 4:30. To say she was nervous was an understatement! Melba likened the way she felt at the moment to the way she felt years earlier when speaking to the board of directors at First Baptist Church, Kilgore, for the very first time to address the need for changes in the Sunday school curriculum. Because she had to address the church board of directors, the pastor and his associate pastor, it had been an incredibly stressful event. Today, she was almost nauseous, and noticed her hands were trembling. How, she wondered, could she talk to her fellow students and all the professors here at S.F.A. (not to mention all the guests and members of the media!) about the meaning of commencement when she, herself, still had so many questions. Right now, the future seemed like a monstrous and frightening entity instead of a profoundly exciting beginning. Trying to remain calm, she talked to her girls about everything they saw on the campus. Details became her refuge as she tried desperately not to dwell on the speech she had committed to memory. She told herself everything would be fine, and she prayed her self-talk would be true…

At 5:30, the graduates arrived at designated areas to line up alphabetically. All the graduate students were placed together at the front, followed by undergraduates receiving honors, followed by all the other graduates. Melba joined those who were receiving honors, and she DID feel proud when the dean of the education department brought her the beautiful satin cords she would wear around her shoulders. The three pairs of purple and white cords that designated her status of Summa Cum Laude were simply spectacular, Melba thought, and the purple and jade green cord for her membership in the Kappa delta PI honor society was a nice extra touch. As she waited for the ceremony to begin, Melba looked around the hallway at the sea of excited, impatient faces of her classmates. She knew some of them by name, others by face. But in reality, Melba mused, most of her fellow graduates were strangers; their paths met on campus, but time for true friendships never existed during all those intense college days. How would they receive a 40 year old woman who was just now receiving her Bachelor's Degree?   In near panic, Melba's old fear of being ridiculed rose to the surface. She nearly passed out, and her heart began to beat so fast she could barely breathe.

At that moment the Orchestra of the Pines began to play the processional music. The line was moving; it was going to happen! Melba's feet moved her forward automatically; she felt hollow inside and could not remember the opening lines of her speech. As the group reached the first rows of seats and those in front of Melba filed in, she felt the urge to run out of the building. "Please, God", she prayed silently, "let me get through this without making a fool of myself. Please let my words be encouraging and inspiring…"

President Steen smiled at the crowd assembled in the Shelton Gymnasium which also served as the college's auditorium and said, "Please be seated."

There was a rustling of papers and graduation gowns as the students took their seats. Dr. Steen looked out at the graduating students as the robed faculty members seated behind him on the stage stood up and applauded. When the professors sat back down, Steen said, "I want to welcome all our guests; you are here today to witness the conferring of hard-earned academic degrees on 421 student Lumber Jacks. I am proud of each one's accomplishments, and I know all the parents, grandparents, families and friends of those assembled here this evening are equally pleased to celebrate the successful completion of a long journey! This is the day that marks the culmination of an academic odyssey and the beginning of a new phase in our graduate's lives. Thank you for joining us in this celebration!"

The room was filled with applause. Having these minutes to quiet her nerves really helped Melba get focused; she felt better. It was nice to see and hear Dr. Steen, and the remembered words he'd said to her just a few weeks ago played through her mind… "We are proud of your accomplishments, Melba. You have earned our recognition and our esteem. Now go home to your family and let them know you are NUMBER ONE!" Melba felt her heart rate slowing. As she dared to look up at the audience seated in the bleachers above the graduates, she saw Clarence and the girls. He was looking at HER; their eyes met, and Clarence touched his fingers to his lips, extending them toward her so subtly that no one but Melba could have noticed. He smiled. Melba realized she would be okay.

Dr. Steen was introducing the next speaker, Reverend John Crockett, the pastor of the respected Christ Episcopal Church in Nacogdoches established over 100 years earlier. Reverend Crockett began his address with a prayer and a reading from the Bible: 1 Corinthians 3:9 "For we are co-workers in God's service; you are God's field, God's building." Crockett's words encouraged each graduate to use his life's work to honor God and help his fellow man. He ended with words from the poem, *Dreams*, by Langston Hughes:

Hold fast to dreams

For if dreams die

Life is a broken-winged bird

That cannot fly.

Dr. Steen returned to the podium and explained how the graduates would be called to accept their diplomas. "I will read the names of each graduate, and the degree granted. Deans from each Department will be at the podium to offer congratulations and hand the diplomas to you. We'll begin now."

Confirmation of graduate degrees was done first. Then the honors graduates were called to the stage, their academic status noted, and their degree confirmed. Melba heard her name read by Dr. Steen, but it seemed his voice was far away and a bit unreal: "Melba Black Winters, Summa cum Laude in the field of Education with a Bachelor of Science Degree" he intoned. Melba stood and walked to the stage.

Dr. Steen smiled at her and shook her hand firmly, whispering, "Congratulations, Melba! It's my privilege to know you; God bless!"

Returning to her seat, Melba observed the long line of graduates as they, too, walked the aisle and accepted their diplomas. The earlier "jitters" had returned in force, and she admonished herself to stay calm. It was almost time for her valediction.

When the last graduate was congratulated and the applause died down, Dr. Steen said,

"It is an honor to welcome back to the podium our esteemed Valedictorian, Mrs. Melba Winters. With a 3.936 grade point, Mrs. Winters has achieved the highest GPA yet earned at Stephen F. Austin. Please greet her warmly!" With those comments from Dr. Steen, Melba stood and walked to the stage.

At the podium, Melba walked up to Dr. Steen and they shook hands. He whispered, "They're going to be inspired!"

With a smile, he moved away, leaving Melba looking out at the crowd of faces that were all trained on HER. She nearly panicked. Then, taking a calming breath, she smiled and started to speak. Suddenly, Melba was focused on her "job"; she knew the next few minutes were a major test and she determined to earn an "A"…

"American writer and philosopher, Ralph Waldo Emerson, wrote the words 'Hitch your wagon to a star' way back in 1904 in his essay 'American Civilization'. Little did he know that more than 50 years later, those simplistic words would continue to harness our thinking and influence our decision-making! I would not be standing here this afternoon if my dad had not listened to Emerson's admonition. Let me explain. My dad was an oil field worker in the tiny town of Damon when I was a child. When oil was discovered in Kilgore during the dark days of the Depression, I overheard Papa and Mama talking late one night. Papa was insisting on a move to Kilgore to find a better life, but Mama was afraid. Papa told her, 'We must hitch our wagon to a star! This is a chance of a lifetime!' So, we packed our sparse belongings and Kilgore became our new home. Kilgore WAS a much better place for our family; we enjoyed a simple but happy life there. Thirty years later, I took my dad's advice and 'hitched MY wagon' to a star, the star of education. But this is just the beginning for me and for each of you, and I challenge consideration of a different bit of advice from Mr. Emerson: 'Do not go where the path may lead. Go, instead, where there is no path and leave a trail.' I am sure that your dreams are more alive today than ever as you contemplate the choices that lie ahead. Our choices will surely determine the kind of trail we will leave, but one imperative for all must be to exercise caution with every choice. The trails we forge will depend on our personal initiative, determination and sense of right and wrong. The fact that women just earned the right to vote when I was a baby still fuels my decisions and colors my personal philosophy about life, tying the choices I make to justice, fairness and equality. Unless I incorporate these values into my life, I cannot make a positive contribution to the human race and, especially, to my fellow female travelers. My goals include working to make positive changes in the roles women are encouraged to undertake as well as endeavoring to advance new opportunities for all men and women, even those who are handicapped or impaired. We do not have the right to prevent others from making their own choices in life or from learning job skills, and we must both support and advocate specialized training to aid our fellow travelers.

The atrocities of World War II speak to the human requirement of honoring the rights of all the world's peoples. The 'Universal Declaration of Human Rights' that was written in 1946 speaks volumes regarding the just and responsible treatment of humanity. Its commission was chaired by our own Eleanor Roosevelt with input from 18 world nationalities, and its content is powerful. We all know that human dignity and worth were denigrated by the Nazis and other Axis powers during the War; this can never happen again. Mrs. Roosevelt's advocacy for worldwide fairness and humanity echo what we must all hold sacred; let's take the United Nations' Human Rights Declaration to heart as we make our individual paths through life. Respect for and observance of human rights and fundamental freedoms without distinction based on race, religion, sex, or language must be our mantra!

What else have I learned during my tenure at Stephen F. Austin? Of utmost importance, I've fully realized the importance of education. I've learned to take the time to reflect daily on the possibilities unlocked by my days here. Psychologist Abraham Maslow's work includes his important 'Hierarchy of Needs' that explains our basic needs must be satisfied before any higher needs can be addressed. The needs, most of you know, begin at the PSYSIOLOGICAL level and include air, water, food, shelter and sleep. When those needs are met, we focus on the need for SAFETY, including protection from the elements, security, order, law, stability and freedom from fear. When safety needs are fulfilled, humans gravitate to a need for LOVE AND BELONGING. These needs include friendship, intimacy, affection and love. When these needs are met, ESTEEM becomes important, including the need for achievement, mastery, independence, status, prestige and self-respect. At the very top of Maslow's Hierarchy is the need for SELF-ACTUALIZATION. Those most elusive needs include realizing personal potential, self-fulfillment, seeking personal growth and peak experiences. Hopefully, all of us have achieved a satisfactory level of esteem and are now poised at the very top of the hierarchy pyramid. According to Maslow, every person is capable of achieving this top level called self-actualization, but our lower needs must be maintained. Maslow noted that only one in one hundred people become fully self-actualized because our society rewards motivation based on esteem, love and other social needs and fails to encourage self-actualization. I challenge each of you to go into the great unknown with your wagons hitched to the stars, searching for and reaching your personal potential, for, as Maslow said, 'You will either step forward into growth, or step backward into safety.' We have received the blessings of a quality education; the rest is up to us! Thank you, my fellow travelers, and God bless your next journey!'"

The applause that followed surprised Melba; she certainly did not think anything she'd said was especially profound. It was nice, she realized, to have this event behind her. She was more-than-ready to move on, and her advice was most-assuredly self-aimed! She smiled once again and turned away from the audience to receive congratulations from Dr. Steen and other faculty members. The realization that she had REALLY graduated was simply exhilarating!

Within minutes, the Recessional March was playing, and the sea of graduates started the parade out of the gymnasium into the waiting arms of loved ones. Clarence and all three girls simply threw themselves at Melba, laughing excitedly and telling her what a wonderful job she'd done. A plethora of congratulations and words of praise came her way as she walked outside with her little family. It felt odd, Melba reflected. To be the object of admiration instead of ridicule felt really nice... Life was good.

EPILOGUE

Melba entered the workforce a few months later as a fourth grade teacher at Pine Tree Elementary School in Greggton, Texas. Those first years as a teacher solidified her determination to take steps on a daily basis to improve life for students, parents and the human condition everywhere. She recognized the importance of public education in America, always reflecting on the doors opened to her due to formal learning. From the first day in her own classroom to the last day she worked as a substitute teacher 31 years later, Melba always agreed with John Dewey's statement in his essay *Experience and Education*: "It is the teacher's business to be on the alert to see what attitudes and habitual tendencies are being created. In this direction he must, if he is an educator, be able to judge what attitudes are actually conducive to continued growth and what are detrimental. He must, in addition, have that sympathetic understanding of individuals as individuals which gives him an idea of what is actually going on in the minds of those who are learning."

Melba's career spanned three decades; her legacy continues on through stories told by former students and those educators who worked with and learned from her. Her contributions to furthering educational opportunities for the mentally and physically handicapped are remembered and sustained. Importantly, Melba achieved her secret dreams and left the world a better place.

- Teacher(4th grade and special education)
- Counselor
- Principal
- Director of Special Education